Britain, the Commonwealth and Europe

Also by Alex May

BRITAIN AND EUROPE SINCE 1945

EMILE NOËL AND THE MAKING OF EUROPE (*editor with Andrea Bosco*)

THE ROUND TABLE, THE EMPIRE/COMMONWEALTH AND BRITISH FOREIGN POLICY (*editor*)

Britain, the Commonwealth and Europe

The Commonwealth and Britain's Applications to join the European Communities

Edited by

Alex May
Research Editor
New Dictionary of National Biography
University of Oxford

First published 2001 by
PALGRAVE
Houndmills, Basingstoke, Hampshire RG21 6XS and
175 Fifth Avenue, New York, N. Y. 10010
Companies and representatives throughout the world

PALGRAVE is the new global academic imprint of
St. Martin's Press LLC Scholarly and Reference Division and
Palgrave Publishers Ltd (formerly Macmillan Press Ltd).

ISBN 0–333–80013–3

This book is printed on paper suitable for recycling and
made from fully managed and sustained forest sources.

A catalogue record for this book is available
from the British Library.

Library of Congress Cataloging-in-Publication Data
Britain, the Commonwealth and Europe : the Commonwealth and Britain's
applications to join the European Communities / edited by Alex May.
        p. cm.
Includes bibliographical references and index.
ISBN 0–333–80013–3
  1. Great Britain—Politics and government—1979–1997.
2. Commonwealth countries—Foreign relations—Europe. 3. Europe–
–Foreign relations—Commonwealth countries. 4. Commonwealth
countries—Foreign economic relations. 5. Great Britain—Foreign
relations—Europe. 6. Europe—Foreign relations—Great Britain.
7. European Economic Community—Great Britain. 8. Great Britain–
–Foreign economic relations. 9. European communities. 10. European
federation. I. May, Alex.

DA589.8 .B737 2000
327'.09171'241—dc21
                                                      00–052416

10   9   8   7   6   5   4   3   2   1
10   09 08 07 06 05 04 03 02 01

Printed in Great Britain by Antony Rowe Ltd, Chippenham, Wiltshire

This volume is dedicated to the memory of our colleague and co-contributor, Dr John B. O'Brien, who died in March 1999. John was for many years Senior Lecturer in History at University College, Cork. Before that he was Senior Research Officer with the Australian Bureau of Census and Statistics, Lecturer at the University of Adelaide and then La Trobe University, Melbourne, and Visiting Fellow at the Research School of Social Sciences, Australian National University, Canberra. He published many studies in the form of both articles and books, on the local history of Cork and Irish history more generally, on Australian history and on the history of the Commonwealth. His study of The Irish Emigrant Experience in Australia *(Dublin: Poolbeg, 1991) was widely acclaimed. He was an active figure in the Irish Committee of Historical Sciences, the Irish Economic and Social History Society, the British Association for the Study of Australia, and the European Association for Studies of Australia. He was also the much loved husband of Catherine O'Brien. He was renowned for his erudition, his wit, and his humanity. He is greatly missed by innumerable colleagues and friends.*

Contents

Preface

This volume has its origins in a conference on 'The Commonwealth and Europe', held at South Bank University in April 1998, and sponsored jointly by the European Institute at South Bank University and *The Round Table*, the Commonwealth Journal of International Affairs.[1] This conference brought together young and established scholars, and former and current officials, to discuss both historical and contemporary issues in the triangular relationship between Britain, the Commonwealth and Europe. Many of the chapters in this volume were given in abbreviated form as papers at the conference. All such papers have been revised in the light of discussion at the conference and further research. A second volume, edited by Shobhana Madhavan, will address the relationship between the Commonwealth and Europe as it has evolved since 1973.

Despite the diversity of approach, the theme of this book is a clear and precise one: the interrelationship between the Commonwealth and Europe in British foreign policy in the period between the end of the Second World War and British membership of the European Community.

The academic study of Britain's relationship with the process of European integration since 1945 and of its evolving relationship with the Commonwealth over the same period has developed enormously. There is now an extensive literature of high scholarly standard by historians, international relations analysts and political scientists in both fields. Nevertheless the extent of cross-fertilization, common focus or even shared interest has until recently been remarkably small. Students of Britain's relationship with western Europe have tended to focus on the 'missed chances' of Britain's reactions to the various proposals for integration emanating from continental Europe, or the continuing difficulties in the relationship after 1973. Students of the Empire/Commonwealth have tended to focus on 'decolonization', viewed either as the emergence of liberation movements in the former colonial world or the contraction for domestic or 'Cold War' reasons of Britain's global power.

This tendency, to compartmentalize Britain's foreign policy into 'European' and 'Commonwealth' policies, has come into question in a number of recent general works. Thus Stephen George and John Young have emphasized the Commonwealth as an important factor in Britain's attitude towards Europe before 1973,[2] and John Darwin has argued for an interpretation of British decolonization which sets Empire/Commonwealth policy firmly in the context of Britain's other foreign policy commitments and goals, including those in Europe.[3] More directly, recent work by Catherine Schenk has focused on the interrelationship between Britain's Empire/Commonwealth and European policies in the field of trade and finance, both before and after the British application.[4] Studies by Stuart Ward and John O'Brien have also illuminated the particular problems of the 'old' Dominions during the first British application.[5]

The contemporary literature abounds with speeches, articles, pamphlets and books on 'The Commonwealth and Europe'; nevertheless, this volume is the first historical (as opposed to contemporary) work directly to address the multiplicity of questions surrounding the interrelationship of these two factors in British policy in the period of Britain's 'turn to Europe'.

While it is difficult to generalize from a wide range of chapters written with different interests and from different perspectives, the contributors to this volume are to a large extent agreed on the centrality of the Commonwealth in British thinking about Europe, and the significance of Britain's European policy for the development of the Commonwealth during this period. They are also to a large extent agreed on the crucial significance of the 1961–63 application, as the moment of acutest debate on Britain's relationship with the Commonwealth and Europe, at all levels of government and political society, in Britain itself, in Europe and in the Commonwealth. As the later chapters argue, the handling of the issues in 1967–68 (and again in 1970–71) showed that much of the heat had left the debate after 1961–63; after 1961–63 European and Commonwealth governments, as well as the British government, adjusted to the new situation created by the application process.

The papers in this volume raise a number of questions about the interrelationship of the Commonwealth and Europe in the period in question. Contributors discuss the nature and extent of both Commonwealth and European sentiment in postwar Britain, the relationship between domestic and party politics and government policy, the motivation behind British policy in the era leading up to the successive British applications, and the extent to which the Commonwealth and Europe were seen as 'alternatives' for Britain. Questions are also raised about the results of other developments in British–Commonwealth and British–European relations and on the wider international stage, the effects on the wider world of the policies pursued by the existing

EEC states, and the impact of British policy towards Europe (and later British membership of the European Community) on the Commonwealth and individual Commonwealth states. In all the chapters in this volume, an attempt has been made to interpret changes in the triangular British–Commonwealth–European relationship in the light of such wider questions.

An overview by Sir Donald Maitland opens the volume, setting the development of Britain's relations with the Commonwealth and Europe in this period within the context of the priorities and trends in British foreign policy from the late nineteenth century until after 1973. The chapter highlights the persistent failure of British governments to recognize, until too late, their overriding interest in the security and stability of western Europe. Only after the successful creation of the ECSC (European Coal and Steel Community), the EEC (European Economic Community) and Euratom (the European Atomic Energy Community) did the government of Harold Macmillan appear finally to have learned this lesson, and only after many setbacks did it fall to Edward Heath to lead Britain into Europe in 1973. The depth of British attachment to the Commonwealth must take some share of the blame for the belatedness of this recognition of Britain's interests, although there were good reasons why the Commonwealth was seen as being of such importance to Britain's foreign policy in the period immediately after the Second World War. During the negotiations for membership of the European Communities which followed, the Commonwealth was perceived as a significant obstacle. Nevertheless reasonable safeguards were eventually secured for the most vulnerable of Commonwealth economic interests. The potential for conflict between Britain's European and its Commonwealth interests was often overplayed. Since 1973, both the Commonwealth and the European Community/ European Union have continued to flourish, in their different ways.

David Russell sets the scene for the chapters which follow, by examining the attitude of the 1945–51 Labour government to the Commonwealth and to Europe. He identifies a persistent gloss on Labour attitudes (which survived beyond 1945–51) which identified the Commonwealth with high-minded and altruistic internationalism, in contrast to the rather sordid self-interest involved in any turn towards Europe. Nevertheless, David Russell argues that such rhetoric was belied by the record of the 1945–51 Labour government. This government's attachment to the Empire and Commonwealth had far more to do with a traditional notion of Britain's national self-interest than with any woolly-minded idealism. The Empire and Commonwealth still mattered to Britain because they potentially provided crucial economic, political and strategic support for Britain's claim to remain a world power, which in turn was deemed essential to the creation of Labour's New Jerusalem at home. While Labour's Foreign Secretary, Ernest Bevin, was not entirely hostile to Europe, his attitude was characterized primarily by a desire to keep European cooperation intergovernmental and functional, and by vague plans for European imperial cooperation. This was an attitude clearly at variance with the aspirations for Europe to be found on the continent, and the fact that Bevin's views were subject to little opposition either within the cabinet or within Britain more generally illustrated the gulf which still existed between the UK and its western European neighbours. While Labour apologists portrayed the Labour government's preference for the Commonwealth over Europe as the result of idealistic internationalism, in fact Labour's policy in this period was characterized by the pursuit of Britain's perceived national self-interest, to which both the Commonwealth and Europe were secondary.

That such a feeling of shared interests between Britain and the Commonwealth was prevalent at the start of the 1950s, but also that this feeling began to diminish as the decade progressed, is illustrated in the chapter by Sir William Nicoll. At the start of the decade, it was clear that the Commonwealth's political and strategic value to Britain was now limited – a point reinforced by the rise of non-alignment in the 'new' Commonwealth, and by the recriminations surrounding the Suez debacle of 1956. Nevertheless, the Commonwealth preference and sterling area systems were still seen by British policy-makers as being of great value to the UK. Attitudes on this point slowly changed, as it was realized that the Commonwealth offered few opportunities for expanding the trade of the UK, as the preference system (particularly in 'new' Commonwealth countries) began to unravel, and as Britain's position as banker of the sterling area came to be seen more as a liability than as an asset in the context of changes in the global trading environment. Peter Thorneycroft's scuppering of a motion to entrench Commonwealth preference at the Conservative Party conference in 1954 was an early sign; the British government's reaction to overtures from John Diefenbaker proposing a study of means of expanding Commonwealth trade three years later was another. Increasingly, British policy-makers saw cooperation with Europe as the most effective means of safeguarding Britain's economic future. There followed a series of initiatives aimed at securing for Britain the best of both worlds – notably in the form of 'Plan G', the plan for a Commonwealth–European free trade area put forward in 1956. The failure of these initiatives paved the way for the British application to join the EEC in 1961. The 1950s were thus a crucial decade, when changes in Britain's relations with its Commonwealth and sterling area partners paved the way for a reassessment of its relations with its western European neighbours.

John O'Brien's chapter illustrates the increasing divergence between the interests of Britain and those of its Commonwealth partners in the late 1950s in the particular case of Australia, which was to prove one of the most vocal critics of Britain's 1961–63 application to join the EEC. Australia had done particularly well out of the 1932 Ottawa agreements and their subsequent renegotiation in 1956, and looked forward to using its Commonwealth preferences as bargaining counters to open up trade with non-Commonwealth countries. The creation of the EEC therefore came as a shock. Having failed to prevent the EEC from coming into existence (through GATT) the Australian government tried in turn to persuade the UK to act on its behalf, then to persuade the Commonwealth to adopt a collective approach in negotiations with the EEC, and finally to persuade the EEC to enter into direct negotiations with Australia by itself. All such attempts failed, leaving the Australian government (and particularly the Department of Trade, under John McEwen) with few positive options. The result was a kind of siege mentality, in which the threat to Australian trade was exaggerated out of all proportion to the actual effect. A more realistic view was articulated by members of the Prime Minister's Department, but, largely for domestic political reasons, failed to make an impact on official Australian policy. Thus the stage was set for the exaggerated and defensive Australian government reaction when eventually, in July 1961, it was announced that the UK would be seeking to join the EEC.

The interrelationship of the Commonwealth and Europe at different levels of British public debate in the period 1956–63 forms the focus of George Wilkes's chapter. Previous interpretations have tended to assume a deep attachment to the Commonwealth in Britain in this period; the Macmillan government's decision to apply to join the European Communities has therefore been seen as the result of a reluctant realization by the government of the need to make concessions on Commonwealth interests in order to achieve success in its application, or else (less charitably) as the result of a conscious decision to 'sell out' on Commonwealth interests to achieve the same goal. George Wilkes puts forward a different interpretation, arguing that Commonwealth sentiment was by no means a fixed or consistent feature of British attitudes in this period; that the Commonwealth entered into the debate on British European policy in ways that were inconsistent and unpredictable; and that it featured in British politics primarily as a pawn in domestic party politics. Thus, on the one hand, it is not possible to characterize 'pro-Commonwealth' sentiment as being 'anti-European' or vice versa, and, on the other, the salience of Commonwealth issues at different times bore less relation to developments in the negotiations in Brussels than to shifts in domestic and internal party politics. This was seen at all levels of the political debate, including Parliament and the political parties, pressure group activity and the press. Disillusionment with the leadership of Harold Macmillan within the Conservative Party, and the desire to make political capital out of the issue within the Labour Party, ensured that Commonwealth issues achieved greater prominence in 1962–63 than was perhaps merited by the intrinsic importance of the points at issue.

The theme of the malleability of Commonwealth sentiment in Britain is picked up in the chapter by Alex May, which examines the interrelationship between Britain, the Commonwealth and Europe in the period of the first application, in an attempt to discover to what extent the Commonwealth and Europe were, and to what extent also they were perceived as being, 'alternatives' for British foreign policy. Before 1961 the Commonwealth was clearly evolving away from the vehicle of British interests which Whitehall intended it to be; nevertheless, there was little sense that Britain faced a 'choice' between the Commonwealth and Europe. Indeed, the 1961 application was motivated in part by a belief that entry into the EEC would, in the long term, strengthen Britain, and therefore its value to the Commonwealth. However, the decision of the Macmillan government to make the satisfaction of Commonwealth interests a 'condition' of British entry gave (a possibly unavoidable) salience to Commonwealth-related issues, making the task of the Brussels negotiators very much harder, giving Commonwealth governments grounds for playing up each and every point of difficulty (though, as a result of the stance taken by European negotiators, the difficulties were in fact greater than either the government suggested or than had been anticipated), and handing the government's opponents a powerful advantage in the domestic political debate. The Commonwealth therefore became an 'obstacle' to British membership of the EEC. De Gaulle's veto spared the Macmillan government the necessity of convincing its Commonwealth partners and domestic public opinion that it was not sacrificing the Commonwealth for Europe; the indications are that it would have faced an uphill struggle in doing so. While the immediate effect of the application was thus to reveal a strong current of pro-Commonwealth sentiment in Britain, the depth and resilience of that sentiment is open to question. Moreover, the longer-term effect of the application was to reveal the divergence of interests within the Commonwealth, to undermine British attachment to the Commonwealth, and to contribute to an increasingly prevalent view in Britain that the Commonwealth was little more than an outdated and at times embarrassing relic of Britain's former imperial glory.

In contrast to the prominence in government policy and public debate of issues relating to the Commonwealth preference system, issues relating to financial arrangements between Britain and Commonwealth countries in the sterling area received little attention during the period of the first application. In their chapter, Michael David Kandiah and Gillian Staerck suggest that this was a serious omission. Sterling area arrangements were still of great importance to some Commonwealth countries – particularly Australia and New Zealand – both in the financing of their trade and in the way they gained access to capital. Potentially, the Treaty of Rome could be interpreted as requiring Britain to impose controls on extra-European capital movements, and even if this proved not to be the case, sterling area arrangements would have been undermined by the requirement to open up British capital, foreign exchange and financial markets to the 'Six'. Nevertheless, the British government decided to downplay the issue, to the extent of being disingenuous about the potential problems. There were several reasons for this. It was clear by the late 1950s that the sterling area was no longer the asset for Britain that it had been immediately after the Second World War; it was hoped that by not drawing attention to the issue Britain might secure favourable arrangements from the EEC, almost by stealth; it was realized that sterling area arrangements would have to change even if Britain did not join the EEC; and there already was increasing cooperation with western European countries on financial matters. Nevertheless, the lack of British clarity on this issue contributed to the suspicion with which some Commonwealth governments – and particularly the Australasian governments – viewed the British application. The issue of sterling area arrangements thus revealed much about the divergence of British and Commonwealth interests by this stage, and about the manner in which the British government sought to proceed with its application.

That the first British application to join the EEC represented in many respects a turning point in both British–European and

British–Commonwealth relations is illustrated by Philip Alexander's chapter on the second application (launched by the Wilson government in 1967). Both the British government and its Commonwealth partners drew important lessons from the first application: for the British government, the lesson was that it could not hope to negotiate on the whole range of issues affecting the Commonwealth, while for the other Commonwealth governments the lesson was that dispositions had to be made to prevent economic disaster in the event that Britain would, as expected, again attempt to join the Communities. A variety of factors ensured that Commonwealth-related issues would not again achieve the same prominence in the application process: the progressive lowering of EEC external tariffs, both as a result of the harmonization of existing tariffs and as a result of international trade liberalization; the negotiation of new and less 'colonial' association arrangements through the Yaoundé Convention; the diversification of Commonwealth trade; the continued fragmentation and diminution of the Commonwealth preference system (illustrated by the Wilson government's 1964 decision to impose a surcharge on all manufactured imports, regardless of origin); the swift failure of Labour schemes for a Commonwealth 'alternative'; the trend towards regionalism in other parts of the world; the increasing willingness of Commonwealth countries to enter into direct negotiations with the EEC; and the political distancing of Britain from the Commonwealth, as a result of the Rhodesian crisis and other factors. While significant problems remained (particularly in the case of New Zealand), there was in general optimism that these could be overcome. Where this was not the case (notably in Australia), concerns were frequently discounted as being the effect of purely domestic party political concerns. Cumulatively, these changes help to explain why it was that the Labour Party – which in 1962–63 had opposed the Macmillan government's application on the grounds of its effects on the Commonwealth – could by 1967 have effected a complete reversal of its policy. While there was still the potential for significant opposition to this move, the Commonwealth featured far less prominently than it had done in 1961–63.

The final chapter in this volume, by Stuart Ward, examines the effects of Britain's turn to Europe on its closest Commonwealth partners, the three 'old' Dominions, Canada, Australia and New Zealand. Before 1961, the relationship between Britain and the 'old' Commonwealth had already suffered a number of crises and setbacks. Nevertheless, there persisted in each of these countries a belief that, ultimately, the interests of Britain and its Commonwealth partners coincided; that any difficulty was merely temporary, and that the commonality of interest was greater than the divergence. Stuart Ward identifies this belief as a reflection of the 'British race patriotism' which still dominated the political culture of the three 'old' Commonwealth states. The 1961–63 application exploded such comfortable beliefs. The application process made clear not only that Britain and its Commonwealth partners had divergent interests, but that Britain was prepared to contemplate entering arrangements which would permanently reorient it away from its old Commonwealth connections. The process was a painful one. In line with the deeply ingrained precepts of British race patriotism, the three 'old' Commonwealth states initially reacted by appealing to common interest, by expressing naive faith in British good intentions, or by claiming that Britain was in danger of acting in an entirely 'un-British' fashion. Increasingly, however, the politicians of the three countries were forced to acknowledge a real divergence of interest, and to look to a future in which a common 'Britishness' was no longer of any relevance. The 1961–63 application was not the cause of such a parting of the ways. The traditional Commonwealth relationship had been in the process of dissolving for many years. Nevertheless the 1961–63 application brought such issues to the fore, and acted as a catalyst for a wholesale re-examination of national priorities, orientations and interests. After 1963, the relationship between Britain and the countries of the 'old' Commonwealth was never the same again. The British turn to Europe was thus an episode of crucial significance for the 'old' Commonwealth – indeed, perhaps of greater significance for the political culture and development of these three countries than for Britain itself.

Notes

1. I would like to thank Professor Andrea Bosco of South Bank University for first suggesting the conference, and then helping to make it possible; the European Commission for providing much of the finance for it; and the editorial board of *The Round Table* for many useful suggestions, and for help in publicizing the conference. I would also like to thank Tim Farmiloe, Karen Brazier, Alison Howson, all at Palgrave and Anne Rafique for bringing this publication to fruition.
2. Stephen George, *Britain and European Integration Since 1945* (Oxford: Blackwell, 1991); John W. Young, *Britain and European Unity, 1945–99* (London: Macmillan Press – now Palgrave, 2000).
3. John Darwin, *Britain and Decolonisation* (London: Macmillan Press – now Palgrave, 1988) and *The End of the British Empire* (Oxford: Blackwell, 1991).
4. Catherine R. Schenk, *Britain and the Sterling Area: From Devaluation to Convertibility in the 1950s* (London: Routledge, 1994); 'Decolonization and

European Economic Integration: The Free Trade Area Negotiations, 1956–68', *Journal of Imperial and Commonwealth History*, 24/3, 1996, 444–63; 'Britain and the Common Market', in Richard Coopey and Nicholas Woodward (eds), *Britain in the 1970s* (London: UCL Press, 1996).

5. Stuart Ward, 'Anglo-Commonwealth Relations and EEC Membership: The Problem of the Old Dominions', in George Wilkes (ed.), *Britain's Failure to Enter the European Community, 1961–63: The Enlargement Negotiations and Crises in European, Atlantic and Commonwealth Relations* (London: Frank Cass, 1997) pp. 93–107; John B. O'Brien, 'Canadian and Australian Responses to Britain's First Application to Join the EEC, 1960–63', in Andrea Bosco and Alex May (eds), *The Round Table, The Empire/Commonwealth and British Foreign Policy* (London: Lothian Foundation Press, 1997) pp. 551–66.

Notes on the Contributors

Philip R. Alexander is a graduate student at St Catharine's College, Cambridge. He is currently completing his doctorate, entitled 'The Commonwealth and European Integration: Competing Commitments for Britain, 1956–1967'. In 1998 he was awarded a Smuts scholarship to undertake research towards his thesis in Australia and New Zealand.

Michael David Kandiah is Director of the Witness Seminar Programme (Institute of Contemporary British History) at the Institute of Historical Research, University of London. His publications include (with Harriet Jones) *The Myth of Consensus: New Views of British History* (London: Macmillan – now Palgrave, 1996) and (with Anthony Seldon) *Think Tanks and Ideas* (2 vols, London: Frank Cass, 1996 and 1997).

Sir Donald Maitland joined the Foreign (later Diplomatic) Service in 1947. He was UK Representative to the United Nations (1973–74), a member of the Commonwealth Expert Group on Trade, Aid and Development (1975), and UK Representative to the European Community (1975–79). He chaired the Independent Commission on World Wide Telecommunication Development (1983–85), is President of the Federal Trust (1987–), was Pro-Chancellor of the University of Bath (1996–2000), and is now Visiting Professor there.

Alex May is a Research Editor with the *New Dictionary of National Biography*, University of Oxford, and Hon. Secretary/Treasurer of *The Round Table*, the Commonwealth Journal of International Affairs. He was formerly Research Fellow at the European Institute, South Bank University. Among his recent publications is *Britain and Europe Since 1945* (London: Longman, 1999).

Sir William Nicoll was an official of the Board of Trade until 1982 (Deputy UK Representative to the European Community from 1977 to 1982), and Director-General of the Secretariat of the Council of the European Community from 1982 to 1991. He has been the Editor of *The European Business Journal* since 1993.

John B. O'Brien was Senior Lecturer in History at University College, Cork. Previously he held appointments in Australia, at the University of Adelaide, La Trobe University (Melbourne) and the Australian National University (Canberra). He published widely on Irish, Australian and Commonwealth history.

David Russell is a Senior Lecturer in History at Bolton Institute. A former journalist, he took his MA at the School of Slavonic and East European Studies, University of London, and now lectures on and researches modern British and European history.

Gillian Staerck is Editorial Research Officer (Institute of Contemporary British History) at the Institute of Historical Research, University of London. She is editor of the IHR's electronic *Journal of International History* and of *Modern History Review*, and her publications include (with Wolfram Kaiser) *British Foreign Policy, 1955–64: Contracting Options* (Basingstoke, Palgrave, 2000) and (with Michael David Kandiah and Christopher Staerck) *British Documents on Far East Asia, 1945–64* (London: Routledge, 1999).

Stuart Ward is a Lecturer in History at the Menzies Centre for Australian Studies, King's College London. He has worked in the field of European integration studies at the European University Institute at Florence, as well as in Commonwealth history at the University of Sydney. He is co-editor of *Courting the Common Market: The First Attempt to Enlarge the European Communities* (London: Lothian Foundation Press, 1996) and editor of *British Culture and the End of Empire* (Manchester: Manchester University Press, forthcoming).

George Wilkes edited *Britain's Failure to Join the European Communities, 1961–63* (London: Frank Cass, 1997), and is currently completing a doctoral thesis at Gonville and Caius College, Cambridge, on British attitudes to the European Communities, 1956–63. He has published articles on the media and European integration, the European Parliament and the 'European-ness' of the Holocaust.

1
Britain, the Commonwealth and Europe: an Overview

Sir Donald Maitland

When touring Australia in 1884, Lord Rosebery, who was later to become British Foreign Secretary, made a speech in Adelaide in which he referred to 'the British Commonwealth of Nations'.[1] This is believed to be the first use in public of the term 'Commonwealth' in the context of a grouping of nations. It was not until 1926 that this concept was more precisely defined. Lord Balfour, a former Prime Minister, who had returned to office in 1922 as Foreign Secretary, described Britain and the Dominions as 'autonomous communities within the British Empire, equal in status and in no way subordinate one to another in any aspect of their domestic or external affairs, though united by a common allegiance to the Crown and freely associated as members of the British Commonwealth of Nations'.[2] Five years later – in 1931 – this relationship was enshrined in the Statute of Westminster – an Act of the British Parliament which conferred on the Dominions of Canada, Australia, New Zealand, South Africa, Newfoundland and the Irish Free State the power to repeal or amend acts of the British Parliament which applied to them. It was this Act of Parliament which created what came to be known as Dominion Status.

At the time of Lord Rosebery's Australian tour Britain regarded itself as a dominant imperial power, and Lord Rosebery's intention was to suggest a way of linking Britain – the 'mother country' – with the new nations created in other parts of the globe by waves of emigrants from the British Isles. Imperial sentiment at the highest political level had been fostered by Disraeli, whose idea it was that Queen Victoria should be made Empress of India – a title she assumed in 1876. Europe meanwhile had been enjoying a prolonged period of peace inaugurated by the Congress of Vienna in 1815. The Crimean War in the mid-1850s, which was a product of one of the misunderstandings which have

1

bedevilled relations between Turkey and its Slav neighbours, was of marginal importance in political terms.

The main preoccupation of the British in the second half of the nineteenth century was competition with other powers over colonization, particularly in Africa. This may explain why, in the early years of the new century, the British government of the day was slow to appreciate the danger posed by the young, irascible, ill-educated, impetuous German Kaiser. Wilhelm II had built up the German navy and frustrated attempts by his rivals elsewhere in Europe to keep his ambitions in check. Too late Britain and France awoke to the danger. In the summer of 1914 German armies marched into Belgium and the world slid into the 'war to end all wars'. Although for centuries it had been a prime objective of English, and later British, foreign policy to prevent the domination of continental Europe by any single power, the lesson was not learned and, a generation later, hostilities with Germany were resumed in 1939. The war which followed – the most destructive in human history – changed the world. But, as the story of the years which have passed since then has shown, not all attitudes have changed with the times.

Like the course of true love, the process of integration in Europe over the past fifty years has not run smooth. There have been notable successes, such as the binding together by the Treaty of Paris in 1952 of the coal and steel industries in western Europe and the decision in 1986 to create a Single Market. Along the way there have also been serious errors. The first of these was the decision by the British government of the day to stand aside when the negotiations began which led to the signature of the Treaty of Rome in 1957 and the formation of the European Economic Community. With the benefit of hindsight the attitude of those in authority in London at that time seems to have been remarkably obtuse. The advice from British embassies in the capitals of the six countries which were to form the new Community was clear; this was indeed the start of an important process which would directly affect British interests. It was also their view that the determination of the six governments was such that they could be expected to make every effort to ensure the success of the venture. In the event, this advice was ignored.

The political miscalculations of the late 1940s and 1950s undoubtedly damaged British interests. However, it is only fair to judge those decisions in the light of the circumstances of the time. Alone among the countries of western Europe, Britain had been neither defeated nor occupied. For over five years the British had sustained their resistance to Nazi Germany in close alliance with the United States and supported by the countries of the Commonwealth. British and Commonwealth forces played a major part in the liberation of Europe in 1944 and 1945, repeating their success in the North African and Italian campaigns. In South East Asia, the main instrument of victory over the Japanese was the Indian Army, officered largely, but not exclusively, by British officers, but manned by every race from the subcontinent.

The strategic direction of the allies' war effort was essentially in Anglo-American hands. Collaboration between the British Prime Minister and the American President, between their military commanders, between the Foreign Office and the State Department and the respective treasuries, reached unprecedented levels. The intimate working relationships established during the war persisted into the immediately following period when the problems of reconstruction, reconciliation and securing the peace were addressed. Several British ministers and their senior advisers in the key Whitehall departments had been personally involved in these events and the habit of consultation and, where possible, cooperation with the United States was deeply ingrained. If the word 'mindset' had been in vogue in the 1940s and 1950s, it would have neatly and accurately described attitudes which had become instinctive. In the same way, the view London took of the Commonwealth was coloured not by delusions of imperial grandeur, but by grateful recognition of the contribution forces from the Commonwealth had made during the struggle for survival. The Commonwealth relationship had stood the test and deserved to be nourished and adapted to changing circumstances. It was understood that the withdrawal from the Indian subcontinent marked the end of colonialism and this raised important questions about the future of the Commonwealth and the colonial empire. This was recognized by the substitution of the name 'Commonwealth Relations Office' for 'Dominions Office' in 1947.

The critical error at this time was the failure once again of the political leadership in London to heed the warning uttered early this century by the American philosopher, George Santayana, in his monumental *Life of Reason* when he wrote: 'Those who cannot remember the past are condemned to repeat it'.[3] In facing the challenges of the postwar world in the 1940s and early 1950s, political leaders in London seem to have been so determined to preserve the platform of common interest and common objectives from which the victory of the allies had been launched that they neglected the critical lessons to be drawn from the events of the 1930s which had led to the war. At Zurich, Amsterdam and elsewhere, Winston Churchill, as leader of the opposition, had advocated the need for unity in Europe; but, when he returned to power as Prime Minister in 1951, he showed little enthusiasm for the idea he had so eloquently propounded. Anthony Eden, his Foreign Secretary, showed similar indifference to developments across the Channel. He had become absorbed in his self-selected role as peace-maker in Trieste, Austria, Indo-China and finally, and disastrously, in the Middle East.

For those who had suffered under the German occupation, analysis of the causes of the war was a main preoccupation. As early as 1943 Jean Monnet had set out his conclusion and his prescription. He was determined that the allies should not only win the war, but also win the peace.[4] His overriding aim was to find a peaceful way of containing the size and strength of Germany at the centre of the continent and his proposals were designed to this end. His formula was not simply the free flow of goods, but a change in the relationship between peoples who would no longer think in national terms but in terms of shared responsibilities.

The steady progress being made by the members of the European Economic Community following the signature of the Treaty of Rome in 1957 persuaded Harold Macmillan, who had succeeded Eden as British Prime Minister in that year, to consider a reversal of Britain's attitude to the European Economic Community. In the summer of 1960 exploratory talks were held in their capitals with the leaders of the six member states. Commonwealth representatives were also consulted. The lack of enthusiasm of the older members of the Commonwealth – Australia, Canada and New Zealand – had been expected, but the opposition of the major Commonwealth countries in the developing world, and notably Nigeria, was a surprise, since they stood to benefit from the Association Agreements contained in Section 4 of the Treaty of Rome.

These soundings persuaded the British government to test the ground with the members of the Community as a whole. The meeting of the Western European Union on 27 February 1961 provided the opportunity. Edward Heath, who had been appointed Lord Privy Seal to act as deputy to the Foreign Secretary, Lord Home, and spokesman on foreign affairs in the House of Commons, said then: '...if the Common Market countries can meet our Commonwealth and agricultural difficulties, the United Kingdom can then consider a system based on a common or harmonised tariff on raw materials and manufactured goods imported from countries other than the Seven [i.e. the EFTA countries], or the Commonwealth'.[5] The ministers from the member states of the Community present at that meeting, as well as the international press, recognized that this statement represented a significant advance on the previous British position.

British embassies in the capitals of 'the Six' reported a general desire for Britain to join the Community. In some member states it was hoped that, given Britain's world-wide interests, its accession would check any inward-looking tendencies within the Community. Reactions in the Commonwealth were predictably less enthusiastic and members of the British cabinet visited a number of Commonwealth capitals in order to explain the general advantages which would flow from British membership of the Community. However, in Australia and New Zealand in particular this message was ill-received. Despite this, the cabinet endorsed Harold Macmillan's proposal that negotiations to join the Community should be opened. This decision was announced in the House of Commons on 30 July 1961 and was broadly endorsed. Such misgivings as were expressed related to the impact on the Commonwealth and on the sovereignty of the United Kingdom.

Edward Heath was charged with the conduct of the negotiations. He formed two delegations to support him – one resident in Brussels to monitor events in the Community, and the other, a high-level peripatetic team, which would advise him at the negotiating table. Among their other duties these two delegations were required to ensure that Commonwealth countries and other interested parties were fully briefed on the progress of the negotiations through their representatives in Brussels and London.

Even before the formal negotiations began a number of prominent personalities in member states of the Community recommended privately that the best course for the United Kingdom would be to accede to the Treaties of Paris and Rome at once and negotiate the appropriate terms afterwards from within. Though well-intentioned, this advice was unrealistic. The problems affecting the Commonwealth and agriculture in particular were not minor, and acceptance in advance of the provisions of the Treaties would have seriously reduced Edward Heath's room for manoeuvre. Apart from this, there was no prospect of Parliament endorsing such a course of action.

As soon as the negotiations began the nature of the issues to be resolved became clear. In accepting the principle of a single external tariff the United Kingdom assumed an obligation to reduce most existing tariffs. This, and the imposition of quotas, created problems for Commonwealth countries as well as some of the colonial territories. On behalf of the countries of the Indian subcontinent, for example,

Edward Heath put forward a strong case for unlimited entry for tea – a commodity in direct competition with coffee – and at the end of the day this was agreed. Although the trade of colonial territories was safeguarded under the Treaty of Rome, for reasons which were never fully explained a number of the larger territories declined to take advantage of the privileges on offer. In due course the Lomé Convention provided essential assistance to the Commonwealth countries among its seventy-odd beneficiaries.

The agricultural trade of the old members of the Commonwealth was the subject of hard negotiation and reasonable terms were agreed in the spring and summer of 1962. However, immediately before the summer recess the French tabled new proposals for a tariff on imports of temperate zone agricultural products, which would have had the effect of maintaining the price of domestic products. This formula seemed to contradict what had already been agreed. This was not a good omen but, when the negotiations resumed after the summer break, steady progress continued to be made.

During the interval in the negotiations a Commonwealth Prime Ministers' Meeting was held in London. On the eve of the meeting Edward Heath discussed tactics with his senior advisers. Also present at this briefing meeting was the Press Secretary at 10 Downing Street, who disclosed that the Prime Minister was not looking forward to the expected onslaught from his fellow Heads of Government. On cue the Indian Prime Minister put forward the case for special treatment for tea, and the Australians asked for parallel treatment for currants from Victoria. However, the principal objections were political. Harold Macmillan argued that the days of the Empire were over and that Britain would acquire more political and economic influence as a member of the Community than outside it; this would be of direct benefit to the Commonwealth. On the main economic issues he was able to satisfy his colleagues that the best possible terms for their trade in the wider market which would become available to them when Britain joined the Community had been secured, and they left London moderately reassured.

The arguments were overtaken by President de Gaulle's veto in January 1963 and the files were put into the pending tray until Harold Wilson, who had become Prime Minister in 1964, and his Foreign Secretary, George Brown, embarked on their tour of the six member states in the early months of 1967. At a meeting of the Council of the Western European Union in July of that year George Brown submitted a second application on behalf of the United Kingdom for membership

of the European Communities. This application was no more successful. In November of that year it too was vetoed by President de Gaulle.
The files went back into the pending tray.

The arrival at the Elysée Palace of President Georges Pompidou in
1969 altered the situation and offered Edward Heath, when he became
Prime Minister in June 1970, the opportunity to pursue his ambition.
One of his first acts was to register the determination of the new government to pursue the effort to join the European Economic Community. With the bitter experience of 1963 much in his mind, the
Prime Minister decided that the first step should be to persuade the
French of the good intentions of the United Kingdom. A confidential
link was established with the Elysée through which ideas and preoccu-
pations could be discussed in parallel with the formal accession negotiations with the Council of Ministers of the Community.[6]

On the United Kingdom side these negotiations were conducted by a
team led by Geoffrey Rippon, the Chancellor of the Duchy of
Lancaster. In the different atmosphere that now prevailed, the points
of difficulty were steadily reduced. For its part, the United Kingdom
was willing to accept the system of Community finance provided that
an adequate transitional period could be agreed, but it was anxious to
ensure that the legitimate needs of dairy farmers in New Zealand and
Commonwealth sugar producers were accommodated. In the end
access to the large market for New Zealand butter and cheese was
agreed on terms acceptable to New Zealand. Likewise, members of the
Commonwealth Sugar Agreement approved the terms negotiated for
their exports. By the middle of May 1971 sufficient progress had been
made through both channels to justify a meeting between the Prime
Minister and the French President. This took place in Paris on 20 and
21 May.

President Pompidou told Edward Heath that, for historical reasons,
France and Britain carried a special responsibility in regard to developing countries. Those in the Commonwealth would enjoy the same
preferential treatment as the former colonies of existing members of
the Community. Pompidou's main anxiety was the position of sterling
as a reserve currency. It was a basic principle that the currencies of the
member states should enjoy equal status. The ultimate goal of economic and monetary union set out in the Treaty of Rome could not
otherwise be attained. Edward Heath agreed that every effort would be
made to reduce the sterling balances, provided that the interests of
those holding the balances were not harmed and that no unacceptable
burden was placed on the United Kingdom's balance of payments.

It was also important that the rate of the pound should be maintained. The understandings reached during these critical discussions at the Elysée Palace were subsequently endorsed by the Community Council of Ministers on 7 June 1971.

When their talks had ended, President Pompidou led Edward Heath into the Salon des Fêtes, where his predecessor had pronounced his veto in 1963. The press were already assembled. When he made clear that there were no longer any obstacles to Britain's entry into the European Economic Community, everyone present understood that they were witnesses to a moment of historical importance. Neither Europe, nor the United Kingdom, nor the Commonwealth would be the same again.

In the years that have passed since then, the producers of temperate foodstuffs in the Commonwealth have found new markets and have forged new relationships. The developing members have taken full advantage of the Lomé Agreements and defend their interests in the councils of the World Trade Organization.

What, then, of the future? The European Union will pursue its way along the path that does not run smooth. The Commonwealth will continue to develop its unique personality and to exercise its influence for good in every corner of the world. The international community as a whole will be the beneficiary. So there is no reason today for the noble and worldly-wise Lords Rosebery and Balfour, or any other architects of the Commonwealth in ages past, to turn in their graves.

Notes

1. See S. R. Mehrotra, 'On the Use of the Term "Commonwealth"', *Journal of Commonwealth Political Studies*, 2/1 (1963) 1–16.
2. Nicholas Mansergh, *The Commonwealth Experience*, Vol. 2, *From British to Multi-Racial Commonwealth* (London: Macmillan, 1982) pp. 27–8.
3. George Santayana, *Life of Reason*, Vol. 1 (London: Archibald Constable & Co., 1905), chapter 12: 'Flux and Constancy in Human Nature'. See Paul-Henri Spaak, *The Continuing Battle: Memoirs of a European* (London: Weidenfeld & Nicolson, 1971), chapter 29.
4. Jean Monnet, *Memoirs* (London: Collins, 1978), chapter 12.
5. *The Times*, 28 February 1961.
6. Stuart Ball and Anthony Seldon, *The Heath Government, 1970–74: a Re-Appraisal* (London: Longman, 1996), chapter 11.

2
'The Jolly Old Empire': Labour, the Commonwealth and Europe, 1945–51

David Russell

In a speech to the Labour party conference in 1962, Hugh Gaitskell put the case for Britain maintaining ties with the Commonwealth in preference to joining the EEC. 'The Commonwealth', he said, 'means something to us and to the world. Where would our influence be in the world without the Commonwealth? It would be much less. And I believe with all my heart that the existence of this remarkable multi-racial association can make a great contribution to the ending of the Cold War'. Gaitskell then added an emotional personal touch:

> If I were a little younger today, and if I were looking around for a cause, I do not think I should be quite so certain that I would find it within the movement for greater unity in Europe. I would rather work for the Freedom From Hunger Campaign; I would rather work for War on Want, I would rather do something to solve world problems.[1]

Gaitskell's remarks – which could have been made by virtually any leading Labour party figure over the past half century – reveal a great deal about the attitudes and assumptions which underpinned postwar Labour thinking about Europe and the Commonwealth, ideas which have influenced much of British thinking to the present day. They are, though, a set of attitudes and assumptions based on a misunderstanding, or perhaps a misrepresentation, of Labour's relations with the Commonwealth and Europe after 1945. For Gaitskell, like British politicians before and since, was not simply stating a preference, but staking a claim for the moral high ground for two key areas of Britain's postwar foreign policy. Is this claim, though, justified by the record? What were the ideas underpinning the British rejection of Europe and the relationship with the Commonwealth, and how powerful have they been?

Underpinning Gaitskell's rhetoric was the assumption that there was an either/or choice for Britain in its relations with Europe and the Commonwealth with, for Gaitskell, the choice being between the dry economics of provincial Europe and the idealism of working to solve the problems of the world within the framework of the Commonwealth. The idea that the Commonwealth, or for later right-wing critics of Europe the 'special relationship' with the United States and the economic internationalism of the global market-place, was inherently a more idealistic frame of reference than Europe was and is a continuing strand [*Example of why*] k of interest in the po... economic success of [...] was argu... nd remarkable for a f... [*Britain chose Commonwealth*] ng was his dismissal [...] l idealism.

Gait... [*Over Europe*] ... more than just his faith in the Commonwealth and his indifference to Europe. There was a deeply cynical and selfish side of Gaitskell's strongly idealistic rhetoric. 'Where', he asked ...edly, 'would any ... be in the world without the Commonwealth? The Commonwealth... it play a role in ending ... It was This 'Third Party' idea was ... d Labour Party dream ... [*Early Years*] ... earlier to Gaitskell's great rival Aneur... Bevan ... ation from the ... government, he argued for a British-led Commonwealth 'third force' ... n international relatic..., to counter the superpower blocs of the USA ... and the USSR. Bevan had outlined his idea in a speech in New Delhi, where it had been crushingly rejected by the Indian Prime Minister Nehru. Gaitskell's attempt to revive the concept the year following the building of the Berlin Wall was even less credible. Gaitskell was not really presenting the Commonwealth as an independent force in its own right, but as the symbol and proof of Britain's Great Power status. The influence to which he referred was not 'the Commonwealth's influence', but, tellingly, 'our influence'.

Alongside this nationalistic strategic view (disguised as internationalism) was an emotional view of much of the Commonwealth as a focus for British charity with high-minded British idealists operating a political and economic soup kitchen for the less privileged (who, presumably, were expected to be duly grateful and defer to British leadership). The Commonwealth was thus presented as the ultimate reason, and moral justification, for Britain's rejection of Europe – the implication being that Britain had, since the end of the Second World War, selflessly rejected national economic benefits available in Europe in favour of a higher moral loyalty to the Commonwealth. The appeal of this argument had been demonstrated the previous year when Harold Wilson, another of Gaitskell's rivals and his successor as Labour leader, dismissed Harold Macmillan's application to join the EEC on the grounds that 'we are not entitled to sell our friends and kinsmen down the river for the problematic and marginal advantage of selling washing machines in Dusseldorf'.[2]

Gaitskell also assumed that the development of the multiracial Commonwealth was, at least in part, a British achievement, and thus reflected Britain's moral superiority in foreign affairs. How true was this? The record of the Labour government in the crucial years immediately after the Second World War, it will be argued, hardly justified Gaitskell's emotional outburst. Gaitskell was, perhaps, continuing the approach established by the Labour government after 1945, of presenting British national self-interest as idealistic internationalism.

Labour's foreign policy after 1945, far from being based on internationalism, as was often claimed and often believed, was founded on a traditional concept of national self-interest. The rationale was clear: Britain was, and had to remain, a Great Power, and therefore had to maintain its Empire as a strategic and political counterbalance to the USA and the Soviet Union. A strong economy was needed to underpin this political ambition and a strong economy, it was assumed, needed the Empire, as a resource base and a market. Labour's domestic agenda and foreign policy were thus linked – with the Empire as the key. Europe, in this analysis, would always be an external factor – an important aspect of foreign policy, but never the central concern. Labour, after 1945, was not looking forward either to European integration or to the multiracial Commonwealth, but back to the days of national self-interest and imperial control.

The driving force behind Labour's foreign policy was Ernest Bevin, surprisingly appointed Foreign Secretary after Labour won the general election in July 1945. Bevin, originally regarded as a purely domestic figure with his long years as a trade union leader, rapidly established himself not simply as the formulator of Labour's view of international affairs but as one of the architects of the postwar order. Two beliefs dominated Bevin's thinking and gave substance to his policies: first, that Britain must remain one of the 'Big Three' Great Powers, with a unique contribution to make to world affairs; and secondly, a deep suspicion of, and passionate ideological opposition to, Soviet communism. This mixture of realpolitik and ideological conviction provided the framework for Britain's relations with Europe and the Empire/Commonwealth.

Bevin, like Winston Churchill, believed in the 'three circles' concept of Britain's international role, with Britain seen as maintaining a unique holding position in world affairs at the heart of the three over-lapping spheres of the Empire/Commonwealth, the special relationship with the United States and Europe.[3] The key point of this concept was not simply that Britain was unique in being involved in all three circles, but that it was at the centre. Britain was the buckle holding together the non-communist world. This Anglocentric view dominated Bevin's thinking and explains the anguished debates in Cabinet over the strings attached to the US loan in 1945, and also Labour's rejection of supranational structures for Europe. For Bevin, as for later governments, Britain was never simply part of a wider international structure, but had a unique role to play.

To later critics (and some supporters) Bevin was essentially a robust imperialist with a strong anti-communist streak. This, though, ignores the attention Bevin paid to European problems immediately after 1945 and the considerable efforts he made – in peculiarly difficult circumstances – to create a distinct British model for the emerging framework of western European cooperation. For Bevin, though sceptical of European integrationist rhetoric and dismissive of the Labour left's idea of a Third Way between the Soviet Union and the USA, was not opposed to the idea of European economic cooperation. Far from being a little Englander, he had always been considerably ahead of most thinking in the Labour movement about international cooperation and the future of Europe. As early as 1927 he had shocked the left at the Edinburgh Conference of the Trades Union Congress by arguing for a European Customs Union, which would create the continental common market enjoyed by American industry.[4]

After the war Bevin was one of the first British political leaders to appreciate the changed international economic framework, and was quick to understand the relationship between economic policy and foreign policy strategy (one of the reasons why he had hoped, and expected, to go to the Treasury when Labour formed the government in 1945). This appreciation of the link between economics and foreign policy – and the importance of Europe – was demonstrated in Bevin's first speech as Foreign Secretary to the House of Commons in August 1945. He argued that lack of trade and lack of security had created a vicious circle in the interwar years. 'Now at last we have found our way to what is, for the time being, security. Therefore, this is the time to break the vicious circle. It is with this in mind that HM Government regard the economic reconstruction of the world as a primary object of their foreign policy.'[5] Europe was the focus of much of Bevin's foreign policy activity immediately after 1945. His dream of breaking the vicious circle within the framework of the security won by the defeat of Nazi Germany proved even more demanding – and necessary – with the onset of the Cold War.

From 1945 Labour's attitude towards Europe contained five key elements. First, there was an appreciation of the parlous economic state of most of the continent. Secondly, there was an early suspicion of the intentions of Soviet foreign policy. Thirdly, there was the specific, and in terms of all European developments central, issue of the future of Germany. Fourthly, there was the question of US intentions towards postwar Europe with Britain anxious to prevent an American retreat into isolationism (as had happened after the First World War). Finally, running through all the other issues and providing the defining aspect, there was the question of British national self-interest.

Bevin's appreciation of the link between economics and foreign policy dictated his policies towards Europe (as they would later towards the Empire), and developed from 1945 to 1947 against the background of Britain's and Europe's economic plight and the growing strategic challenge of the Cold War. Bevin's appreciation of the dual nature of the challenge facing Europe was demonstrated at the 1945 London Conference of Foreign Ministers, when he famously clashed with Soviet Foreign Minister Molotov. From then on, until the creation of the Marshall Plan in 1947, Bevin worked to encourage the nations of western Europe to help themselves, without waiting for an American lead. Crucially, though, according to his biographer Alan Bullock, 'he never believed that western Europe was strong enough to provide for its own security or recovery without American help'.[6]

By 1947 it was clear that the idea of British leadership of Europe was neither economically nor politically possible. Against the background of a serious financial crisis, which threatened Labour's domestic programme, Bevin enthusiastically seized the opportunity presented by US Secretary of State George Marshall's proposals for a European Recovery Programme. Marshall made his famous speech at Harvard University on 5 June. From 12 July Bevin chaired a conference on European economic cooperation, attended by representatives from 14 nations. By the autumn a new infrastructure for west European cooperation and reconstruction had been created.

Even at this stage, the British government was not prepared to abandon its own distinct view of international cooperation. The new structure 'was always carefully tailored to the British view that economic cooperation should be multilateral and functional in approach rather than a kind of economic integration as urged by the Americans and the French'.[7] Bevin opposed the American idea of a strong supranational executive to oversee the aid programme. The United States wanted the executive to be made up of economic ministers. The British representative, though, was not a minister but a Treasury official, Sir Edmund Hall-Patch, who had been seconded to the Foreign Office and was directly responsible to Bevin. Crucially, Oliver Franks, generally regarded as one of the leading figures in the Foreign Office, had been moved from Paris to become the British Ambassador in Washington. The switch of the high-flying Franks at that vital stage of European development underlined Bevin's determination to maintain Britain's independent role – and for that to be clearly understood both by Europe and the United States.

The establishment of the Marshall Plan ended the first stage of Labour's European policy. The Labour government had since 1945 attempted to balance the growing strategic challenge of the Cold War with the immediate crisis of European reconstruction, while maintaining a distinct independent position. The fundamental – and ultimately insoluble – problem was Britain's continuing economic weakness. From the acceptance of the US loan in 1945 to Chancellor Hugh Dalton's 'annus horrendus' of 1947, it had become increasingly clear that Britain lacked the immense financial resources needed to maintain its global imperial position, confront the Soviet Union in the Cold War, reconstruct the domestic economy, carry out its New Jerusalem social agenda – and lead the economic reconstruction of western Europe. In its changing relations with Europe, Britain did not lack interest or ideas. It lacked money.

These economic constraints did not, however, end Labour's determination to pursue a distinct foreign policy. On the contrary. With the political and economic framework of western Europe now apparently settled (in a way acceptable to Britain), Bevin now turned his attention to the future of the Empire.

It would be wrong to suggest that Labour took reluctantly to its imperial role, or that it was forced upon it by the onset of the Cold War. Labour demonstrated a remarkably strong ideological and emotional commitment to the Empire. Despite its history, the party was never alienated from the idea of Empire. It saw the Empire as 'ours' (a great national achievement and legitimate source of patriotic pride) rather than 'theirs' (the creation of a social and political order the Labour party had been formed in order to overturn). Surprisingly, the left wing of the party, though critical of the leadership over the Cold War and Britain's position in the postwar world, never produced a thorough-going critique of the government's imperial role. At a time of immense change in international relations Labour failed to produce a distinct 'socialist' imperial policy, nor did it begin to develop an alternative philosophy defining the role of the Empire. The leadership slipped comfortably into the imperial robes of previous Conservative governments, while the left wing focused on the Cold War and the domestic agenda. What criticism there was from within the Labour movement came from outside the party in government – from the colonial development lobby in the Fabian Society, from the books of Leonard Woolf and others, and from the one-man campaign for colonial independence of Fenner Brockway.

Underpinning this ideological position was an unexpected depth of emotion. One of the striking features of the Labour government's attitudes towards its imperial legacy and the challenges of postwar European developments was the emotional imbalance between the two areas. Labour never enthused about Europe either politically or culturally. Clement Attlee, in a preface to a history of the Labour party in 1948, stressed the party's peculiarly British identity and its lack of links with the continental socialist tradition.[8] The contrasting (and racially highly selective) identification with Empire and Commonwealth was made clear in a party publication, *European Unity*, in 1950: 'In every respect except distance we in Britain are closer to our kinsmen in Australia and New Zealand on the far side of the world than we are to Europe'.[9] This important and revealing comment demonstrated the duality (and hypocrisy) of imperial ties: emotional personal links with the old white Commonwealth but, by implication, traditional imperial attitudes of ownership towards the nonwhite colonies. Herbert Morrison's remark to *The Times* in 1946, that 'we are friends of the jolly old Empire and we are going to stick to it', reflected the party's emotional commitment to its imperial legacy.[10]

Perhaps surprisingly for a party which prided itself on its internationalist outlook, Labour had produced little in the way of policy or philosophy towards the Empire or Europe when it took office in 1945. The election manifesto was dominated by the domestic agenda, with only a passing reference to 'the planned progress of our colonial dependencies'. The lack of an alternative policy towards the Empire reflected the widely held view in the party that Labour would continue

Britain's control of the colonies for the indefinite future. Arthur Creech-Jones, the future Colonial Secretary, had underlined Labour's imperial position in a speech in the House of Commons the previous year. 'Britain today is in the colonies and she cannot withdraw', he said, 'nor do I think that she should'.[11] The realpolitik behind Labour's imperialism was clearly and enthusiastically articulated by Bevin, when he addressed the Party's pre-election conference in May 1945:

> You will have to form a government which is at the centre of a great Empire and Commonwealth of nations, which touches all parts of the world and which will have to deal with every race and every difficulty, and everyone of them has a different outlook on life. I would ask the conference to bear this in mind. Revolutions do not change geography, and revolutions do not change geographical need.[12]

The importance of Bevin's imperial commitment was that it was not simply the elevation of traditional foreign policy realpolitik over social- ist idealism, but that it reflected his deep conviction that the pursuit of Labour's New Jerusalem domestic agenda was linked to the continua- tion of Britain's world role. 'Bevin', as P. S. Gupta has argued, 'had been persuaded that the building of a welfare state in Britain was consistent with, and indeed necessarily linked with, the maintenance of Britain as a world power'.[13] For Labour, the assumed international framework for the domestic economy was the traditional one of the Empire as a resource base and market, not the new one of European cooperation.

Bevin's defence of Britain's imperial role was, as ever, blunt and unapologetic. It would, though, be wrong to see Labour's new imperial- ism as simply Bevin's policy – an aspect, perhaps, of his Cold War stance. None of the other leading figures in the government had a rad- ical conception of Britain's place in the postwar world. 'None of them', John Darwin has argued, 'regarded with distaste the continuation of Britain's colonial empire or objected to Britain's pursuit of an indepen- dent great power position based on her pre-war spheres of influence outside Europe'.[14] Labour never saw Britain, either emotionally or intellectually, as a post-imperial power needing to redefine its identity in a new Europe. Stafford Cripps, like others in the party, apparently underwent an intellectual sea-change during the war, moving from anti-imperialism to nationalism. As Chancellor of the Exchequer from 1947 to 1950 he would preside over 'the economic integration of the Empire/Commonwealth, in the form of the sterling bloc, with all the enthusiasm of a pre-1914 Chamberlainite Tory'.[15]

The war years had been a key factor in reviving imperial enthusiasm and converting some Labour figures to the virtues of Empire. It was perhaps also a key factor in deepening existing suspicions of European involvement. The secretary of the Fabian Colonial Bureau, and one of the Labour movement's leading thinkers on colonial matters, Rita Hinden, said in 1944: 'I was a rabid anti-imperialist at one time but one cannot ignore the fact that there is a certain sympathy, an intangible something, which holds the British Empire or Commonwealth together and which cannot be wholly explained in terms of material advantage'.[16] It would, however, be a mistake to assume that Labour's postwar attitude towards Empire stemmed simply from the memories of the war. Labour's imperialist roots ran very deep.

Labour had been thinking about creating a more 'progressive' colonial structure before the war, the aim being to replace the traditional imperial framework with a 'socialist' colonial relationship. However, the important point with regard to Labour's vague musings about the future of Empire is that independence was not seen as an option. A radical minority, represented by people like the journalist H. L. Brailsford, had developed an anti-imperialist critique, especially with regard to India, but this did not influence the party leadership. Labour's central concern was not colonial independence, or even development, but the role the colonies could play in helping the British economy. In 1929 the Labour government introduced the Colonial Development Act (taken straight from the Conservative election manifesto). Despite the title, the Act was designed not to develop the colonies but to help the British unemployment problem.

Radical ideas for imperial development or cooperation were rejected or ignored. Oswald Mosley argued in the House of Commons in 1930 for a Commonwealth economic plan to tackle the developing economic crisis: 'a systematic planning organization to rationalize the machinery of imperial trade, to put through a big merger, to unify a lot of small businesses into one highly centralized organization to insulate these islands and this Commonwealth from the shocks of world conditions'.[17] Revealingly, Mosley's radical proposals were rejected by Ramsay MacDonald not because of their impact on the future of the Empire/Commonwealth, but because they threatened British living standards. This concern with national self-interest was reflected at the same time by Bevin who, supporting the TUC's memorandum calling for the control of the supply of raw materials within the Empire, warned:

> I see expenditure of millions of pounds going for the development of areas where native races have not yet begun to be industrialized.

You talk about the coal trade. Ought there not to be some control against the possible development of coal in Tanganyika which might come into competition with coal from here?[18]

Bevin's concept of Labour imperialism had its roots, therefore, not in the postwar era, but in his response to the domestic economic problems of the 1930s. As early as 1930, John Kent has argued, Bevin 'could not discuss imperial economic matters without a political reference to what was to dominate his post-war thinking': the idea that Britain was not finished as a great power and that the Empire would provide the means of restoring its position.[19] Another strand in Bevin's evolving prewar attitude towards Empire was his concept of Europe's role. Bevin had floated the idea of European imperial cooperation in 1938 when he wrote in his Union journal:

The great colonial powers of Europe should pool their colonial territories and link them up with a European Commonwealth instead of being limited British, French, Dutch or Belgian concessions as is now the case. Such a European Commonwealth, established on a European foundation, would give us greater security than we get by trying to maintain the old balance of power.[20]

The idea of European imperial cooperation was one of Bevin's favourite ideas immediately after the end of the war and contrasted with the federalist and integrationist ideas for the future of Europe being advocated by Jean Monnet and others.

In 1938, Bevin attended a conference in Australia organized by Chatham House and the Australian Institute of International Affairs. This was to prove a turning point in his thinking about Empire and its relationship with Britain's economic prospects. On his return he talked enthusiastically about the potential of the Empire, viewing it not (as one might expect from a socialist) in terms of a political problem, but as a source of huge economic potential for Britain. It was then that Bevin made the link between Britain's domestic economic problems and its status as a world power. From then on he would argue that the Empire was crucial for the economic well-being of Britain as well as being the main component in Britain's global political position.

The lack of intellectual opposition to Bevin's view was remarkable, given the ferment in the party over most other issues after 1945. A key factor was the long-standing belief, shared by many in the Labour party as well as Conservatives, that Britain drew her economic and political strength (and to some extent her identity) from the Empire. John Darwin has argued that this attitude among Britain's political elite dates back to the publication of J. R. Seeley's influential *The Expansion of England* in 1883, with its Whiggish view of the growth of England from island state to world power.[21] The Labour leadership's acceptance of this view of British history was, perhaps, reflected in Clement Attlee's choice of Arthur Bryant as his favourite historian. Europe, in contrast, was seen instinctively as an economic rival and an area of potential conflict.

The one man who might have made a difference was Aneurin (Nye) Bevan, one of the few leading Labour figures to have made explicitly anti-imperial speeches. When Churchill made his famous defence of Britain's imperial role in his Mansion House speech of 1942, declaring that he had 'not become the King's First Minister in order to preside over the liquidation of the British Empire', it was Bevan who launched an anti-imperialist attack in the Commons. 'If members opposite think we are going through this in order to keep their Malayan swamps, they are making a mistake', he warned – not a sentiment shared by the rest of the party leadership.[22]

Bevan's biographer, John Campbell, has suggested that had Bevan been Foreign Secretary 'he would certainly have made more explicit his support for anti-colonial liberation movements in the Empire for which Bevin had little sympathy'.[23] After his resignation from the government, Bevan showed his interest in developing an alternative foreign policy when he floated the idea of the Commonwealth becoming a 'third force' in world affairs. In an address to the Indian Parliament in 1953, Bevan argued that the creation of a third force led by the Commonwealth would lead to a realignment in world affairs and force the Soviet Union and the United States 'to see wisdom'. Interestingly Bevan, who prided himself on his internationalist outlook, never saw Europe as developing such a world role. The more realistic Nehru, the Indian Prime Minister, rejected the idea as fanciful and dangerous. Talk of a third force 'frightens and embarrasses people', he said, adding, pointedly, that the cause of peace was best served 'without too much shouting'. On his return to Britain, Bevan revealed the national self-interest at the heart of his talk of a 'third force' when he urged the Labour party to 'put itself at the head of those forces which are genuinely concerned to mediate between the two great power blocs'.[24]

During the government reshuffle in 1950, Bevan wanted to move to the Colonial Office. The idea was rejected by Attlee, for reasons (according to Hugh Dalton) which reveal a great deal about the true nature of Labour's imperial policies. Bevan, Dalton wrote, 'was not to be trusted (a) not to waste money, and (b) not to be carried away by his colour prejudice, pro-black and anti-white'.[25]

If Bevan's inability to influence imperial policy is easily explained, the role of the Prime Minister, Clement Attlee, is more of a mystery. Although he staunchly supported Bevin's foreign policy line (especially over the Cold War, where Bevin's suspicions and distrust of the Soviet Union chimed with his own sentiments), Attlee at times hinted at a potentially very different attitude towards the Empire and Commonwealth from the one his government eventually took.

Attlee's involvement with Empire began in 1927, when he was a member of the Simon Commission on Indian constitutional reform. India remained at the centre of his imperial attitudes when he became Prime Minister. He remained, according to Kenneth O. Morgan, 'an old India hand; he retained his veneration for the Crown and the Imperial connection for all his socialism'.[26] Attlee's concept of empire and commonwealth was never clear-cut. Despite his emotional identification with the old India he was realistic about accepting partition and an accelerated timetable to independence. Towards the rest of the colonial legacy he demonstrated a mixture of hard-headed realism, romanticism, indifference and an element of genuine racial idealism rarely demonstrated by his colleagues. While Bevin and the military chiefs dreamed of new Imperial bases, Attlee penned 'pungent Cabinet papers which called for Imperial retreat and the removal of outlying British bases in the new era of long-range air power'.[27] Yet, in 1949, it was Attlee who raised the question of creating an Army of Africa to replace the Indian Army.

The possibility of Attlee creating an alternative philosophy and policy towards the Empire and thus, by implication, towards Europe was first raised with the response to the Atlantic Charter of 1941. The Charter, described by Wm. Roger Louis as 'essentially a press release not a formal document',[28] posed problems for Britain's traditional imperial stance. Article 3 stated that all peoples should have the right to choose their own form of government. Churchill, not surprisingly, chose to interpret this as applying only to Europe, not as a questioning of the legitimacy of the European colonial empires.[29] Attlee, though, offered a very different interpretation. He was, by coincidence, addressing a group of west African students the day after the Charter was released. 'Our enemies, the Nazis', he declared, 'set up a monstrous and ridiculous racial doctrine. They declare themselves to be a master race to which the rest of us are inferior, and if they assert that claim in respect to Europeans you may be quite assured they will apply it to everyone else – Asiatics, Africans and everyone'. In language quite distinct from that of Churchill, or indeed many of his colleagues among the Labour leadership, Attlee talked of 'us', British and Africans, when he attacked the Nazi concept of the master race. He went on to argue that the principles of the Atlantic Charter applied to all the peoples of the world, not simply Europeans. 'It was', comments Louis, 'a significant public indication that the Atlantic Charter might have consequences reaching far beyond Europe'.[30]

Attlee further developed his questioning of the future of the Empire at a ministerial meeting in 1942 held to formulate government policy for the Far East. Attlee stood out against the traditional imperialist line being argued by Anthony Eden (Foreign Secretary), Lord Cranborne (Secretary of State for Colonies) and Leo Amery (Secretary of State for India), and, for the first time, raised the issues of the economic cost of a postwar empire and the role of domestic public opinion. Challenging the traditional assumption that the Empire was politically popular as a symbol of patriotism, he doubted whether the British public would be prepared to pay the price of the postwar colonial development and defence schemes being mooted. 'The people of this country', he argued, 'would not wish to have the exclusive privilege of paying for the defence of all these territories at the expense of their own standard of living and for the benefit of certain privileged classes'. The alternative to the continuation of the Empire in its existing form, with consequent high defence costs and impact on domestic living standards, was to create a new form of international colonial cooperation. 'Instead of national armaments he favoured an international force and a general sharing of the burden of defending these colonial areas. This could be achieved by international control and administration of these territories'.[31]

Attlee was not suggesting colonial independence as an alternative to Empire. He was, though, arguing for a profoundly different form of colonial order to the one his government inherited in 1945 – and very different from the one his government presided over. At a time when Churchill and Bevin were seeking ways to maintain the Empire in its traditional form, Attlee, alone among postwar political leaders, was sounding a note of scepticism about the strategic purpose of the Empire and the willingness, or ability, of the British people to meet the costs. In a memorandum in September 1945, he opposed the idea of expanding the Empire by including Italian colonies as trust territories as had happened with German and Ottoman territories after the First World War. 'After the last war', he wrote, 'we acquired large territories. The world outside, not unnaturally, regarded this as a mere expansion of the British Empire. Trusteeship will appear to most people as only old mandates writ large'. Apart from his ideological opposition to imperial expansion and his concern about the cost of over-ambitious global commitments, Attlee was one of the first (and very few) British politicians to appreciate that the strategic value of the Empire had changed with the rise of air power and the development of atomic weapons.

> Quite apart from the advent of the atomic bomb, which should affect all considerations of strategic area, the British Commonwealth and Empire is not a unit that can be defended by itself. With the advent of air warfare the conditions which made it possible to defend a string of possessions scattered over five continents by means of a fleet based on island fortresses have gone.[32]

A set of policies built on these sceptical (and in terms of the impact on the British economy, more realistic) foundations would have given the Labour government a distinct post-imperial philosophy while, potentially, leading to a new attitude to Europe. Why Attlee, so tenacious in other areas, moved away from his initial radical position can, perhaps, best be explained in terms of the practical foreign and domestic political and economic crises the government was confronted with. The parlous state of the economy after the war may have persuaded Attlee that, as Bevin argued, the colonies were Britain's only resource base. This traditionalist view of the economic importance of the colonies was a continuing major obstacle to any change in British attitudes towards Europe. More important, though, was the gradual hardening of the Cold War. Attlee, no less than Bevin, was determined that Britain would play its full part – and the Empire, despite his earlier doubts, increasingly appeared to be a strategic asset rather than an economic and political cost. Another important factor was Attlee's patriotism and constitutional conservatism which, perhaps, steadily diluted his earlier radicalism.

The question of what kind of imperial and Commonwealth policy a Labour government motivated by the ideas Attlee articulated during and immediately after the war would have produced thus remains intriguing if unanswerable. Instead, the Labour government which took power in 1945 embarked upon a deliberate policy of 'new imperialism'. The basic driving force behind this policy was a traditional view of British national self-interest. In 1948 the Cabinet Secretary, Sir Norman Brook, advised Attlee that the government's policies towards the Empire/Commonwealth fell within the normal definition of imperialism.[33] That reality, though, was something Labour was acutely uneasy with. To square the circle of being a progressive socialist movement presiding over a traditional Empire, Labour developed a rationale of social and economic development for the colonies which, in turn, led the government (including even the generally robust and unapologetic Ernest Bevin) into the double-talk and special pleading reflected more than a decade later in Gaitskell's rejection of Europe.

Labour went to great lengths to stress that its colonial role was profoundly different from the old imperialism – an indication, perhaps, of its continuing unease. Ernest Bevin declared in 1948 that 'we have ceased to be an imperialist race; we dominate nobody'.[34] The party's handbook for speakers for the same year claimed that '[i]n all the areas under our control we have abandoned the old type of capitalist imperialism', and (in a sentence which sums up the contradictions of Labour's entire approach) that 'Imperialism is dead but the Empire has been given new life'.[35] Nevertheless the conservatism, and underlying racism, of Labour's postwar attitude to Empire was foreshadowed in a remark by the deputy leader Herbert Morrison in 1943: 'It would be ignorant, dangerous nonsense to talk about grants of full self-government to many of the dependent territories for some time to come. In those instances it would be like giving a child of ten a latch-key, a bank account and a shot-gun'.[36] Labour had clearly been affected by the wartime revival of Imperial enthusiasm which had an impact on even the most unlikely enthusiasts. Labour's commitment to an imperial policy after the war was spelled out at the Party's pre-election conference in May 1945, when Bevin put forward the classic realpolitik argument that 'revolutions do not change geographical need'.[37] Bevin was, as Lord Listowel observed, 'at heart an old fashioned imperialist, keener to expand than contract the Empire'.[38]

Bevin's central belief that Britain was, and had to remain, a great power, and that this meant retaining the Empire, was underpinned by three other linked ideas. First, he was one of the first British politicians to link the continuation of Empire with Britain's role in the developing Cold War. As early as 1945, in a debate in the House of Commons, he described the Soviet Union's demand for a place in the Mediterranean as 'coming across the throat of the British Commonwealth'.[39] The idea that the Empire/Commonwealth was threatened by Soviet ambitions, and that it had a vital role to play for the western allies, became one of Labour's justifications (especially in dealings with the Americans) for its continuation.

Secondly, Bevin was acutely conscious of the anti-imperial stance of the United States. The future of the empire was, from the earliest days, one of the most contentious aspects of the 'special relationship'. American opposition to imperialism on ideological grounds had been clear in the 1930s and during the war had developed into a critique which saw imperialism as politically wrong, a source of international conflict, and a potential brake on postwar world economic progress. The feeling that the war was being partly fought to save Britain's colonies was summed up in the American joke that SEAC (the South East Asian Command) really stood for Save England's Asiatic Colonies. Bevin was determined that Britain would retain its great power status and maintain control of its own foreign policy. The Empire, he believed, was the guarantor of Britain's status and – unlike Europe and the Cold War – a sphere of political and economic activity outside the control or influence of the United States.

Thirdly, Bevin reversed Attlee's old scepticism about the cost of Empire and the potential impact on Labour's radical domestic agenda by presenting an imperial policy as a necessary foundation for domestic economic recovery and progress. Far from being Disraeli's millstones, the colonies were presented as a vast untapped reservoir of markets and raw materials.

The end of the Raj has sometimes been thought of as the beginning of the end of Empire, or at the very least the start of post-imperial thinking in the Labour government. Indian independence has been hailed, in retrospect, as one of the Attlee government's great progressive achievements. The reality is very different. Although the Labour government was prepared to move further and faster towards a settlement than the Conservatives, the final result of full independence for the two states in the old Raj was not Labour's original intention. Far from wishing to preside over full independence, Labour's hope in 1945 was to create a new Dominion settlement under which a united India would accept internal self-rule while maintaining a close and subservient economic, military and foreign policy relationship with Britain.

The Labour government was anxious to maintain Britain's strategic position in the Indian subcontinent and, far from welcoming independence, went to considerable lengths to try to find alternative solutions. In the end, Labour's dream of an all-India government remaining under the British defence and foreign policy umbrella failed because of Britain's military and financial weakness, the rapidly deteriorating position in India, and growing pressure from a United States unhappy with the thought of Britain maintaining any imperial role. The final blow to Britain's plans came not with independence, but with partition. Crucially, 'the first and greatest casualty of partition would be the Indian Army. This was one of the reasons why the Attlee government was so reluctant to sanction partition'.[40] Far from being a triumph for Labour's diplomacy, the end of the Raj was a shattering blow to the government's entire Imperial policy. Partition, the breaking up of the Indian Army and the refusal of India and Pakistan to lock themselves into economic and military ties amounted to 'the graveyard of Labour's hopes'.[41]

The loss of the Raj, however, did not lead to a lack of interest in the Empire or the development of a post-imperial policy by Labour. On the contrary, it was followed by a determined attempt to reposition and develop the remaining Empire. 'Britain's decision to quit India was not intended to mark the end of Empire', as John Gallagher has argued. 'Quitting India has to be seen in the light of the simultaneous decision to push British penetration deeper into tropical Africa and the middle east'.[42]

The depth of Labour's commitment to its imperial legacy is reflected in Gallagher's claim that 'not until the 1940s was there a serious version of imperialism in tropical Africa'. Africa, became the centre of attention for Labour's 'new imperialism'.[43] In 1949 Attlee asked the Colonial Office and the chiefs of staff if it would be possible to raise an African army to replace the army of India.[44] To Bevin Africa was the philosopher's stone that would solve Britain's domestic economic problems and restore her international financial and political standing. In 1948 Bevin (dubbed the Imperial Micawber by Gallagher) waxed emotional about the potential: 'If we pushed on and developed Africa we would have the US dependent on us, eating out of our hand, in four or five years'.[45]

The two architects of Labour's policy were Bevin, who was the main driving force behind Labour's strategic vision for a revived Empire, and the Colonial Secretary Arthur Creech-Jones, who devised and articulated the policy of social and economic development of the colonies which provided the moral justification for the 'new imperialism'. Their argument was that the apparent continuation of Britain's traditional strategic and political role was more than balanced by Britain's altruistic role in the social and economic development of the colonies. Was there ever a balance, though? How far was Britain prepared to go in promoting economic and social development in the colonies if this led to demands for matching political developments, or clashed with the interests of the British domestic economy?

The idealistic (if patronizing) interpretation of Labour's colonial policies was provided by Creech-Jones in a debate in the Commons in 1947, when he presented the government's version of Lord Milner's 'civilising mission': 'We are in the general service of the colonial peoples. We hope that there will be a common appreciation of our efforts, that they are able, by our service, to make a contribution to the larger life of mankind'.[46] Behind this idealistic claim, though, was a policy of imperialism which saw the Labour government ignore and attempt to stall growing demands for political change and consistently manipulate colonial economic development in the interests of the British economy – at times to the clear disadvantage of the colonies themselves. 'The basic fact', as David Fieldhouse has argued, 'is that between 1945 and 1951 Britain exploited those dependencies that were politically unable to defend their own interests in more ways and with more serious consequences than at any time since overseas colonies were established'.[47]

The sterling area continued through into the 1950s as a device for supporting the pound against the dollar – to the disadvantage of colonies such as Malaya and the Gold Coast, who were compelled to build up balances in London thanks to their dollar earnings. Britain's policy of price controls and bulk buying also penalized the colonies. The gap widened between the world price and the price paid to the colonies for their raw materials (except for the 'white dominions', who were able to demand the world market price). Finally, the much-heralded financial investment in Britain's colonies was remarkably modest – under the colonial development and welfare acts investment totalled only £8 million per year from 1946 to 1951, while during the same period colonial sterling balances rose in London by £150 million and, by 1951, West African marketing boards held £93 million on deposit in London. In those five years the colonies were lent or given £40 million by Britain but had been forced to lend, or tie up in London, £240 million. 'This', as Fieldhouse has commented, 'was disinvestment on a grand scale', the 'most accurate assessment of the extent of British imperial exploitation'.[48]

One long-term negative impact of Britain's economic approach to the colonies was that they missed out on the Korean War commodity boom, which could have allowed some of them to cash in on rising raw material prices and lay the foundations for future development. This chance was lost because of the economic framework maintained by the Labour government: a modern form of social imperialism which cushioned the British consumer from the real costs of world prices and postwar reconstruction, at the expense of colonial development.

Later Labour apologists have suggested that the various comments by Bevin, Herbert Morrison, Hugh Dalton and other ministers of the time represented the reactionary views of the old guard in the Party, not the idealism of the rank and file. They have pointed instead to the 'progressive' rhetoric of Creech-Jones and his supporters in the Fabian Colonial Bureau who were, it has been argued, attempting to create a socialist policy for the colonies. On the fundamental issue of independence, though, there was little real difference between the old imperialists and the 'progressives'. Fenner Brockway's was an isolated voice in 1946 when he attacked the government's colonial policy, arguing that 'the colonial peoples do not desire Britain to be good to them. They desire freedom to decide their own good'.[49] The limitations to Labour's progressive social development approach were made clear by Rita Hinden of the Fabian Colonial Bureau when Kwame Nkrumah called for 'absolute independence'. Dr Hinden (seen as one of the radical thinkers behind Labour's approach, and far removed from Morrison's jingoism) replied that 'British socialists are not so concerned with ideals like independence and self-government but with the ideal of social justice. When British socialists look at the Eastern Europe of today they ask themselves whether independence in itself is a worthwhile aim'.[50]

The long-standing claim that Britain sacrificed its own economic interests in Europe because of loyalty to the Commonwealth can therefore be dismissed. Dean Acheson believed that Britain's objections to the Schuman Plan stemmed from its view of national economic self-interest not because of Commonwealth ties.[51] P. S. Gupta agreed and pointed out that while rejecting the Schuman Plan in Europe the Labour government in 1950 was also lukewarm about plans for Commonwealth economic cooperation.[52] Labour after the war did not hold back from Europe because of loyalty to the Commonwealth, nor did it set out to replace the Empire with a multiracial Commonwealth of independent states. It was motivated, in both areas, by a strong sense of national self-interest. Europe and the Empire were objects of British policy – and, despite the rhetoric, always secondary.

Notes

1. Ioan Davies, 'The Labour Commonwealth', *New Left Review*, 22 (December 1963) 75.
2. Alan Sked and Chris Cook, *Post-War Britain: A Political History*, 4th edn (Harmondsworth: Penguin, 1993) p. 170.
3. For a discussion of Bevin's foreign policy, see Alan Bullock, *Ernest Bevin, Foreign Secretary* (Oxford: Oxford University Press, 1985), and John Kent, *British Imperial Strategy and the Origins of the Cold War, 1944–1949* (Leicester: Leicester University Press, 1993).
4. Bullock, op. cit., note 3 above, p. 103.
5. Ibid., p. 104.
6. Ibid., p. 541.
7. Kenneth O. Morgan, *Labour in Power, 1945–1951* (Oxford: Oxford University Press, 1984) pp. 271–2.
8. Sked and Cook, op. cit., note 2 above, p. 71.
9. Anne Orde, *The Collapse of Great Britain: The United States and British Imperial Decline, 1895–1956* (London: Macmillan Press – now Palgrave, 1996) p. 170.
10. *The Times*, 12 January 1946.
11. David Goldsworthy, *Colonial Issues in British Politics, 1945–1961* (Oxford: Oxford University Press, 1971) p. 14.
12. P. S. Gupta, *Imperialism and the British Labour Movement, 1914–1964* (London: Macmillan Press – now Palgrave, 1975) p. 281.
13. Ibid., p. 284.
14. John Darwin, *Britain and Decolonisation: The Retreat from Empire in the Post-War World* (London: Macmillan Press – now Palgrave, 1988) p. 71.
15. Ibid., p. 72.
16. Wm. Roger Louis, *Imperialism at Bay, 1941–1945: the United States and the Decolonization of the British Empire* (Oxford: Oxford University Press, 1977) pp. 15–16.
17. Davies, op. cit., note 1 above, p. 77.
18. Ibid., p. 77.
19. Kent, op. cit., note 3 above, p. 121.
20. John Saville, *The Politics of Continuity: British Foreign Policy and the Labour Government, 1945–1946* (London: Verso, 1993) p. 94.
21. Darwin, op. cit., note 14 above, p. 73. For a discussion of the impact of Whig history on British official thinking, see Edwin Jones, *The English Nation: The Great Myth* (London: Sutton Publishing, 1998), chapter 7, pp. 218–47.
22. John Campbell, *Nye Bevan and the Mirage of British Socialism* (London: Weidenfeld & Nicolson, 1987) p. 120.
23. Ibid., p. 194.
24. Michael R. Gordon, *Conflict and Consensus in Labour's Foreign Policy, 1914–1965* (Stanford, CT: Stanford University Press, 1969) p. 54.
25. R. D. Pearce, *The Turning Point in Africa: British Colonial Policy, 1938–1948* (London: Frank Cass, 1982) p. 96.
26. Morgan, op. cit., note 7 above, p. 193.
27. Ibid., pp. 192–3.
28. Louis, op. cit., note 16 above, p. 122.
29. Mansion House Speech, 1942.

30. Louis, op. cit., note 16 above, p. 125.
31. Ibid., pp. 192–3.
32. Ibid., p. 549.
33. Kent, op. cit., note 3 above, p. 151.
34. Stephen Howe, *Anticolonialism in British Politics: The Left and the End of Empire, 1918–1964* (Oxford: Clarendon Press, 1993) p. 144.
35. Ibid.
36. Louis, op. cit., note 16 above, p. 14.
37. Gupta, op. cit., note 12 above, p. 281.
38. Peter Hennessy, *Never Again: Britain, 1945–1951* (London: Jonathan Cape, 1992) p. 233.
39. Saville, op. cit., note 20 above, p. 98.
40. John Gallagher, *The Decline, Revival and Fall of the British Empire* (Cambridge: Cambridge University Press, 1982) p. 145.
41. David Fieldhouse, 'The Labour Governments and the Empire-Commonwealth, 1945–1951', in Ritchie Ovendale (ed.), *The Foreign Policy of the British Labour Governments, 1945–1951* (Leicester: Leicester University Press, 1984) p. 91.
42. Gallagher, op. cit., note 40 above, p. 144.
43. Ibid., p. 145.
44. Lawrence James, *The Rise and Fall of the British Empire* (London: Little, Brown, 1994) p. 533.
45. Gallagher, op. cit., note 40 above, p. 146.
46. Davies, op. cit., note 1 above, p. 82.
47. Fieldhouse, op. cit., note 41 above, p. 95.
48. Ibid., p. 98.
49. Pearce, op. cit., note 25 above, p. 124.
50. Ibid., pp. 110–11.
51. Gupta, op. cit., note 12 above, p. 301.
52. Ibid., p. 300.

3

Britain and the Commonwealth in the 1950s

Sir William Nicoll

At the opening of the decade after the war, the symbol of the Commonwealth was a column four abreast with its head at the Cenotaph and its tail in Princes Street, Edinburgh. This was the tally of the dead of the UK, Empire and Commonwealth armed forces since 1914. Twice what was called British outside Britain had joined in the war declared by the country called Britain.

What was this Commonwealth? Unlike most international gatherings, it had no charter or constitution. These were not considered the English way of doing such things. More tellingly, no charter could have been drafted without endless anguish ending in wearisome banality: better to use the symbolism of a monarch rebranded 'Head of the Commonwealth'. The British government, which paternalistically organized most Commonwealth gatherings throughout the 1950s, imposed upon itself severe restraint in its Commonwealth dealings. It has been said that there was a tacit understanding that the content of all Commonwealth gatherings was a search for consensus, that is, a minimum. When consensus was manifestly unattainable, as it was right at the creation in the Kashmir dispute, the subject was dropped from the agenda. There it stayed, as those who venture to intervene find out to their discomfiture.

It has also been said that for most of the 1950s, the Commonwealth had not much to say to itself about world security and foreign policy. The old Commonwealth was in the Western camp; the biggest of the new nations, India, was not. It was also preparing the doctrines of Panch Shil and the policy of non-alignment proclaimed at the Bandung conference in 1955. Non-alignment was compatible with membership of a Commonwealth without foreign policy and with rapprochement with the Soviet Union, especially when the Bulganin–Khruschev diarchy offered tempting trade deals, with easy financing and the transfer of technology and training for investment in heavy industry under India's derivative Five Plans, drafted by Professor Mahlanobis, who applied his knowledge of meteorology to economic development as scientific adviser to the Cabinet.

So what was the substance of the Commonwealth connection which British governments of the 1950s and beyond regarded as one of the 'pillars' or 'circles' of their external relations? There was trade. Britain's trade with the Commonwealth was an inheritance from the mercantilism of a past era. In 1660 Charles II directed, in what would today be called the mission statement he sent to the Councell of Trade:

> 11. You are to consider the generall State and Condicion of our forreigne Plantacions and of the Navigacion, trade and several Commodityes arising thereupon and how farr theire future improvement and prosperitie may bee advanced by any discouragement, imposicion and restraint upon the inportacion of all goodes or Commodityes with which those Plantacions do abound and may supply these our kingdoms.[1]

That is to say, a preferential import regime. Three centuries later, we still wanted cheap imports, especially food, which in cost of living terms give us international competitive advantage. As my old respected chief, Douglas Jay, put it: 'The higher food import prices [he was attacking EEC membership] together with the abandonment of subsidies on our home-produced food, would force up living costs and prices of all our exports, with loss of exports throughout the world'.[2]

We likewise wanted to hold onto our privileged access to traditional markets: it was now called Commonwealth preference. There was unrelenting US pressure to abandon the economic expression of colonialism against which they had themselves rebelled. It appears in the communiqué from the Atlantic Conference of 1941 with the commitment: 'they will endeavour, with due respect to their existing obligations [note the British reservation], to further the enjoyment by all peoples of access on equal terms to the trade and to the raw materials of the world which are needed for their prosperity'.[3] The US kept up the pressure for equal access. In the conditions attached to the postwar loan they tried to bring an end to discrimination at large, with the attack focused on sterling convertibility, of which more below. But Commonwealth preference hung on. There were two respectable supporting arguments.

Whitehall economists believed postwar that primary products were likely to remain scarcer and dearer than they had been in the 1930s. The shortages which developed during the Korean War and which occasioned the setting up of the Ministry of Materials were evidence. There was a theory that the earth's resources were finite. This suggested that the UK interest was in maintaining close ties with the Commonwealth, with its ample resources of primary commodities and dollar earning potential. European integration would lead to specialization in manufacture for the European market, which would weaken the capacity for saving or earning dollars. *Ergo*, links with Europe must not weaken links with the Commonwealth. There was perhaps the additional flavour or aftertaste of Fabian concepts of development and partnership, as expounded by the Colonial Research Bureau in its advocacy of development corporations. They never recovered from John Strachey's ill-starred groundnuts scheme in Tanganyika.

The second argument for upholding preferential trade arrangements within the Commonwealth was their possible value as negotiating currency, one of the reasons for the 1932 general tariff. The mandarins of Whitehall might have doubts about their material benefits to Britain, but they looked forward, in retrospect rather overoptimistically, to the prospect of trading preferences away in return for reductions in the then restrictively high US tariffs. If the US was so worked up about unequal access, then it must pay to see it go.[4]

The trade argument itself was powerful. In 1949–50, 53 per cent of British exports went to the Commonwealth, and 46 per cent of its imports came from there.[5] (In 1998, 55 per cent of our import trade in goods and 58 per cent of our export trade in goods was with the EU.) The 1949–50 export share was roughly the same as prewar; the import share a little higher. Canada suffered, more or less willingly: Britain practised dollar discrimination and forced it on the rest of the sterling area. We then did twice as much trade with the Commonwealth as we did with OEEC members. But there were strains. The Indian subcontinent was strapped and imposed import licensing restrictions, without preference. India was not even paying new money for some of its imports. It was perfectly properly running down, except by conversion into dollars, the half a billion or so of sterling balances which had largely accumulated from local Crown procurement during the war (£10 billion at 2000 prices). As long as they were not drawn down, the sterling balances of all the Commonwealth countries which had them were cheap loans for the British Exchequer. Throughout the 1950s the UK's net liabilities to the rest of the sterling area were steady at around £2½ billion at prevailing prices.

At the beginning of the 1950s, and with the sole exception of Malaya, Britain and the Commonwealth countries were each other's most important bilateral trading partners. To take a few figures: over 50 per cent of the imports into Australia, New Zealand and British West Africa came from Britain, over 40 per cent of South Africa's and 25 per cent of India's and Pakistan's. On the export side, 73 per cent of New Zealand's went to Britain, 66 per cent of British West Africa's, 56 per cent of Northern Rhodesia's, 40 per cent of Southern Rhodesia's, 39 per cent of Australia's, down to 16 per cent of Pakistan's exports. Alongside the trading links there were the hefty investments, in primary industry, in commodity production and in manufacture. Barclays, Grindlays, Lloyds and Hong Kong and Shanghai were ubiquitous in retail banking, from monumental halls to shacks in African villages. British insurers had branches in all main towns. British publishers gave on the flyleaf branch addresses in Toronto, Sydney, Bombay, Johannesburg.

But already in the mid-1950s perceptions were changing. In anticipation of possible mood swings, the floor at the Conservative Party Conference of 1954 sought to pass a motion which would have entrenched Commonwealth preference as a fixture in economic policy. The motion was seen off by Peter Thorneycroft, then President of the Board of Trade and later one of the early Europhiles. The significance of the political head of the Department deemed to be profoundly attached to the traditional Commonwealth trade links opening his mind to new thinking should not have been underestimated.

It would be an exaggeration to suggest that there was a worked-out Commonwealth trade policy. The 1957 initiative is an example. John Diefenbaker, a.k.a. Dief the Chief, had a fixation about Canadian dependence on the USA. In 1957, at the Commonwealth Conference in London, he proposed a study of Commonwealth trade expansion, and talked about a target of increasing trade exchanges with Britain by 15 per cent. The study was undertaken, but was sidetracked by the British suggestion that Dief's purpose would be best served by an Anglo-Canadian Free Trade Area. Was this serious, or was it a spoiling manoeuvre? If the latter, as it more probably was, it worked. The free trade area and the expansion plan were stillborn. It was at the meeting of Commonwealth Finance Ministers in 1958 to follow up Dief's suggestion that an interconnection between Britain's economic relations with the Commonwealth and with Europe, which was to dominate British policy for years to come, became explicit. The communiqué said:

The Commonwealth Ministers recognised that the establishment of an outward-looking Free Trade Area in Europe would broaden the advantages to be derived from economic integration in Europe not only by the United Kingdom but by all the other participants. *This was regarded as important as it would contribute to agreed Commonwealth policies of expanding world trade* [emphasis added].[6]

Diefenbaker had his revenge in the negative Ottawa communiqué issued during the Macmillan government's charm offensive of 1961, when Commonwealth leaders were told of the British decision to explore the terms of possible membership of the European Communities.[7]

The other subject which engaged most of the Commonwealth and much of its meetings was the management of what were then called the 'gold and dollar reserves of the sterling area', most of which were banked in London. Membership of the sterling area, with the privileged access which it gave to the British financial market, matched by the influence which this handed to British governments, did more than anything else to hold the Commonwealth together. But it also imposed costs on the British economy in the form of constant pressure on the reserves. It was an extra complication in Britain's other involvement in monetary arrangements of the European Payments Union, which reconciled fixed exchange rates with bilateral balances. Such ideas as bringing the rest of the EPU into the sterling area were considered but dismissed as fanciful.

In 1952 the Treasury brought forward the 'Robot' plan for a float of the pound, partial convertibility of current sterling earnings, and the blockage (euphemistically called 'funding') of most of the sterling balances. The centre of the scheme should be familiar to us today. The strain was to be taken by the exchange rate and not by the reserves. In the Cabinet discussion 'Robot's' champion, Rab Butler, the Chancellor, was disarmingly frank: 'It would be a shock to the Commonwealth members of the sterling area and might bring one or two of them to the point of deciding to leave the Sterling Area altogether'.[8] It would certainly have been a shock to Commonwealth Finance Ministers, who only a few weeks before had been discussing other financial and budgetary measures to reduce imports from outside the area. The plan died. The devastating attack on it came from the Lord Privy Seal, Lord Salisbury, who said that it would create very great political difficulties and was against the policies pursued for the previous twenty years.[9] The Commonwealth factor was not the only negative argument, but it was a cogent one. The 'Robot' interlude helps to illustrate British solicitude for the Commonwealth during most of the 1950s, from which it was an unusual departure. It was deeply ingrained into Whitehall that it must take account of Commonwealth interests in all its doings with external implications.[10]

The invitation to join the discussions in 1950 of a European Coal and Steel Community – which explicitly was to be the foundation of a European Federation, and which was interpreted to imply a pre-commitment to the Schuman Plan – had to be measured against the realities of trading and financial interest, as well as the psychological perceptions of what Britain was in the world. The latter was caught by Lord Home when in 1985 he wrote: 'The British public was still too near to the glory of Empire to accept the role for Britain of just another country in Europe'.[11]

In 1952, with the change of government in Britain, Harold Macmillan showed his European credentials by seeking reconsideration of attitudes towards the Schuman Plan and the European Defence Community then being elaborated. In his memoirs, he quotes extensively and approvingly from a memorandum which Lady (Juliet) Rhys Williams, with some overstatement, sent him in 1953:

> Britain cannot possibly remain a world power on the present basis. The Commonwealth is non-existent, except as a Coronation pageant...It is only by dominating Europe now that [Britain] can continue to appear sufficiently strong to command the respect of the rest of the world, including the Dominions, and before long, the Colonies too. The Sterling area can disappear overnight if Britain ceases to be a world power on a recognisable scale, and much if not all of our overseas trade can disappear at the same time...Far from shedding her Empire, she will hold it to her because she will be strong enough to act as a magnet, which is not the case today.[12]

Like Butler, Macmillan was seen off by the imperialism or 'tepid Europeanism' (Macmillan's words) of Lord Salisbury: 'We were not a continental nation, but an island power with a Colonial Empire and unique relations with the independent members of the Commonwealth. Though we might maintain a close association with the continental nations of Europe, we could never merge our interests wholly with theirs'.[13] But the wind of change was already blowing strong. Decolonization was in the logic of history. Most of it, the subcontinent excluded, lies outside the period of this chapter: Ghana in 1957, Nigeria in 1960, Gambia in 1963. The effective decolonization of another British zone of influence, the nationalization of the Suez Canal in the watershed year of 1956, the humiliating aftermath and later revelations of duplicity and complicity[14] permanently changed Britain's worldwide relationships. The Commonwealth had been at best cool towards Eden's actions, and India vehemently hostile.[15] In the Ceasefire Resolution in the General Assembly of the UN on 2 November 1956, only Australia and New Zealand voted with Britain, France and Israel.

My own first-hand experience of Commonwealth diplomacy was gained in India in the second half of the decade. We charted in what we called 'Sovindreps' the growing Soviet infiltration into an India which was happy to receive it, especially as the counterweight against the US backing, including arms supplies, of Pakistan. We saw there in 1959 an event which only a few years before would have been unthinkable: a considered British government decision, enthusiastically supported by the CRO – normally the apologist for a Commonwealth country – to suspend export credit insurance in our trade with India. It would have reverberated through world financial markets to India's grave detriment. Only the powerful intervention of our man in Delhi, Malcolm MacDonald, and my boss, the Senior Trade Commissioner, Gerald MacMahon, secured a reconsideration. Already the Commonwealth star was waning in the Westminster sky. My first job on reporting for duty in Delhi had been to 'top and tail' a communication to the Indian Ministry of Foreign Affairs reporting on the meeting of the Six at Messina in June 1955 and the British government's detachment from it. By the close of the decade the Macmillan government came to the conclusion that the dictum which Churchill had pronounced in 1930 was no longer sustainable: 'We are with Europe, not of it'. The 1930 Foreign Office minute on the Briand plan for a European Community could not hold either: '... what would seem necessary would be careful study of the course of events coupled with a discriminating sympathy for all such reorganisation of Europe as is not in unjustified contravention of British rights and interests, of the peculiar and indissoluble connexion of the British Isles with the world wide territories of the British Empire ...',[16] and so on; it was the doctrine of 'cordial caution' towards new plans for an ever closer union. We hear it still today as some kind of third way between Europhilia and Euroscepticism.

By 1959 the attempt to maintain the Commonwealth trade link, one of the binding forces of the structure, but simultaneously to enter into a free trade with the new European Community, the so-called Plan G, had shown itself to be a chimera. The next imagined option would be to be a member of the Community, but with special safeguards for Commonwealth trade. That vision was rudely dispelled by President de Gaulle in delivering his veto on the first application: 'England in effect is insular, she is maritime, she is linked through her exchanges, her markets, her supply lines to the most diverse and often the most distant countries...'[17] The ten years from the British refusal to commit its fortunes to European integration and its decision to pursue the Commonwealth role which it had found after the loss of Empire ended with Britain moving towards its first unsuccessful attempt to enter into what the Treaty it had declined to sign called a 'destiny henceforward shared'[18]... in Europe.

Notes

1. W. Cunningham, *Growth of English Industry and Commerce*, Part II (Cambridge: Cambridge University Press, 1917) p. 913.
2. Douglas Jay, *After the Common Market* (Harmondsworth: Penguin, 1968) p. 62.
3. Winston Churchill, *The Second World War*, Vol. III, *The Grand Alliance* (London: Cassell, 1952) p. 353.
4. The contention that Commonwealth preference was going out and that there would be equal access to the larger Commonwealth markets was not brought forward in the EEC's 1973 GATT Article XXIV negotiations, noticeably with the USA, following the transition of the British tariff to the Common Customs Tariff.
5. All historical statistics are taken from *The Sterling Area, an American Analysis* (Economic Cooperation Administration, Special Mission to the United Kingdom, 1951).
6. Treasury Press release, in Miriam Camps, *Britain and the European Community, 1955–1963* (Oxford: Oxford University Press, 1964) p. 128n.
7. Ibid., pp. 341–51.
8. Sir Edwin Plowden, *An Industrialist in the Treasury* (London: André Deutsch, 1989) p. 150.
9. Conclusions, 28–29 February 1952, Public Record Office, Kew, London (PRO), T 236/3242, CC(52).
10. 'We must always bear in mind our relationship with the Commonwealth and its value as a stabilising factor in the free world...': Paper for Cabinet committee meeting, PRO, CAB 134/1820, EQ(60) 33.
11. Edmund Dell, *The Schuman Plan and the Abdication of British Leadership in Europe* (Oxford: Clarendon Press, 1995) p. 299; Plowden, op. cit., note 8 above, p. 172.
12. Harold Macmillan, *Tides of Fortune, 1945–55* (London: Macmillan Press – now Palgrave, 1969) p. 476.
13. Kenneth O. Morgan, *The People's Peace* (Oxford: Oxford University Press, 1990) p. 134.
14. On the affair of the Sèvres memorandum, see Avi Shlaim, 'Collusion at Suez', *International Affairs* 73/3 (July 1997) 509, and Edward Heath, *The Course of My Life* (London: Hodder & Stoughton, 1998) p. 177.
15. Selwyn Lloyd, *Suez 1956* (London: Jonathan Cape, 1978) p. 227.

16. T. C. Salmon and W. Nicoll, *Building the European Union* (Manchester: Manchester University Press, 1997) pp. 14–15.
17. Press Conference, January 1963, ibid., p. 88.
18. Preamble to the Treaty of Paris establishing the European Coal and Steel Community.

4
The Australian Department of Trade and the EEC, 1956–61

John B. O'Brien

The lines of Australia's response to post-1956 trade developments had been set as far back as 1932, following the success of the Australian negotiators at the Ottawa Conference. The Department of Trade, the successor to these negotiators, wholly endorsed the approach taken at Ottawa and were convinced that such an approach would continue to pay dividends for years to come, thereby placing Australian trade policy within an Ottawa time warp that was ultimately to prove quite sterile. John McEwen, the Minister for Trade, believed that the tried technique of bartering trade preferences was still the answer in 1956 to all Australia's trading problems.

The success of the 1956 renegotiation of the Ottawa agreement, which confirmed Australia's traditional access to the British market without having to concede as many preferences as hitherto in its own market to British exporters, opened new fields for McEwen and his staff. Now the Ottawa system could be extended to non-Commonwealth countries, to the mutual benefit of Australia and whatever 'fortunate' country it chose to solicit. However, for that design to work, it was vital that an international free trade system be promoted. There was no country more dedicated to the concept of free trade than Australia, as long as it did not apply to itself. Australia would only benefit from preferential trade if its customers in its preferential markets were forced to operate on free trade terms, preferences being only effective when selective. McEwen readily endorsed the 1952 Commonwealth collective approach which sought to broaden Commonwealth trade to include dollar area countries, and which thereby implied liberalizing world trade. Nevertheless, when an independent British Commonwealth Committee examined the progress of the scheme in 1958 it found that 'so far as the reduction of discrimination against dollar imports is concerned, Australia has tended to lag behind other Commonwealth countries', because the 'Australian licensing system remains sharply discriminatory against dollar area imports'.[1] The formation of GATT in 1947 was a windfall for Australia. Recalcitrant countries could now be hauled before that body and forced to purge their anti-liberal misdemeanours.[2] But not Australia. From the outset McEwen made it quite clear that Australia's existing discriminatory preferences were exempt from GATT.[3] Then, in 1958, when about to court non-Commonwealth countries with preferential baits, he was emphatic that 'negotiations with European countries and with the countries of South-East Asia would be broadly outside GATT'.[4] Thus, with the rest of the world moving towards freer trading and with Australia commanding an arsenal of preferences that could now be spread more widely, McEwen confided to his Cabinet colleagues in 1957 that the time was ripe for a major breakthrough in Australia's external trade.[5] He did not foresee or anticipate the impact which the creation of the EEC in 1957 would have on world trade or the way in which existing trade patterns would be transformed.

So accustomed had McEwen and his government colleagues become to the existence of the Commonwealth trading bloc that they were totally blind to the possibility of a rival bloc or blocs appearing. They were convinced that the Commonwealth bloc would remain the sole trading entity in the world, with Britain as its centre and Australia basking in the security which it provided. Those outside that privileged sphere were relegated to mere shadow boxers waiting for a partner of substance to emerge from the Commonwealth – Australia itself being among the more eligible. Thus, when confronted first by the six EEC countries, then by a possible 17-member Free Trade Area, next by the seven EFTA countries, then by a possible Nordic Common Market, and finally by the possibility of a Common Market for Latin America, McEwen and his Department were, to say the least, confused if not totally disorientated. R. W. B. Clarke of the British Treasury wrote to Sir Henry Lintott of the Commonwealth Relations Office in November 1957 that he had got the impression from Sir Edwin McCarthy, the Australian High Commissioner in London, that in Canberra there existed 'quite considerable confusion and indeed chaos in the Australian administration on this series of questions'. He went so far as to suggest either that the British Trade Commissioner in Canberra be recalled and trained to instruct the Australians on the intricacies of the EEC, or that Australian civil servants be sent to London 'for two or three weeks to receive indoctrination first hand and then to return and for this process to be repeated every few months'.[6] This did not eventuate. When questioned in the

Senate nearly two years later about the implications for Australia of the Common Market, Senator Spooner, Leader of the Government in the Senate, confessed that he 'experienced difficulty in answering questions relating to the European Common Market because of its complexities'. He then referred to eight countries being involved, although he could only recollect the names of six.[7]

It was galling for McEwen and his colleagues that just when the pattern of international trade with all its inherent contradictions seemed to favour Australia, the terms changed. However, because of tradition and also because of an inability to understand or cope with the altered environment, the Department of Trade did not change, preferring instead to follow proven paths, despite the altered international trading topography. For that reason all Australia's efforts to cope with such a novel situation were doomed to failure, and indeed could not have been expected to succeed. Exchanges of preferences on a bilateral basis found scant support in the trading environment of the mid-1950s.

McEwen's first response to the establishment of the EEC was to have it dismantled. He dispatched a note to Brussels in the Australian government's name, condemning the creation of an exclusive trading bloc in Europe sharing preferences among themselves to the exclusion of outside suppliers,[8] failing to acknowledge that 'the Six' were in many ways merely refining the Ottawa system itself. In that note, he deplored 'the level of the common external tariff and the administration of quantitative restrictions and other non-tariff controls on trade'. The EEC ignored McEwen. He next resorted to GATT, and again, on his own initiative, sought to haul the Six before a 'special session of that body'.[9] This was also unsuccessful, mainly because GATT was not prepared to oppose the EEC and took refuge behind procedural and technical barriers. This was despite the fact that, according to the Sub-Committee of the Commonwealth Liaison Committee on European Trade Relations, there was 'no doubt of the incompatibility of a great deal of what the EEC had in mind with Article XI of GATT' (or for that matter with Article XXIV 5a, which 'required that the duties of the common tariff proposed by countries forming a Customs Union shall not on the whole be higher than the general incidence of duties applicable in the constituent territories prior to its formation').[10]

In fact, most of the EEC countries had already managed to opt out of their obligations under GATT. Germany, for example, was 'unwilling to promise any date for the removal of the restrictions in respect of basic agricultural products, a range of manufactured foodstuffs made from these and a range of fruit and vegetables'. Instead it merely pledged at the fourteenth session of GATT in May 1959 'to use her best endeavours to remove such restrictions at the earliest possible date and meanwhile endeavour to improve conditions of access to the German market for all contracting parties'.[11] Luxembourg was recognized to have special problems because of its very small area and 'was accorded a waiver of indefinite duration'. France and Italy had been granted 'waivers' from GATT obligations because of balance of payments difficulties at the ninth session in March 1955.[12] Belgium and the Netherlands, 'while ceasing to claim balance of payments justification for restrictions', nevertheless blatantly persisted with their restrictive practices. The fact that in March 1955, at the time the so-called 'hard core waiver decisions' were being negotiated, the US was granted a waiver of indefinite duration and with no effective limitations in respect of the restrictions which it operated as part of its system of agricultural support, obviously weakened the hand of GATT in its dealings with other and smaller countries. It is therefore understandable that the Sub-Committee of the Commonwealth Liaison Committee on European Trade Relations should have concluded in 1959 that 'the progress made in the GATT in dealing individually with the problem of quantitative restrictions on imports of agricultural products into certain individual countries of the EEC has been disappointing and raises doubts about the results which might be expected when other members of the EEC emerge from balance of payments difficulties'. McEwen therefore had to be content with the innocuous outcome of the autumn 1958 thirteenth session of GATT, which merely appointed three committees to investigate the problem – an illuminating case study in the operation of Parkinson's Law, if nothing more. Committee 1 was established to make recommendations for the holding of further GATT Conferences or tariff negotiations on a multilateral basis; Committee 2 was charged with examining the problem of agricultural protectionism as it affected international trade in agricultural products; and Committee 3 was concerned 'with other measures for the expansion of trade'.[13]

Having failed to prevent the formation of the EEC, the Australian government reverted to its proven policy of exchanging preferences, using Britain first of all as an agent in negotiations with EFTA, then inviting the Commonwealth to enter into dialogue with the EEC, and finally initiating direct negotiations on its own with individual EEC countries. It was ironic that just after Australia had cut some of its strings with Britain following the 1956 renegotiation of the Ottawa Agreement, it should find itself once more on its old mentor's lap. However, McEwen believed that the EEC could only be contained and

Australian markets in Europe protected if Britain could entice the six into a wider European arrangement from which agriculture was excluded. In a speech to the Liberal Party Council in October 1957, Menzies highlighted the advantages of a 17-member Free Trade Area, indicating that 'if the scope of the EFTA is confined to industrial goods, almost all the Commonwealth preferences can be maintained and at the same time the essentials of association with the European Economic Community can be achieved'.[14] So enamoured were the Australians with the possibility of the 17-member Free Trade Area that McEwen himself was prepared to make agricultural concessions, albeit minor ones, to ensure its success.[15]

This initiative also came to nought. Foreshadowing de Gaulle's dramatic intervention in January 1963, the French soon pulled the carpet from under the British. In a broadcast of November 1958, the French Minister for Information, Monsieur Soustelle, announced that 'France was not prepared to consider the formation of a Free Trade area on the basis of the British proposals'.[16] This the Australian Department of External Affairs interpreted as a clear indication of the divergence between those inside and outside the EEC on the political as distinct from the economic targets of the Common Market. McEwen was palpably disappointed, leading to a temporary cooling in British–Australian relations. When the United Kingdom raised the matter of a separate EFTA of seven countries, Australia's initial response was to distance itself from any new negotiations. At a meeting of Commonwealth officials in London in May 1959, the Australian representative informed the British 'that the position now so far as we are concerned is one of a "clean slate"'.[17] The fact that the EEC would not be party to these new negotiations was a further reason to engage another body such as the seven in pursuing that objective. Instead McEwen proposed that the Commonwealth itself be invited to assist the British in its dealings with the EEC.

Again, McEwen was to be frustrated – not because of EEC opposition, but rather because of Britain's and certain other Commonwealth countries' objections. The initiative had come from the New Zealanders and in welcoming their move McEwen had informed the cabinet in June 1959 that he was attracted by 'some form of Commonwealth association with the European Community which might involve some modification in Commonwealth preferences in return for better access to European markets'.[18] He next cabled Menzies, then in London, 'to put to the U.K. the idea that there should be a thorough examination of the possibility of negotiations between the Commonwealth and European countries'.[19] He could well have anticipated a frosty response from the

British to that proposal. During the 17-member Free Trade Area negotiations in 1957, the British refused Australia 'a voice in the negotiating arena' because, according to Sir Edwin McCarthy, 'they, the British, fear that to allow Commonwealth countries to get too close to the EFTA negotiating body might embarrass the U.K. in their negotiations'.[20] McEwen was to experience a similar rejection in 1959. He reported to his cabinet that outside of New Zealand 'other Commonwealth countries have not given it wholehearted support'.[21] In fact the United Kingdom and Canada were positively hostile to the idea, with the United Kingdom advising that the 'outer Commonwealth should look after their own interests vis-à-vis the six through the GATT and direct negotiations with the six'.[22] So much for Commonwealth cohesion or British sympathy or support for Australia's trading dilemma.

There can be no doubting McEwen's resentment or even pique at that rebuff. His cherished preferences were no longer being appreciated, and McEwen himself was left in the role of the unrequited suitor. His attitude towards EFTA hardened and he informed cabinet that 'at least at this stage he was not prepared to give it any general blessing'. More surprisingly, he was now opposed to 'a wider free-trade area if it eventuated'.[23] He even questioned the legality of EFTA, asking 'how the United Kingdom could justify EFTA in GATT since some features of the EFTA draft plan appeared to be just as much in conflict with GATT as those features of the Rome Treaty which we have been attacking'.[24] Thus with his 'preferences' rejected by Britain, rejected by EFTA and also rejected by the Commonwealth, McEwen had no option but to solicit individual EEC countries directly. They also rejected him. The only country even to acknowledge his gesture was Germany, but it only offered to listen further to Australian objections in the event of German discrimination against Australian goods.[25]

Thus, by the time of Britain's momentous decision in July 1961 to join the Common Market itself, Australia found itself stuck in a series of blind alleys where it was being marginalized internationally. Assessed in terms of the personnel involved, in distances travelled, in the number of reports produced, in the hours spent at conferences and especially in the frustration of all concerned, not to mention the monetary cost, the price was indeed high. However, what was worse was that Australia's traditional bargaining tool, the exchange of preferences, was being exposed as a paper tiger, and the Department of Trade could not countenance any other approach.

All this begs the basic question: was Australian trade really threatened by these European developments? It must be made clear that

Australian preferences in the British market were not at stake during this period, even if Australian suspicions on that score were never fully allayed by British assurances. In a series of public statements, British ministers confirmed the Ottawa preferential system. As early as September 1956 the British Chancellor of the Exchequer advised the Australians that 'U.K. interests outside Europe, particularly with the Commonwealth, meant that the U.K. could not in any circumstances join the European Customs Union'.[26] At the Commonwealth Prime Ministers' Meeting in June 1957, Thorneycroft stated that it was the 'firm intention of the United Kingdom government not to agree to include agriculture' in the proposed Free Trade Area, and that that 'had always been made plain to the six countries'.[27] In summing up at that conference, Macmillan was even more emphatic when he stated that 'if the essential safeguards [for the Commonwealth] could not be obtained from the [17-member] EFTA, the United Kingdom would be compelled to stand aside from the European arrangement'.[28] Finally, on a visit to Canberra in February 1958, Macmillan re-emphasized that 'it was not the intention of the United Kingdom to make agricultural concessions' to the EEC.[29] Accordingly, Australian concerns through-out this period were with continental Europe, with the six EEC countries in particular, and not with the United Kingdom. Australian trade policy must therefore be assessed on those terms.

The value of Australia's exports to the EEC countries in 1957–58 was £146 million: just short of Canada's total of £150 million and well below the United Kingdom's of £500 million. However, of the three countries, Australia sold a higher proportion of its exports to the EEC: 22.3 per cent, as against 15 per cent for the United Kingdom and 9 per cent for Canada. Further, of these exports, Australia obtained free entry for a much larger proportion of its products. Eighty-eight per cent of its exports were admitted free of tariffs to the EEC, as against 22 per cent for Canada,[30] the main reason being that wool and sheepskins, which accounted for the bulk of Australian exports, were not subject to tariffs in the EEC. Thus, at most, only 12 per cent of Australia's exports to the EEC were affected by possible tariff restrictions. Even then, the Sub-Committee of the Commonwealth Liaison Committee on European Trade Relations discounted a portion of the 12 per cent, arguing that 'in 1957–58 there were grounds for anxiety for Australian exports totalling only £8.3 million, representing approximately 5 per cent of her total exports to the EEC', whereas in previous years there would have been grounds for anxiety for approximately '0.1% of Australian total exports to the EEC'. By far the largest share of these problematic exports to the

EEC was accounted for by barley and wheat. Australian exports of barley to the EEC in 1957–58 amounted to £3.1 million, or 41 per cent of Australian barley exports to the world. Greater concern was expressed about the future of wheat exports, even though in 1957–58 Australia exported no wheat to the EEC countries. The average of the three previous years was approximately £4 million, about 10 per cent of total Australian world exports of wheat. This anxiety about wheat appears to have sprung from the German 29 per cent *ad valorem* duty on Australian wheat, contrary to the GATT binding rate of 20 per cent. Thus it should be apparent that only a small minority of Australian exports were threatened by EEC developments. In fact the bulk of them could possibly benefit.

McEwen himself was forced to admit in a Cabinet submission of 13 May 1960 that only £15 million of Australia's 1958–59 exports to the EEC were affected by EEC tariffs: wool, sheepskins, lead, zinc and metals were not subject to any duty under EEC proposals. McEwen accordingly conceded that 'our trade is unlikely to be greatly affected'.[31] On the contrary, the Commonwealth Liaison Committee on European Trade Relations concluded that 'exports of wool and sheepskins to the EEC countries can be expected to increase if the creation of the EEC leads to higher living standards and hence to a growing demand for the raw materials of the textile industries'.[32] Even in 1948–49 EEC countries were buying 37 per cent of Australian wool as against 34 per cent by Britain; in 1963–64 EEC purchases were 28 per cent as against 16 per cent by Britain, with Japan taking 29 per cent. The value of Australian greasy wool exports to the United Kingdom in 1956–57 was £106 million; to the EEC countries it was £170 million. In 1948–49 wool exports accounted for 42 per cent of all exports. In 1951 they were 64 per cent, and in 1963 they were 34 per cent.[33] Thus any improvement in the sales of wool and sheepskins would have had a major impact on the Australian balance of trade.

These possibilities were not lost on the Prime Minister's Department, the only Australian government department to take issue with the Department of Trade. As early as February 1957, even before the signing of the Treaty of Rome, the Prime Minister's Department had raised strong objections to the Department of Trade's line of action. In a letter to the Secretary of the Department of Trade, A. S. Brown, Secretary of the Prime Minister's Department, upbraided him for his department's unilateral response to the Common Market proposals of the Messina countries. 'We consider', he wrote, 'that a government to government message was of such significance that it would have been preferable for it to have been discussed in cabinet'. The message itself, he suggested, 'conveyed the impression that we were inclined to take a selfish viewpoint wherever our interests were concerned', which in his view was misguided because 'we cannot exclude the possibility that at some later date in these developments we might be prepared to overlook some possible short-term losses in markets in the interests of contributing to the development of a strong and stable European Community'. He was also critical of the Department of Trade's recourse to GATT, which he considered 'overemphasised'. Inevitably, in his view, 'GATT will be called on to pass judgment on the plan but it would be unfortunate if before we had resolved our overall attitude there should be any possibility of the plan bogging down in a special session of the contracting parties where there could be some danger of losing sight of the fundamental purpose of the plan'.[34] In his subsequent submission to the Prime Minister, Brown was even more emphatic. He stressed that 'the political strategic aspect and the wider trade aspect should not be neglected. Even on the narrower aspect of trade in agricultural commodities, the risks do not seem to be very substantial'. In respect of GATT he advised that Australia 'should encourage effective liaison with the community but not endeavour to put them through the hoops'.[35]

The Prime Minister's Department followed up this attack in March 1957 with a trenchant memorandum written by Peter Lawler, which accused the Department of Trade of being fixed myopically on the agricultural aspects of the EEC, and of ignoring the welcome which the United States and Canada had given it on political grounds and also the other trade advantages which in the Prime Minister's Department's view did exist in the new arrangements. The Department of Trade, it alleged, was 'moping with imagined fears about wilting trade opportunities'. While Lawler acknowledged that the EEC was largely self-sufficient in certain agricultural products – for example supplying 84 per cent of its own bread grain needs, 75 per cent of its beef and veal and 90 per cent of its butter – it was not self-sufficient in the commodities that most affected Australia, namely wool and sheepskins. The Prime Minister's Department calculated that 'a 2% increase in wool sales' would be the 'equivalent of a 10% increase in Australian sales of other items to the six'. 'If the European Community and the Free Trade Area lead to economic expansion in Europe', that should enhance Australia's overall export opportunities even if 'a few marginal items might get hit'. Anyway, it argued, 'the changes involved in the Common Market will be staggered over a number of years'. Accordingly, the Prime Minister's Department cautioned against confrontation with the EEC;

it recommended a 'nod and a wink' approach to GATT surveillance on the grounds that 'if we faced similar pressures, for example, the sale of New Zealand butter in Australia, would we be as enthusiastic about GATT investigations?' Finally it argued that Australia should offer 'a public and Free Trade Area', as both the US and Canada had already done.[36]

In the opinion of the Prime Minister's Department, the future lay with the regional economic blocs then appearing all over the world. Lawler later argued that 'there was no mistaking that the regional approach to a solution of trade payments problems was in the ascendancy. The European Economic Community was established. The Free Trade Area was being devised; the Nordic Common Market stood ready to be put into operation and serious work was proceeding on a Common Market for Latin America'.[37] Accordingly, the Prime Minister's Department strongly recommended that Australia follow New Zealand's example and associate itself with a widely expanded Free Trade Area, or if that failed with the EEC itself.[38] The Department also recommended that Australia should accredit an official to the EEC Commission in Brussels.[39] While the Prime Minister's Department agreed that its approach was somewhat unorthodox, it maintained that 'as our present approach is certain to be unfruitful and even damaging there is therefore merit in seeking an alternative' – 'with closer economic co-operation with Europe as the best means of promoting our trade and other interests'.[40]

Emanating from such an important source as the Prime Minister's Department, it might have been expected that these ideas would have carried some weight. The opposite, however, was the case, for the very simple reason that the Prime Minister does not appear to have had much influence himself. On trade matters, Menzies was no more than McEwen's spokesman, and that was accordingly reflected in the lowly ranking of his department in that sphere. As has been noted, McEwen acted as if he alone was the Australian government – a sort of political organ-grinder. He composed and sent aide-memoires in the government's name without consulting anybody, and he even instructed Menzies on the appropriate responses when the latter was in London. He was to continue to do so with even greater frequency in the early 1960s.

Equally influential was McEwen's departmental head, John G. Crawford. Writing to Clarke of the Treasury in December 1957, Sir Edgar Coagan of the Board of Trade noted that 'the key to the problem at the Australian end is to carry Jack Crawford with us'. He advised that the British civil service should take the unprecedented step of 'sending personal messages to Jack Crawford, in addition to any message which is sent to the Government', because of his belief that Crawford 'reacts quite especially to direct personal messages'.[41] This view was endorsed by Sir Henry Lintott of the Commonwealth Relations Office, who in a letter, also to Clarke, confirmed that he agreed 'that Crawford is the key to our problem at the Australian end'.[42] Harry Gray, the British Trade Commissioner in Canberra, also maintained that Crawford had been upset by other government departments being involved in trade matters, especially by the 'recent decision to hold regular meetings with Commonwealth High Commissioners in London'.[43] The outcome was that R. W. B. Clarke wrote to Lintott at the end of December 1957 recommending that Sir Frank Lee and Sir Rasley Rowan be appointed letter writers to Crawford, because of their personal relations with him.[44] However, Lintott now demurred. 'Such a course', he said, 'was likely to make our relations with other governments unnecessarily complicated'. In addition, 'it could easily create jealousies amongst those to whom messages were not sent'.[45] McEwen and Crawford did not need these assurances; their dominance in the Australian public service was unassailable. At an interdepartmental meeting in June 1957 all departments, including External Affairs and Primary Industry, endorsed the Department of Trade's position, although the Treasury was ambivalent, recommending that Australia should take a passive role in respect of the proposed Treaty of Rome, 'listening' rather than intervening.[46]

Accordingly there was no effective check on the direction of Australian trade policy between 1956 and 1961. The Prime Minister's Department did not matter. Years later, in his documentary history of *Australian Trade Policy*, Crawford was to question the 'competency' of these observers, who in his view were 'ignorant of further technological developments in European agriculture so that in cereals, sugar and dairy products, imports could be expected to diminish greatly and even disappear'.[47] Again he missed the point made by his critics, who had never denied that fact, but who had placed these products within the context of total EEC imports, where the losses would be compensated for by the gains. More convincing, however, was the political argument, not alluded to by Crawford: namely that these minority crops were located in politically sensitive regions in Australia. This was the perceptive conclusion of J. D. B. Miller in 1976, who wrote that 'Rural electorates all over Australia but especially in sugar, fruit and dairying areas had an overwhelming interest in preserving special access'. For the Country Party these special interests 'could be represented as a matter of life and death since if that Party were unable to ensure them the special protection they had been accustomed to, there would be little reason for the separate existence of a rural non-Labour Party and the Liberal Party might overrun what had formally been Country Party strongholds'.[48]

Thus the pattern of Australian trade responses was set by a combination of tradition, the blinkered vision of McEwen, Crawford and their departmental officials, and sectional political interests. It was accordingly a partial response that tended to ignore the wider implications, and so, as has been seen, was doomed to failure. But because it had been hyped up as Australia's response to a greater challenge than in fact existed, the disillusion was even more pronounced. This also provides some explanation for the near-panic in government circles in Australia in July 1961 when Britain itself decided to join the Common Market, thereby posing a genuine threat to Australian export trade. Menzies was to refer to that as the greatest challenge of his political career, even dwarfing the Second World War. Government departments were left floundering. The legacy of the shadow boxing of the previous six years that had been mistaken for the real thing now came to haunt the Department of Trade, initially nearly paralysing the government response to these new and more serious developments. This panic is neatly captured in a memorandum of July 1961 which recommended that Australia's response to Britain's intention to seek membership of the EEC should be

> to avoid either saying or giving the impression that we can be counted on ultimately for support as long as a few recognisable concessions are made in our direction and on the other to avoid saying or giving the impression that we are opposed almost immovably to the initiative by Great Britain – for the present we reserve our position. We are not supporting. We are not opposing. And we are not neutral or indifferent. We will have views, but not yet.[49]

Notes

1. National Archives of Australia, Canberra (AA), A4926/XMI, Vol. 47.
2. McEwen's Cabinet Submission, 12 September 1957, AA, A4926/XMI, Vol. 34.
3. Minutes of Interdepartmental Meeting on the European Common Market and Free Trade Area, held in Department of Trade, 20 June 1957, AA, A1838/2 791/4/11, Pt. 3.
4. July 1958, AA, A4926/XM, Vol. 23.

5. February 1957, AA, A571 56/1237, Pt. 3.
6. November 1957, Public Record Office, Kew, London (PRO), DO 35/8383.
7. Australian Senate, 30 April 1959.
8. AA, A1838/2 791/4/11, Pt. 2.
9. AA, A1209/23 57/5119, Pt. 1.
10. Report of the Sub-Committee on European Trade Relations, August 1959, AA, A1838/2 724/1/9/2, Pt. 2.
11. Ibid.
12. Ibid.
13. Ibid.
14. G. Menzies, Address to the Liberal Party Council, 21 October 1957, PRO, DO 35/8382.
15. Cabinet Meeting, 17 September 1957, AA, A4926/XM1, Vol. 34.
16. Department of External Affairs to Australian High Commissioner, London, January 1960, AA, A1838/2 81/3/2, Pt. 5.
17. McEwen's submission to Cabinet, 8 June 1959, AA, A1838/2 724/1, Pt. 14.
18. Ibid.
19. McEwen to Menzies, 4 June 1959, AA, A1838/2 724/1, Pt. 14.
20. Sir Edwin McCarthy to Canberra, 16 July 1957, AA, A1838/2 791/4/11, Pt. 3.
21. McEwen's submission to Cabinet, 16 September 1959, AA, A5818/2, Vol. 8.
22. Ibid.
23. Ibid.
24. Ibid.
25. AA, A1838/2 724/1/9/2, Pt. 2.
26. AA, A1209/22 57/5119, Pt. 1.
27. Australian High Commissioner in London to Canberra, 4 July 1957, AA, CRSA 1310/1 56/3/1.
28. Ibid.
29. Meeting between Mr Macmillan and Australian Cabinet in Canberra, 11 February 1958, PRO, DO 35/8382.
30. These and the following statistics are to be found in AA, A1838/2 724/1/9/2, Pt. 2.
31. McEwen's Cabinet submission, 13 May 1960, AA, A5818/2, Vol. 16.
32. AA, A1838/2 724/1/9/2, Pt. 2.
33. Quoted in J. G. Crawford, *Australian Trade Policy, 1942–1966* (Canberra: Australian National University Press, 1968) pp. 574–5. Also, Australian Bureau of Statistics, *Overseas Trade, 1956–7*, Bulletin No. 54, p. 539.
34. A. S. Brown to J. G. Crawford, 5 February 1957, AA, A1838/2 791/4/11, Pt. 2.
35. AA, A4926/XM, Vol. 23.
36. Ibid.
37. Ibid., 11 July 1958.
38. July 1958, AA, A4926/XM, Vol. 23.
39. L. Hibbs (British Trade Commissioner, Canberra) to Miss D. M. Wilde (Board of Trade), 20 August 1959, PRO, DO35/8383.
40. July 1958, AA, A4926/XM, Vol. 23.
41. Sir Edgar Coagan to R. W. B. Clarke, 2 December 1957, PRO, DO35/8383.
42. Sir Henry Lintott to R. W. B. Clarke, 10 December 1957, PRO, DO35/8383.
43. Sir Edgar Coagan to R. W. B. Clarke, 2 December 1957 in which he refers to Gray's information, PRO, DO35/8383.

44. R. W. B. Clarke to Sir Henry Lintott, 19 December 1957, PRO, DO35/8383.
45. Sir Henry Lintott to R. W. B. Clarke, 30 December 1957, PRO, DO35/8383.
46. Interdepartmental Meeting on the European Common Market and Free Trade Area, held in Department of Trade, 20 June 1957, AA, A1838/2 791/4/11, Pt. 3.
47. Crawford, op. cit., note 33 above, pp. 272–3.
48. J. D. B. Miller, *The EEC and Australia* (Canberra: Nelson, 1976) p. 78.
49. Memorandum, 6 July 1961, AA, A571/95 1961/791, Pt. 9.

5
The Commonwealth in British European Policy: Politics and Sentiment, 1956–63

George Wilkes

In the late 1950s and early 1960s, the discrepancy between British rhetoric about the overriding importance of Commonwealth links and the British government's steady retreat from guarantees for Commonwealth interests in negotiations with other Europeans became increasingly evident. Those historians of the British decision to join the European Community who have tried to provide explanations for this discrepancy can roughly be divided into two tendencies. The successive governments of Anthony Eden and Harold Macmillan both presented a picture of themselves as reluctantly compromising on their deep attachment to the Commonwealth, and this has been followed by most historians commenting on the subject.[1] A few more critical observers, on the other hand, either from the Commonwealth or Britain, have seen British pro-Commonwealth rhetoric as a sop to public opinion while the government 'sold out' on the interests of the Commonwealth.[2] Both of these views rely on an assumption that British attitudes to the Commonwealth in this period were deeply entrenched and consistent features of British European policy debate, an assumption which will be seen in the course of the present chapter to be untenable.

The complex reality of British attitudes to the Commonwealth in the 1950s and 1960s by no means escapes all of these writers. Nevertheless, as long as their chief intent has been to provide a straightforward judgment of British European policy, this complexity has failed to make a substantive impact on their basic approach. The relative lack of attention given to the impact of public attitudes to the Commonwealth by specialists tracing the relationship between Britain and the European Community is perhaps not particularly surprising. If there had been more attention given to attitudes to the Commonwealth in studies of

British foreign policy in general, then this omission would be less excusable, but this area has not been a priority for research here either. Undoubtedly there is also something behind this of the disinclination to consider the role of public opinion in foreign policy-making of the old 'realist' school among international relations specialists, still dominant in the study of international history today (as contested as it is in international relations circles). Since even works on British Commonwealth policy have given remarkably little attention to the attitudes of British public opinion leaders,[3] we can only hope here to open up a new research agenda, and to underline its significance in the study of British policy. At the same time, the research for the present chapter was motivated by the conviction that the available evidence does suggest a number of specific conclusions which do not fit neatly into the rubrics of the 'sympathetic' and 'unsympathetic' approaches to Britain's Commonwealth and European policy.

What follows is an overview of the impression given by the public and private records now available, offering a third interpretation based on changing approaches to the Commonwealth within the British government and on the impact of changing attitudes elsewhere in the British political elite. 'The Commonwealth', with all the interests and peoples that implied, provoked an unpredictable response from government and public alike, and foremost among the causes of their shifts of opinion over Commonwealth issues was the impact of party politics. At a number of critical junctures, this pushed policy-makers into striking more cautious stances than were made necessary by the state of Commonwealth relations, or by relations with Britain's other international partners, or even by the government's domestic political situation. At other times, ministers were quite ready to throw caution to the wind. After outlining the shifts in the attitudes of political parties, the press and interest groups, which complicated the government's policy calculations, the chapter will revisit the question of how far policy-makers' approaches to the Commonwealth were actually constrained by their perceptions of the international situation rather than by domestic politics alone.

Parliamentary and party politics

History has forgotten many of the pro-Commonwealth opponents of the Conservative 'turn to Europe', though not the influence which they exercised in swaying the Conservative and Labour party leadership against a more forthright approach to the nascent European Community. A closer examination of the Commonwealth rhetoric of party leaders and back-benchers suggests that their changing approaches to the issue were affected as much by domestic party politics as they were by shifts in European and Commonwealth relations abroad.

Within the Conservative Party, outspoken anti-Europeans were weak in number and influence throughout the period before 1963. On the backbenches, they were largely on the right wing of the party and were passionate 'imperialists' or 'Commonwealthers', at least insomuch as they were passionate about Britain's international influence and responsibilities. A connection between European and Commonwealth policy was only natural, since changes in Britain's European relations would inevitably affect Britain's position within the Commonwealth. In 1956 as in 1963, there was nothing automatic about the identification of the turn to Europe with a retreat from Empire. Leading members of the right-wing Suez Group opposed to the scaling-down of Britain's worldwide military operations were strongly pro-European – the most well-known being Julian Amery – while others were determinedly anti-European. The majority had no fixed position on Britain's relationship to the nascent European Community, even where – like John Biggs-Davison – they were professedly 'pro-European' in the Churchillian sense.[4] And yet over the course of this period a sizeable element of the Conservative right wing shifted against association with Europe on the terms outlined by their government, increasingly citing the Commonwealth as their chief objection.

In 1956, a handful of Suez rebels in the Commons formed the small 'Expanding Commonwealth Group' in an attempt to reverse the impression that the Conservative right wing was defending an imperial status quo without presenting any alternative vision for the development of the Commonwealth. Initially, the group was not cohesive on Europe. This is clear from the records of Early Day Motions tabled in the Commons during the early summer of 1956: members of the group signed motions both for and against British membership or association with the Common Market then under negotiation among the Six. In early 1956, one central figure in the group, Sir Patrick Maitland, published a proposal that the Western Europeans be brought into the Commonwealth, a suggestion which had been floated by leading Conservatives in the framework of the Council of Europe in 1952. In the heat of the Suez Crisis later that year, Eden and Macmillan, then Chancellor of the Exchequer, made vague gestures of support for a Commonwealth–Europe condominium in the hope of strengthening their support on the right of the party, as we will see later.

The perception that Macmillan was in tune with the mood of the Conservative right wing evaporated once he became Prime Minister in January 1957. By mid-1957, the Suez rebels, having lost their battle over the retreat from Suez, had become rebels without a cause, or at least without the cause with which they had set out. Macmillan's 'betrayal' of the right over Suez and then over Cyprus sent the Expanding Commonwealth Group into renewed rebellion and key members lost the Conservative whip. In this context, the group began to see an exclusively European association as a further betrayal of their Commonwealth vision, and the Conservative right solidified further around an anti-European position.[5]

Trouble in the party over decolonization continued in 1957, the right having turned its attention from Suez to Africa and Cyprus in particular. The new policy of rapid decolonization was supported by a large majority of Conservatives[6] and Macmillan and his government felt little need to make concessions to pressure from discontented backbenchers. The rebels therefore spread their attention to other issues. Working through the Expanding Commonwealth Group, they turned their fire against British entry into an exclusively European economic framework, whether it was called a European free trade area or a common market. Relations with the Commonwealth were thus still a crucial test of any European arrangement for many on the Conservative right, and the freedom to liberalize trade further within the Commonwealth was given a central place in the campaign to reverse the weakening of links between members of the former Empire.

In diary entries written in August and October 1961, Macmillan pointedly referred to this anti-European hard core as persistent troublemakers – 'the disgusted group', 'the usual grumblers', 'frondistes', using relations with Australia, Canada and New Zealand as a cover for their rebellion.[7] Beyond this small group, opposition to association with the EEC on purely economic grounds was relatively weak among Conservative MPs. A few protectionists in the party defended preferential trading tariffs within the Commonwealth ('Commonwealth preference') as a cover for their broader anxieties about international competition, but – except where agricultural produce was concerned – forthright declarations of the merits of Commonwealth protectionism were very few indeed.[8]

The impact of right-wing opposition to Macmillan's European policy was more than offset by initiatives from the 'One Nation' group on the left of the Conservative Party in favour of 'joining' the Common Market, first in 1956 and then in 1961.[9] There were also a number of

Conservatives who sought a substitute for the Empire in joining Europe, though this was only discussed in the vaguest terms at the time.[10] Other right-wing pro-Europeans sought to use Europe as a prop for the Empire, rather than as a substitute. In 1961, a few pro-European right-wingers still called themselves 'imperialists', and a handful of MPs prominent in the debate over association with the EEC stressed that the overseas Empire and Commonwealth was 'European' too.[11]

Within the Conservative Party, there had been little attempt to relate the developing inclination towards European Community membership to Commonwealth economic policy. The Conservative Party committees responsible for scrutinizing Commonwealth policy – the Commonwealth Policy Committee and the parliamentary party's Commonwealth Affairs Committee – gave the issue little attention.[12] The same was true of the party bureaucracy. At least two studies have suggested that the Conservative Party inside and outside Parliament was converted to the argument for membership of the EEC by July 1961, largely on the ground that it would help the Conservatives to win the next election.[13] Those who have argued the case have pointed chiefly at the influential Conservative Research Department (CRD), though the CRD in fact seems to have given the issue a low priority. The head of the economic department, sceptical of the merits of the case for joining the EEC, argued that a Commonwealth–EFTA alternative was worth exploring, strengthening Britain's negotiating hand and countering the weakening of Commonwealth trading links which joining the Six was likely to provoke.[14] The head of the CRD, Sir Michael Fraser, seems from the CRD files not to have been very involved in work on the issue at this stage.

From 1960 until the decision to seek negotiations with the Six was made in mid-1961, opposition from senior Conservatives on the left of the party, notably Rab Butler and Reginald Maudling, proved more serious than opposition from backbenchers on the right. Butler's attachment to the Commonwealth made less impact on his position than his anxiety about the fate of British agriculture. Maudling, however, and the Chancellor of the Exchequer, Derick Heathcoat Amory, were more focused on global trade liberalization as a long-term economic strategy, and for them at least the treatment of the Commonwealth was at this point a major test of any European association.[15] Once the Cabinet had decided to open negotiations for EEC membership, Maudling, Amory and Butler publicly supported the application, and at least by late 1962 also supported it in private.[16]

From the outset, the impact of Community membership on the Commonwealth was given more attention in the speeches of Conservatives who favoured membership than it was in those of their anti-Market adversaries. During the Commons debate of 2–3 August 1961, for instance, the Commonwealth issue received most attention from pro-Community or non-committal Conservatives who emphasized that there was no question of a 'choice' between Europe and the Common-wealth, and very little attention in the speeches made by Conservative 'anti-marketeers' (as they were now most commonly called).[17] While there were some anti-Europeans with strong personal connections to the Commonwealth, this was equally true for many of the most out-spoken pro-Europeans. In order to counter anxiety about the applica-tion these pro-Marketeers perhaps not unnaturally tended to make more of a point of their personal knowledge of overseas Common-wealth perceptions of Britain's European relations.[18]

Macmillan's attempt to steer his party and the country towards European Community membership faced the opposition of only one senior Cabinet rival, Rab Butler. In public Butler actively supported Macmillan's European policy. In private he was known to be a poten-tial leader for discontented Conservatives, and there is still today some debate among his contemporaries about the extent to which he used his position as chair of the Cabinet Common Market Negotiations Committee to stiffen the government's demands at Brussels. By July 1962, however, he had recognized that the Conservatives' electoral for-tunes were tied to reaching an outline agreement at Brussels that could be sold to the Commonwealth Prime Ministers' Conference called for September and thereafter to the British public.[19] Ironically Butler's decision was not made on the basis of negotiations over the interests of Britain's farmers, the problem about which he was most concerned and which was not dealt with until the autumn of 1962. Indeed, major questions about Commonwealth trade were also left open at that stage. Butler could have reversed his position again if occasion demanded, but the fact that he had given public backing to the deal reached thus far implied a longer-term commitment to the EEC application. It was a commitment he had made, then, on the basis of his assessment of the domestic political prospects of the Conservative Party as much as on the likely terms which could be obtained at Brussels.

The distance between the Conservative backbenchers opposed to EEC membership and the senior party figures most likely to swing their way was a major constraint on the impact of the Conservative anti-Marketeers within the party during the negotiations. By the end of 1961, leading party strategists had begun to become more active in their public support for the application, a strategy spearheaded by the party chairman, Iain Macleod. The records of the party's backbench and extra-parliamentary committees record no open rebellion at that level in 1962 or early 1963. Even during the period of controversy over the impact of the application on the Commonwealth in the months leading up to the Prime Ministers' Conference, all of the members of the extra-parliamentary Conservative Party Commonwealth Affairs Committee bar one appear from committee records to have continued to support the EEC membership bid. The developing backbench rebellion prompted by the by-election disasters of the government in early 1962 did not have any noticeable impact on backbench attitudes to the negotiations over the Commonwealth.

Outside the Cabinet and Commons, the most senior Conservative Party grandees also steered clear of confrontation with the government. Winston Churchill's views on the potential damage to the Commonwealth were a subject of some debate, but his poor health would have prevented him from rallying opinion among Conservatives in Parliament even had he wished to.[20] The most senior party figure who might have swung his colleagues against the application was Lord Avon (Anthony Eden), the former Prime Minister whose long experience at the Foreign Office still gave him the respect of many of his colleagues. Initially, Eden held his fire, hoping to use whatever influence he might carry with de Gaulle to improve the prospect of Britain's negotiating goals being met at Brussels. Once concessions began to be made by the British negotiating delegation, however, Eden swung against Macmillan's bid, believing that Macmillan was willing to split both the Commonwealth and the Conservative Party.[21]

For most of this period, and in particular during the negotiations over the Commonwealth, backbench Conservative anti-Marketeers refrained from engaging in open warfare with the government. The conflict between pro- and anti-Marketeers was waged in the Commons with notable restraint, the anti-Marketeers being careful that the numbers of MPs they signed up to Early Day Motions only just matched the numbers of signatures on the pro-entry motions to which they felt constrained to respond.[22] Only at the end of October 1962 did the hard core of pro-Commonwealth opponents of the application in the parliamentary party coalesce into what some of them loosely referred as the 'Common Market Committee', largely drawn from the MPs associated with the Expanding Commonwealth Group.[23] By December the Committee had drawn up a policy document, published in the New Year, which pressed for an alternative based on more free trade with the Commonwealth.[24]

In mid-December 1962, the Expanding Commonwealth Group and the Common Market Committee judged that the progress now being made in the negotiations also demanded a more open challenge than they had previously deemed necessary. The policy document was used as the basis for an Early Day Motion placed on the order books on 13 December which attracted 49 signatures (as against the usual 30), most notably that of the chair of the party's parliamentary agricultural committee, Sir Anthony Hurd.[25] For the anti-Marketeers, this was a major success, a number of fairly senior figures within the party having put their names to a document urging the government to drop the Common Market application in favour of a Commonwealth alternative. Nevertheless, what motivated most of the first-time signatories was very clearly not the Commonwealth issue – they were looking for a means to express their anxiety at the latest concessions in Brussels over the terms on which domestic British agriculture would join the Common Agricultural Policy. The party leadership and the media also appear to have taken it in that spirit. The 'revolt' was not followed by any debate or follow-up campaign and the episode did not attract the attention of observers either at the time or subsequently. It seems highly likely that the episode was more a calculated move to strengthen the hand of the British negotiators dealing with agriculture at Brussels than an expression of Commonwealth patriotism. Even the pro-Commonwealth opposition within the party was slow to make capital out of their apparent strength, no doubt aware that the entry bid would only provoke further rebellion if a deal at Brussels made the threat of European Community membership more immediate.

The overwhelming domestic political interest of the Conservative government in a successful negotiation played a major role in turning Commonwealth considerations into pawns in a domestic political game. The difficult progress of the negotiations in Brussels over the course of 1962 was therefore largely viewed by Conservative opinion-formers through the prism of the coming election. This was made all the easier where decision-makers believed the Commonwealth issue was not a major problem in its own right. In mid-1962, Conservative back-bencher Maurice Macmillan (the Prime Minister's son) noted that 'the pro-Commonwealth feeling strong in the House of Commons is not really very strong in the country, and ought not to be allowed to turn the centre against the Common Market before the true conditions are known'.[26] By late May 1962, the Conservative Research Department was working on an election strategy to which the application was central, but in which a wide range of Commonwealth interests might have to be sacrificed for the sake of Community membership. Brendan Sewill, head of the CRD's economic department and still privately concerned about the wisdom of the European application, came up with a counter-argument. If terms were 'shifting', he wrote, '50 or so Conservatives could vote against the government, which would be forced to go to the country in the autumn of 1962. If we stay out it would look better for us to be the ones pushing for Commonwealth safeguards'.[27] When the negotiations over the Commonwealth reached the point where major concessions had to be considered, ministers took a similar view.[28]

If the Labour Party were going to choose an issue on which to oppose the Macmillan government's application, it was going to be the Commonwealth – British agriculture figured even lower on Labour's political agenda. The left and right wings of the Labour Party both included an unusually high proportion of committed anti- and pro-Marketeers, the 'antis' stronger on the left, pro-Marketeers on the right. The anti-Marketeers focused on the Commonwealth, those on the left giving a patriotic Commonwealth spin to their anti-imperialist rhetoric, those on the party's right combining support for Commonwealth preference with free trade arguments against joining Europe. Roy Jenkins, already an ardent pro-Marketeer, mischievously pointed out in *The Spectator* that Labour's anti-Marketeers were 'neo-imperialist'. Over-whelmingly the anti-Marketeers saw the Commonwealth as a source of agricultural and other primary products, not industrial goods. Their doomsday predictions about EEC membership also ignored the prospects for expanding trade between the Commonwealth and Europe.[29]

Labour's pro-Marketeers often had little or no Commonwealth experience or inclination. Similarly their supporters in the largest trade unions – mirroring the concerns and aspirations of Britain's big industries – were more concerned with the dynamic growth of the markets of the EEC than with the entirely undeveloped Commonwealth markets which dazzled the left. Pro-European arguments for Community membership in the Labour Party consequently centred on Britain's own interests and influence, not on good terms for the Commonwealth. Broadly convinced of the benefits of EEC membership, the pro-Market tendency on the left was nevertheless not as insistent as many pro-Marketeers on the right of the dangers of exclusion from the Common Market. Many pro-Marketeers, like the majority of the party and trade union movement, were not disturbed when Hugh Gaitskell, the Labour leader, united the Labour Party against the terms secured by the Macmillan government at the party conference of October 1962.

Gaitskell's decision to oppose the Macmillan application has often been presented as a response to the terms for Commonwealth trade agreed in Brussels in early August 1962.[30] In fact, he had begun to make up his mind before then. In July 1962 he told the editor of *The Guardian*, Alistair Hetherington, that nothing should be done to break up the Commonwealth. On the other hand, it might be that the Commonwealth was already breaking up. Only if it did should the UK join the Common Market.[31] His own family background in the Indian subcontinent may have coloured his view of the Commonwealth's potential.[32] When the Indian High Commissioner in Brussels, K. B. Lall, suggested that the deal being worked out at Brussels for Indian tea imports was unfair, Gaitskell made it one of his main objections even though in public Indian diplomats had already accepted the terms agreed for Indian trade.[33] Gaitskell's sincerity has never been questioned by his colleagues and biographers, but the depth of Gaitskell's Commonwealth attachment does appear from his private conversation and public speeches to have been somewhat restricted. Over the course of his parliamentary career, Gaitskell had not shown a particularly strong interest in the Commonwealth. In conversations with *The Guardian*'s editor, Gaitskell warmed to Nehru's five-year plan, which he feared the trading arrangements agreed at Brussels would not encourage, but he did not show a broader concern for the maintenance of Commonwealth preferences. His famous 'thousand years of history' speech at the Labour Party Conference in October 1962 was also rather vague on what exactly he believed would be lost for the Commonwealth in the European deal and did not offer a clear alternative vision of the future for the new Commonwealth. Indeed, Gaitskell was at his most passionate in lauding the Old Dominions, Australia, Canada and New Zealand, for the sacrifices they had made for Britain in the past, particularly in the First World War. Gaitskell's speech was clearly aimed to please the Labour left. In tone and content, however, it aligned him far more closely with the vague Commonwealth sentiment of other senior Euro-agnostics[34] on the Labour front bench, notably Harold Wilson, Denis Healey and James Callaghan.

Gaitskell's turn against the application, ostensibly related to his own Commonwealth objections and often laid at the door of his wish to unite the Labour Party, was more closely linked to his mistrust of the domestic political motivation of the Macmillan government. From early on, Gaitskell had refused to treat the application as a bi-partisan policy, and made a point of forgoing ministerial briefings on the negotiations that would have restricted his ability to attack the government freely. In early 1962, the increasing commitment to the application on the part of Conservative Party figures like Party Chairman Iain Macleod provoked Gaitskell into responding, at this stage still stressing his own balance on the issue.[35] By early summer, Gaitskell had decided the issue was of critical electoral importance. This explains his intemperate behaviour at the meetings of European Socialist leaders in July and his attempt to pit the European Socialists against their Commonwealth counterparts in September. Almost immediately thereafter, he announced that he was opposed to the application proceeding on the terms agreed in Brussels, demanding a general election if this was not redressed – a move which Macmillan interpreted as motivated by domestic political considerations.[36] Gaitskell's conference performance was designed to outflank what he saw as Macmillan's electorally motivated European diplomacy. By the time of the party conference, then, Gaitskell viewed the issue in a larger domestic political frame than simply healing old wounds within the Labour Party, which were in any case now by and large no longer a serious threat to his electoral prospects.[37] His premature death in January 1963 changed the dynamics of internal party politics considerably, elevating Wilson to the position for which he had last been thought a serious contender during the battle over unilateral nuclear disarmament of 1960.

The Commonwealth was by contrast not a major element in the divide within the Liberal party. The anti-European Liberals tended to be as opposed to Commonwealth preference on 'free trade' grounds as they were to European tariff regimes. Nor were pro-Europeans in the party noticeably less idealistic about the Commonwealth than they had been in previous decades. After the collapse of the negotiations at Brussels, pro-European Liberals overwhelmingly backed a motion at the party assembly in favour of 'Commonwealth integration', advocating many of the reforms which, taken up by the government, ultimately did set the Commonwealth on a new course in the mid-1960s. Reinforcing this consensus that Liberal European policy need not raise questions about its Commonwealth policy, the party's relative weakness was accepted by a number of doubters and confirmed anti-Europeans as a reason not to air their views in public. Towards the end of 1962 the Liberal leader, Jo Grimond, privately entertained doubts about whether the terms agreed for the Commonwealth were good enough.[38] He nevertheless stuck loyally to the party's pro-Community line, distancing himself from Gaitskell and from the prospect of a Lib–Lab pact in the process.

The impact of party politics on press coverage

The impact of association with the European Communities on the Commonwealth exercised editors and specialist journalists throughout the period. However, when the crunch came in the summer of 1962 few publications treated the Commonwealth as much more than a pawn in the domestic political game – the fanatically 'pro-Empire' *Express* being the most notable exception. To the rest of the British press, the Commonwealth was a pretext for taking a stance towards the negotiations more than a commitment demanding any clear response from editors.

From 1956 onwards, the editorial attitudes of the press faithfully reflected the broad partisan and factional lines dividing the parliamentary parties over Europe, and their attitudes to the Commonwealth dimension of European policy reflected this too.[39] At the two extremes, the right- and left-wing press were vociferously pro-'Commonwealth' and anti-European, a position which the *Express* maintained throughout the period but which *The Daily Herald* abandoned when it passed from the hands of the trade unions to the ownership of Cecil King. Centre-right and centre-left newspapers all supported the free trade area from late 1956, *The Guardian* going so far as to suggest the initiative might provide an opportunity to review the 'obsolete' system of Commonwealth preference.[40] When in 1960 and early 1961 the issue of full membership of the European Communities began to gain support in Britain, the publications of the centre-left were the first to come out in favour – without giving much attention at all to potential problems relating to the Commonwealth. The mainstream Conservative broadsheet papers waited until the intentions of the government were clearer, laying particular emphasis on the impact EEC membership would have on the Commonwealth. The more populist tabloids were less timid than the broadsheets, and quickly became active and committed partisans of the 'pro-' and 'anti-Market' causes. The *Express*, quick to detect a conspiracy, had been spurred into action against the government's rapprochement with the Six in July 1960 after news of a civil service report recommending closer alignment with the EEC was leaked. In the spring of 1961 the *Express* embarked upon a self-conscious campaign in response to the pro-entry campaigns launched by the centre-left *Mirror* Group, which now included *The Daily Herald*. Lambasting the leadership of both main parties for sitting on the fence, the tabloids paid more attention to those backbenchers committed for or against Common Market membership. The *Herald* launched its campaign for entry into the Communities with articles by two Atlanticists, Desmond Donnelly and Woodrow Wyatt, both on the right of the Labour Party, both of whom dismissed the Commonwealth as an economic or political alternative to a European partnership.

Similarly a handful of Conservative anti-Marketeers were involved in Lord Beaverbrook's 'pro-Commonwealth' campaign in the *Express*.[41]

When the crunch came over the terms for the Commonwealth in the entry negotiations in 1962, press editorials were a source of some anxiety to the Conservative leadership. However, what at first appeared to be an issue on which the Conservative loyalist press might break away from the government soon turned out to be the subject of a division on party lines. The publications most likely to break ranks were the Beaverbrook press. In the summer of 1962, Beaverbrook declared that the 'Empire' bias of the *Express* would override his loyalty to the Conservative Party for as long as the government persisted in trying to join the Common Market. On a few occasions, the *Express* went so far as to support anti-European candidates competing against the Conservatives in the increasingly difficult by-elections of 1962. The paper even turned on those Conservative anti-Marketeers who like Peter Walker were campaigning for the Conservatives.[42] At the end of 1962, Beaverbrook also met with Gaitskell in an attempt to find common ground on the issue between the *Express* and the Labour leader.[43] Privately, however, he claimed that his flirtation with Labour would not affect his support for the Conservatives in a general election.[44] Macmillan had already noted the support which the *Express* gave him on a few occasions during the crucial debates over Commonwealth relations in September and October 1962. With the *Express* group preparing to re-examine its forthright opposition to the government in the event of an election, the rest of the Conservative fold was unlikely to be any less accommodating. Thus, though *The Times* did move to a slightly more sceptical position over the effect of membership on the Commonwealth during the Commonwealth Prime Ministers' Conference of September 1962, on the whole it remained a loyal supporter of the government's negotiating stance.

Gaitskell's shift against the application in mid-1962 had a similar effect on the highbrow broadsheets of the centre-left. In the summer of 1962 *The Observer*, edited by David Astor, began to criticize the government's approach to Europe. This was partly because it claimed a poor deal had been reached for the Commonwealth, though *Observer* editorials made clear that it still believed on balance the case for entering the Community was stronger. Astor's growing opposition to the prospect of entering the EEC under the Conservatives was more closely related to the belief that Macmillan might strike a nuclear deal with de Gaulle that would destabilize East–West relations. Gaitskell criticized the EEC application on this same ground in a letter to the US President,

John F. Kennedy, in December 1962. The suspicion that personal loyalty to Gaitskell was a critical factor behind Astor's shift did not escape some pro-Marketeers, despite the criticism of Gaitskell's extreme position that now crept into *Observer* editorials.[45] Gaitskell's impact on *The Guardian* was somewhat clearer and rather less equivocal. *The Guardian* moved against the application shortly after Gaitskell's conference speech, ostensibly because the terms for the Commonwealth were inadequate. *The Guardian's* editor, Alistair Hetherington, later wrote that the newspaper's shift was based on the independent conclusions of his Common Market reporter, Leonard Beaton.[46] The private notes which Hetherington took at the time suggest otherwise. Hetherington's shift appears to have been made on the basis of the arguments put to him in private meetings by the Labour leader. Hetherington himself then put these same arguments to the Liberal leader while at the same time sanctioning a general shift in *The Guardian's* editorial stance.[47]

The impact of party politics on pressure group activity

Few of the main bodies that represented British industry managed to remain aloof from the party political battle in forming their own approaches to the European issue. If this was true for the stances taken by the representatives of the main economic interest groups in Britain, it was all the more true of many of the various groups established to argue for or against association or membership of the European Economic Community. As with the main political actors involved in the European debate, industrial representatives and campaigning groups gave rather uneven attention to the Commonwealth. Not a few observers were convinced that 'the interests of the Commonwealth' were little more than a cover for the interests of British industry and agriculture.

The staff of the most influential industrial lobbying group, the Federation of British Industry (FBI), acknowledged that Commonwealth preference was a dwindling asset to British industry. In 1957 the FBI's European affairs specialist, Peter Tennant, argued that the UK government's use of the Commonwealth to support the exclusion of agriculture from the Free Trade Area was a transparent excuse for protecting British farmers. 'The Continentals', he wrote, 'do not mind us playing the Commonwealth card, but they do object to us claiming God put it there'.[48] In late 1962 he again emphasized that Commonwealth trade would not be jeopardized by entry into the Community.[49] On the other hand, many FBI Grand Council members were firmly convinced of the need to maintain Commonwealth preference, so the

FBI's public statements tended to be cautious. The FBI did at least welcome the Free Trade Area plan and the EEC membership application. One industrial group was fiercely opposed to both: the Commonwealth Industries Association (CIA), a partisan group of Conservative MPs and small British companies with strong Commonwealth connections. Other lobbies for Commonwealth trade took a balanced approach to both of Britain's European initiatives, welcoming them while insisting on safeguards for Commonwealth traders.

The preservation of Commonwealth interests was one of the chief grounds on which the National Farmers' Union (NFU) opposed European agricultural integration throughout the period. The ardently pro-Commonwealth speeches of NFU president Harold Woolley in early 1961 and 1962 have prompted at least one observer to the conclusion that Woolley's own Commonwealth 'sentiment' was a major cause of the NFU's hostility to the application.[50] The NFU's increasing resort to assertions of the unity of British and Commonwealth agricultural interests speaks volumes about the union's increasingly embattled attempts to gain special exemptions from the Common Agricultural Policy. After the Brussels negotiators had moved on from the Commonwealth to British agriculture, the NFU rejected the terms negotiated at Brussels without even referring to the Commonwealth argument.[51] Perhaps the shift in NFU tactics can be explained simply by the fact that the negotiators in Brussels were now focusing on British agriculture, not on the Commonwealth. But this was also a tacit acceptance of the real divergence between British and other Commonwealth agricultural interests, an acknowledgment perhaps that the Commonwealth argument was not an essential part of the NFU's case, or possibly that the NFU did not expect its defiance to be able to alter the shape of the deal over Commonwealth agricultural trade reached in Brussels.

The pro-European campaigning groups all approached the Commonwealth issue with caution, largely because they aimed to attract as wide a range of supporters within Britain as possible. The two pro-European organizations most active in the debate over ties with the nascent European Communities were the 'Britain in Europe' group, established in 1956, and its explicitly pro-entry successor, the Common Market Campaign, established in May 1961. Both gathered committed federalists together with industrial representatives, trade unionists, businessmen and parliamentarians from all of the main political parties with the purpose of arguing the case for strengthening ties with the Common Market as much as possible. The tone of these groups was set by the desire of the federalists to appeal to as wide a cross-section of pro-Europeans as possible, and these organizations were thus always chaired by a prominent public figure (Lord Salter, then Lord Gladwyn) who was not known to be a federalist. Gladwyn, a diplomat by career, maintained throughout the debate over joining the Communities from 1961 to 1963 that joining the Communities would be as good for the Commonwealth as it would for Britain.

Caution over the Commonwealth meant it was relatively rare that a pro-European argued that the days when the Commonwealth was a force to be reckoned with were over. Instead pro-European campaigning concentrated on countering the claim that there was a 'choice' to be made between the Commonwealth and Europe. The argument sometimes heard in the Commons to the effect that the Commonwealth was no replacement for a European trading association did not feature in the literature of the main pro-European lobbying groups. Britain in Europe and the Common Market Campaign consistently preferred the argument that European trade liberalization would strengthen Britain and would therefore be good for the Commonwealth. In 1958 Britain in Europe commissioned a study to prove this was true of the European free trade area, published after the plan's demise, which had considerable influence in the preparation of government opinion before the decision to apply for EEC membership was taken.[52] The pro-Europeans then paid little attention to the subject until late 1962, as Peter Tennant noted,[53] when the Common Market Campaign finally saw it had to counter the arguments of the anti-Europeans over the precise terms of the deal being negotiated over Commonwealth trade. Because of the speed with which negotiations were altering these terms, the pro-Europeans were unable to produce a definitive economic analysis comparable to Britain in Europe's study of the free trade area. Until such time as this were possible, their rough estimates had to compete with the far more alarmist calculations of Cambridge and London university economists dedicated to the anti-European cause, many of whom were convinced that the 'new' Commonwealth held out a promise of economic expansion which the developed European countries could not match.

In 1961 Labour MPs involved in the Common Market Campaign established a 'Labour Common Market Committee'. The bulk of the Labour left had always suspected that the European project was little more than a party political weapon in the armouries of the Conservative and Liberal parties. There were bound to be special difficulties then in eliciting support for European Community membership on the left, and it was at this constituency that the Labour pro-Europeans aimed.

Because of this, the Labour CMC was unlikely to be more radical over the Commonwealth than its all-party sponsor, the Common Market Campaign, was. Some of the parliamentarians and trade unionists involved in the campaign were personally convinced that developing trade with the EEC was now more important than developing trade with the Commonwealth, but the Labour Common Market Committee could not reflect their enthusiasm.

The United Kingdom Council of the European Movement (UKCEM) had been an active supporter of the free trade area plan and the European Free Trade Association but was less involved in promoting the Macmillan government's membership bid, and the expected effect on the Commonwealth was one of the main factors behind the shift. The UKCEM was also the most determinedly anti-federalist member of the European Movement, though in view of de Gaulle's ascendancy within the Community this was only a side issue in the public debate in Britain. The fact that prominent members of the Council such as Denis Healey personally opposed entry into the Community on the basis of the foreseeable effects on the Commonwealth was therefore more significant in preventing the UKCEM from taking any position on the application, as Council members noted at the time.

The main anti-European groups were more sharply divided on party political lines than the pro-European organizations were, and this was also reflected in their approaches to the Commonwealth. Though all of the anti-European campaigns focused heavily on the political cohesion of the Commonwealth and on the system of tariff preference that linked the Commonwealth countries on an economic level, their consensus ended there.

The Anti-Common Market League (ACML), connected with some prominent right-wing Conservative backbenchers, made 'the Commonwealth' the main theme of its attack on the Macmillan government. However, when the ACML attacked European Community membership on the grounds that it would weaken the economic and political cohesion of 'the Commonwealth and Empire', they were primarily concerned with relations with the 'Old Dominions' and not with trade with the Asian or black African Commonwealth member states. ACML campaigners, a number of whom were associated with the new right-wing 'Monday Club', had previously been involved in campaigning against withdrawal from the African empire and against changes in UK trade that would raise the price of foodstuffs imported to Britain, one of the main threats which they saw in the weakening of the Commonwealth trading system. John Paul, director of the ACML, was a former member of the Cheap Food League, a campaign uniting modern-day mercantilists on the right of the Conservative Party with classic free traders on the right of the Liberal party in support of the cheap food regime at the heart of the Commonwealth trading system. In so far as the desire for low prices constituted an argument against European Community membership, it was only really applicable to grain, dairy and meat imports from the 'Old Dominions' rather than to the former African dependencies, from which raw materials and food-stuffs were not to be subjected to high tariffs by the EEC anyway. What grated most for the ACML was the impression that, for dubious economic gains, the Macmillan government was voluntarily surrendering Britain's role as linchpin of the economic and political system that was supposed to link the Commonwealth and Empire. The ACML campaign attracted considerable support in the country at large, but its wild rhetoric about the government's betrayal of Empire and Commonwealth gained it little support among Conservatives in Parliament.

Opponents of the 'betrayal of the Commonwealth' on the left were chiefly drawn from a number of avowedly anti-imperialist groups: the Forward Britain Movement, spearheaded by a group of left-wing trade unionists, the 'New Left', a young group of Marxist intellectuals who published *The New Left Review*, the Tribune group (which published *Tribune*), and the 'Victory for Socialism' group, a parliamentary group with a pool of support in the labour movement. Like the ACML, these groups underlined their support for Commonwealth trading preferences, though unlike their right-wing counterparts they gave equal attention to the 'new' Commonwealth in Africa and Asia and to the 'Old Dominions'. Beneath a veneer of anti-colonialist rhetoric, a clumsy approach to transforming the economic relations between the First and Third Worlds made much of the left's material an easy target for Roy Jenkins and other pro-Marketeers. The left-wing anti-Europeans did not mount a defence against pro-European criticisms that their arguments about 'complementary economies' would condemn the rest of the Commonwealth to trading raw materials in exchange for manufactured goods on unfavourable terms.[54] For the left, the greatest bogey was First World capitalism, and the only real basis for a socialist Third World policy was the rejection of an alliance with a European 'capitalist club'.

The small number of Liberal opponents of the Common Market application who created their own campaign, Keep Britain Out, had cut their teeth on years of campaigning against a preferential economic association with Europe on the ground that it was a 'protectionist' club which contravened Liberal free trade principles. The campaign was led by Oliver Smedley, once a Vice-President of the Party and a central figure in the Cheap Food League and other similar campaigning groups. 'Keep Britain Out' made little headway within the Liberal movement, despite the considerable appeal of Commonwealth schemes within the party, in part because the British farming communities which fell within the party's traditional constituency felt no greater threat from the Common Agricultural Policy than they did from their Commonwealth competitors.

The popular appeal of the Commonwealth was clearly a fact accepted by both pro- and anti-Market campaigners. But most informed opinion-leaders in Britain were also keenly aware of the conflicts between domestic and Commonwealth interests, and the ease with which these conflicts were often brushed over must have made much of the material published by the two sides in the public debate appear very unconvincing.

Government policy and party politics

The shift from a 'bipartisan' European policy to a more forthright identification of the Conservatives' electoral interests with success in the Brussels negotiations had potentially far-reaching implications for Commonwealth policy. It had taken a long time to reach this position, and during both the free trade area discussions and the first membership bid, the Conservative government erred on the side of caution in resisting compromise with the other Europeans over Commonwealth preference. Only in late 1961, after the application was lodged, did the government realize it would have to make a major shift away from Commonwealth free trade, and even then for the sake of domestic and Commonwealth opinion the British still made a drama out of each and every concession the Six demanded.

The publicly 'bipartisan' free trade area plan launched in 1956 prompted a fair amount of domestic political intrigue, much of which touched on the effects of the plan on the Commonwealth. The Cabinet at this time was dominated by a generation of politicians convinced that Britain's attachment to the Commonwealth would be endangered by closer links with other Europeans – a fear that Labour's chief spokesman on the issue, Shadow Chancellor Harold Wilson, appeared to share. In a Cabinet meeting in September 1956, Eden introduced the free trade area plan and noted that there was encouraging support for links with the Common Market within the Conservative Party: 'although the Conservative Party had traditionally been a Commonwealth party, the younger generation were conscious of a need for new policies'.[55] Aspirations for Commonwealth–European arrangements persisted among ministers and many officials in 1956, and even in 1958, long after it should have been clear that very few of Britain's international partners would accept them.[56] All of these arrangements were rejected by Whitehall, with the sole exception of the Canadian proposal for a free trade association, and even this was only accepted in the knowledge that the Canadians could not go ahead with it at the time.[57] It seems very likely, though this has not yet been proven, that the Anglo-Canadian free trade association was a decoy fired off by the Macmillan government to distract pro-Commonwealth opinion in Britain from the implications of the European free trade area.

To the consternation of a number of civil servants, the idea of a Commonwealth–Europe union was taken up by Eden in 1956 in the context of discussions over strengthening the French government during the Suez crisis.[58] In public, Macmillan initially also attempted to cloak the free trade area plan in dreamy language about a Commonwealth–Europe arrangement. (In internal government memoranda he had already recognized that the aspiration to deal with both Europe and the Commonwealth as a single economic bloc was unrealistic,) particularly in view of the likelihood of American opposition, but Macmillan chose a visit to Washington, DC in September 1956 to announce this 'Commonwealth–Europe' free trade scheme.[59] Coming at a time of acute tension within the Conservative Party over the Suez crisis, the choice of the venue for the press conference was surprising – Macmillan seemed to be more concerned by the Conservative right at home than by his American hosts. In Cabinet he introduced the free trade area plan by telling ministers he favoured a European–Commonwealth meeting on the subject, chaired by Winston Churchill.[60] No steps were taken in this direction, and it is not clear whether Macmillan's stance in fact helped to assuage the opposition of Cabinet ministers like Lord Salisbury who argued the plan would have a negative impact on the Commonwealth.[61] Salisbury was gradually dissuaded from opposing the free trade area project at the end of 1956, but soon after the appointment of Macmillan as Prime Minister in 1957 he resigned in protest at the Macmillan government's acceleration of the retreat from Empire.

The Cabinet as a whole took a more cautious line over making compromises on Commonwealth trade in the free trade negotiations than their officials did. This was partly a function of the Cabinet's role in resolving interdepartmental conflicts involving the Commonwealth Relations Office, the Colonial Office and their rivals, making it natural for Cabinet decisions to rein in the more radical steps towards Europe that might affect Commonwealth trade urged by the Board of Trade and other departments. It was also a product of the conservatism of many ministers. David Eccles, one of the more 'pro-European' ministers, believed as late as May 1958 that a free trade area could be established without affecting Commonwealth preferences, a position which had long since been abandoned by his officials and which was already the subject of agreements negotiated with the Six.[62]

Much of this conservatism was a product of the personal inclinations of individual ministers rather than a response to serious evaluations of Commonwealth opinion or of popular opinion, or a reaction to real pressures from industrial or agricultural representatives. The intransigence of British and Commonwealth opinion to anything suggesting a diminution of the role of the Commonwealth in British foreign policy was taken for granted. In the event, Commonwealth member states exerted little pressure during either the free trade area negotiations or the negotiations establishing the European Free Trade Association, despite a good deal of initial caution from Commonwealth representatives over the ultimate implications of Britain's new European orientation. Parliamentary and public opinion, as we have seen, was confused over the effect of the free trade area, and was easily led by the government with respect to Commonwealth ties. The main area in which the NFU was able to garner support against government concessions among its industrial partners was the identification of the interests of Commonwealth and British agriculture, though FBI support for the NFU stance had weakened by 1959.[63] There was, then, no great pro-Commonwealth reaction against a European initiative. Nevertheless, the Conservative leadership remained far more cautious during the initial phases of the free trade area plan than some of their advisers felt was helpful: the key party official responsible for the issue, for instance, believed a more forthright public campaign would help the British initiative.[64] By the time the government began to consider entering the Communities, there was still no clear sign that there would be a public reaction against making concessions on Commonwealth trade. The main obstacle within Britain to the decision to apply for European Community membership was thus the government's repeated insistence that it could not sign the Treaties of Rome without damaging the Commonwealth. The assertion would return to haunt the government in 1962, when it was clearer that the Six were not ready to make the concessions to the Commonwealth on the scale that the Cabinet had hoped they would.

Unsympathetic observers have sometimes asserted that the first EEC membership application was made not because the government was convinced it was good for Britain, but chiefly for electoral reasons, a government in office for the third consecutive term desperate for ideas to maintain public support.[65] The archival evidence does not support this position, and one strong reason to doubt this was the case lies in the continued anxieties of Conservatives at every level of the party over the Commonwealth. Macmillan's diaries show that he was quite aware how widespread this anxiety was – he nevertheless felt he could cope with a certain amount of anxiety in the absence of a rival within the party ready to challenge him directly.[66] If the first negotiations for EEC membership succeeded, the potential impact on the Commonwealth was likely to be of prime electoral importance to the Conservative government. It would not have made much electoral sense to try to sell Common Market membership to the public if the government's electoral calculations were not based on a belief that the terms agreed for the Commonwealth would be defensible.

A shift in ministerial attitudes to the Commonwealth in 1960–61 was a critical factor in the Cabinet's decision to move towards a European application ahead of some of the Conservative Party's key constituencies. Already in July 1960, shortly before Macmillan began more actively to steer the Cabinet and Whitehall towards a major European initiative, the Commonwealth Secretary, Lord Home, came out in favour of joining the Community.[67] The main opposition to a shift at this time came from the President of the Board of Trade, Reginald Maudling, and from the Chancellor of the Exchequer, Derick Heathcoat Amory, both arguing that Commonwealth trade was the main obstacle to joining the Communities.[68] A Cabinet reshuffle two weeks later left Maudling in office but replaced Amory with Selwyn Lloyd, a loyal colleague of Macmillan who as Foreign Secretary had more than once taken a firm stance in favour of close association with the Six. Home became Foreign Secretary, and was replaced at the Commonwealth Relations Office (CRO) by veteran pro-European Duncan Sandys who now oversaw the implementation of a sea change in attitudes to the EEC within the CRO, despite fierce resistance from senior officials in the department.[69] Over the course of late 1960 and early 1961, the Cabinet's opposition to concessions on Commonwealth interests reversed.[70] The decision to negotiate was also made in the knowledge that much of the Commonwealth preferential system would come to an end in any new EC–Commonwealth trading arrangement.[71]

The Cabinet's cautious approach to concessions on Commonwealth interests was translated into a theatrical defence of unrealistic and even petty Commonwealth desiderata in early 1962, a drama which the Six were relied upon to understand.[72] Only the last-minute deputation of Heath to negotiate a package deal with the foreign ministers of the Six in January 1963 belatedly promised to overcome the difficulties which had been reached by the negotiating teams at Brussels.[73] A few critics have concluded from this that the government overestimated the strength of pro-Commonwealth opposition to 'joining Europe' in British domestic politics.[74] On the other hand, if the British government's approach to the negotiations encouraged domestic opposition on Commonwealth grounds, Macmillan believed he could live with it. Indeed, when Gaitskell turned against the application, he was playing a political game to which Macmillan positively warmed. The Prime Minister hoped for nothing more than an election fought on an issue that made the Conservatives seem forward-looking and the Labour Party appear stuck in the past.[75] The evidence suggests that Macmillan only became confident in his calculation that the Conservative approach would appeal more to British public opinion in 1962, well after the negotiations had been formally launched.

Over the course of the negotiations, Cabinet ministers increasingly swung round to the belief that the Conservatives' electoral fortunes were tied to the conduct of the negotiations. Now, in spite of the clear obstacles to the government's initial negotiating objectives, the Conservatives decided to commit themselves more firmly to the results of the negotiations. Once the negotiations were underway the European issue gradually gained a higher and higher profile in the Cabinet's public relations and electoral strategy. A key figure behind the shift was the Party Chairman, Iain Macleod, whose first concern was to take up position against the government's political opponents, whether Labour, Liberal or Conservative. Though Macleod would not have wanted to commit the party to a losing cause, his calculations apparently had little to do with the immediate prospects of success at Brussels. At the very time Macleod made his stance known in January 1962 the Six were negotiating a deal on the Common Agricultural Policy which put pay to British hopes of an easy negotiation on terms favourable to UK and Commonwealth agriculture.

A similar shift in Macmillan's public approach to the issue was also heavily influenced by domestic considerations. In July 1962, Macmillan spoke to the Conservative Party Chairman's Strategic Advisory Committee. The key to winning the next election, he told them, was to turn 'the European thing into a great thing'; just as the last election had been won by announcing the arrival of the affluent society, so the European application would carry the Conservatives to success in the next election.[76] In September at the party conference Macmillan was more forthright in his defence of the case for Common Market membership than he had yet been. And speaking in Liverpool during a by-election at the end of 1962 the Prime Minister proclaimed for the first time that he was convinced that Britain should enter the Community on the terms that had thus far been agreed. Privately, Macmillan appears by this time to have been quite unconvinced that de Gaulle would allow the negotiations to be concluded successfully. But at least if the negotiations collapsed, it would have been clearly beyond his control. Macmillan's shift from a more cautious approach to the application was based on the shift in Cabinet and Conservative Party opinion in favour of reaching a deal at Brussels on Commonwealth trade short of free entry for Commonwealth goods. The prospect of major concessions on Commonwealth trade at the turn of 1963 was not blocked at home, it was torpedoed by the French insistence at Brussels that the negotiations be suspended indefinitely.

Conclusions

Between 1956 and 1963, the effects of European policy on the Commonwealth received an unpredictable and inconsistent response from British public opinion and from the British government. Where the Commonwealth moved to the centre of the debate over Europe, this was often a product of party political calculation rather than a direct reflection of deep Commonwealth sentiment or any clarity over the effect closer ties with the other Europeans would have on the Commonwealth.

If, as this chapter suggests, the strength of Commonwealth rhetoric in 1962 was largely a product of party politics, then what does this suggest about the increasingly minor role of the Commonwealth issue in British debate over joining the European Community in the decade which followed de Gaulle's 'non' in 1963? While Wilson was still raising the issue of New Zealand butter in the 1970s, and Mrs Thatcher still raised the Commonwealth as an obstacle to closer integration with Britain's European partners in the late 1980s, the anti-European campaign had already shifted away from the Commonwealth issue by 1970. The standard explanations of this trend look at the relationship between the British government and its Commonwealth partners, not at domestic politics in Britain. It may well be that the Commonwealth was no longer a central issue because the leaders of the campaign against Common Market membership in 1962 – the National Farmer's Union, the Conservative right and the Labour left – had other more pressing concerns and no longer saw their own interests were served as well by vague appeals to Commonwealth unity.

Notes

1. Miriam Camps, *Britain and the European Community, 1955–1963* (London: Oxford University Press, 1964), e.g. p. 338. Research on British foreign policy under Bevin in the immediate postwar period has been even more forthright in affirming the strength of British Commonwealth sentiment. See, for example, Michael Blackwell, *Clinging to Grandeur: British Attitudes and Foreign Policy in the Aftermath of the Second World War* (Westport, CT: Greenwood Press, 1993), *passim*, and John Kent, *British Imperial Strategy and the Origins of the Cold War, 1944–49* (Leicester: Leicester University Press, 1993), esp. ch. 4.
2. G. St J. Barclay, *Commonwealth or Europe* (St Lucia: University of Queensland Press, 1970) pp. 147ff, 159, 201ff; Stuart Ward, 'Anglo–Commonwealth Relations and EEC Membership: The Problem of the Old Dominions', in G. Wilkes (ed.), *Britain's Failure to Enter the European Community, 1961–63: The Enlargement Negotiations and Crises in European, Atlantic and Commonwealth Relations* (London: Frank Cass, 1997) pp. 93–107.
3. See esp. W. David McIntyre, *The Commonwealth of Nations: Origins and Impact, 1869–1971* (Minneapolis: University of Minnesota Press, 1977), esp. pp. 442–6, 461–2; John M. MacKenzie, *Propaganda and Empire: the Manipulation of British Public Opinion, 1880–1960* (Manchester: Manchester University Press, 1984), esp. pp. 1ff. The contents of the *Journal of Imperial and Commonwealth History* reflect the continuing lack of interest in British public opinion among contemporary historians of the Commonwealth.
4. See, for example, J. Biggs-Davison, *The Walls of Europe* (London: Johnson, 1962), *passim*.
5. A useful study by Sue Onslow, *Backbench Debate within the Conservative Party and its Influence on British Foreign Policy, 1948–57* (London: Macmillan Press – now Palgrave, 1997), deals with the imperial and European strands of Conservative backbench opposition to the Macmillan government at this time, though without attempting to relate the two themes to each other.
6. John Ramsden, *The Making of Conservative Party Policy: The Conservative Research Department since 1929* (London: Longman, 1980) pp. 213–14.
7. Diary entry for 5 August 1961, quoted in H. Macmillan, *At the End of the Day* (London: Macmillan Press – now Palgrave, 1973) p. 26. See also diary entry for 20 December 1961, ibid., p. 46.
8. Interventions of Harry Legge-Bourke and Gerald Nabarro, *Hansard*, 5th Series, 12 and 26 November 1956, vol. 560, col. 61, and vol. 561, cols 112–16, 648–9.

9. In July 1956, 'One Nation' parliamentarians spearheaded the placing of an Early Day Motion on the agenda of the House of Commons urging the government to 'join' the Common Market. A similar motion was then put by a group of Labour MPs. In 1961, the pro-Market and pro-integration case was pressed publicly by the extra-parliamentary Bow Group and its widely-read publication, *Crossbow*, and by 'One Nation' parliamentarians such as Gilbert Longden (see Longden's speech of 28 June 1961, *Hansard*, 5th Series, vol. 643, cols 528–36). For more details, see G. Wilkes, 'Britain and the European Community, 1956–63', forthcoming PhD thesis, University of Cambridge.

10. For comment on 'substitute imperialists', see Leonard Beaton, 'Heirs of the Imperialists in search of New Loyalties', *The Times*, 9 January 1969, p. 8; Geoffrey Edwards, 'Britain and Europe', in Jonathan Storey (ed.), *The New Europe* (Oxford: Westview Press, 1990) pp. 209–11; Martin Holmes, 'The Conservative Party and Europe', in M. Holmes (ed.), *The Eurosceptical Reader* (London: Macmillan, 1996) p. 115; Ramsden, op. cit., note 6 above, p. 214; Ronald Butt, 'The Common Market and Conservative Party Politics, 1961–62', *Government and Opposition*, 2/3 (April–July 1967) 374–6.

11. Biggs-Davison, op. cit., note 4 above, *passim*.

12. Fairly isolated references to debate over the issue can be found in the Conservative Research Department papers (CRD), file 2/34/8, particularly on the meeting of the Canada Group of April 1960, Canada and the Commonwealth, Conservative Commonwealth Committee (CCC) 178; Conservative Central Office papers (CCO), file 507/1/1, notes on the meeting of the Conservatives' parliamentary Commonwealth Affairs Committee, 27 April 1961, Conservative Party Archives, Bodleian Library, Oxford. For more discussion, see G. Wilkes, 'Britain and the European Community, 1956–63', forthcoming PhD thesis, University of Cambridge.

13. Nora Beloff, *The General Says No* (Harmondsworth: Penguin, 1963) p. 95, and Beloff, *Transit of Britain: a Report on Britain's Changing Role in the Post-War World* (London: Collins, 1973) p. 172; Wolfram Kaiser, *Using Europe, Abusing the Europeans* (London: Macmillan Press – now Palgrave, 1996) p. 146.

14. See B. Sewill to R. Maudling, 3 March 1961, CRD file 2/8/11, Conservative Party Archives, Bodleian Library, Oxford; interview with Brendan Sewill, 1998.

15. Cabinet conclusions for 13 July 1960, Public Record Office, Kew, London (PRO), CC(60)41, CAB 128/34.

16. See, for example, Maudling's speech winding up the first day of the Commons debate of August 1961, *Hansard*, 5th Series, vol. 645, cols 1480–606. Butler spoke on behalf of the government at the party conference of October 1961, and chaired the Cabinet committee responsible for negotiating with the Six thereafter.

17. *Hansard*, 5th Series, vol. 645, cols 1480–606, 1651–777.

18. Ibid.

19. Minutes of the meeting of the Chairman's Committee, 17 July 1962, CRD, file 2/52/8, Conservative Party Archives, Bodleian Library, Oxford; private memorandum of 23 October 1962, Butler papers, Trinity College, Cambridge, file G38. See also Ramsden, op. cit., note 6 above, pp. 219–20.

20. Macmillan (op. cit., note 7 above, p. 24) noted in his diary (5 August 1961) that Churchill had been in and out of his office throughout the August

1961 Commons debate, and claimed that a successful application would have 'crowned' his work as founder of the European Movement. Macmillan's implication that Churchill was broadly in sympathy with the application was not backed up by any firmer support from Churchill, whose secretary replied to a letter from Macmillan's foreign affairs adviser that he did not think 'Sir Winston has any very decided views on the Common Market question'. PRO, PREM 11/3788. A report that Churchill opposed the betrayal of the Commonwealth was carried to the press by Viscount Montgomery in August 1962, and was subsequently denied by Churchill's secretary.

21. Correspondence with Robin Turton, file 23/64 (*passim*), Avon papers, University of Birmingham.
22. See Robin Turton to Anthony Eden, 18 October 1962, file 23/64, Avon papers, University of Birmingham.
23. Records of the meeting of 31 October 1962, file 23, papers of John Biggs-Davison, House of Lords Records Office, London.
24. 'A Policy for Britain Outside the Six', 8 December 1962, typed MS, file 23, papers of John Biggs-Davison, House of Lords Records Office, London.
25. Four then withdrew their names from the motion. Further details in Ronald Butt, 'The Common Market and Conservative Party Politics, 1961–62', *Government and Opposition*, 2/3 (April–July 1967) 378–9.
26. Paper for the Conservative Party Chairman's Committee, CRD 2/52/7, Conservative Party Archives, Bodleian Library, Oxford.
27. 'The Common Market and the Election', Brendan Sewill, 25 [*sic*] May 1962, AC/1, for the 24 May 1962 meeting of the Auxiliary Committee (which was to report to the Manifesto Committee), in file marked 'David Dear's Auxiliary Committee', CRD 2/52/10, Conservative Party Archives, Bodleian Library, Oxford.
28. See below, 'Government policy and party politics'.
29. *The Spectator*, 7 July 1961.
30. Philip Williams, *Hugh Gaitskell* (London: Jonathan Cape, 1979), ch. 25.
31. Discussion with Alistair Hetherington, editor of *The Guardian*, 26 July 1962, Hetherington papers, file 3/17, London School of Economics archives (LSE).
32. George Brown, *In My Way* (Harmondsworth: Penguin, 1970) p. 211.
33. Discussion with Alistair Hetherington, 11 September 1962, Hetherington papers, file 3/15, LSE, and the testimony of Lord Roll in Eric Roll, *Crowded Hours* (London: Faber, 1985) p. 126.
34. Compare Brian Brivati, *Hugh Gaitskell* (London: Richard Cohen Books, 1996) pp. 412–15.
35. Notes by Alistair Hetherington on meeting with Jo Grimond, 6 November 1962, Hetherington papers, file 3/9, LSE.
36. Macmillan's diary, 9 September 1962, in Macmillan, op. cit., note 7 above, p. 130.
37. Brivati, op. cit., note 34 above, pp. 412–15.
38. Off-the-record discussions with Alistair Hetherington, editor of *The Guardian*, 25 July and 6 November 1962, Hetherington papers, files 3/18 and 3/9, LSE.
39. For more on the relationship between press, broadcasting and party political approaches to European Community at the time, see George Wilkes,

'Britain and European Integration, 1948–1975: Political Roles of the Media', in Jan Servaes and Rico Lie (eds), *Media and Politics in Transition: Cultural Identity in the Age of Globalisation* (Leuven: Acco, 1997) pp. 175–94.

40. *The Manchester Guardian*, 4 October 1956.
41. See, for example, Lord Beaverbrook papers, House of Lords Records Office, and Peter Walker, *Staying Power: An Autobiography* (London: Bloomsbury, 1991) pp. 31–2.
42. See, for example, ibid., pp. 32–3. On Beaverbrook's withdrawal of support for Macmillan and the Conservative government, see *Time & Tide*, 2–9 August 1962.
43. Beaverbrook to Gaitskell, 6 December 1962, and Gaitskell to Beaverbrook, 12 December 1962, file C/139, Lord Beaverbrook papers, House of Lords Records Office.
44. Beaverbrook papers, file C/139, and John Junor, *Listening for a Midnight Tram* (London: Chapmans, 1990) p. 123.
45. See the shift in stance in *Observer* editorials between 26 August and 16/23 September 1962; interview with Christopher Layton, 16 May 1992.
46. Alistair Hetherington, *Guardian Years* (London: Chatto & Windus, 1981) pp. 176ff; see also Hetherington's notes on his discussion with Reginald Maudling, 12 November 1962, file 3/13, Hetherington papers, LSE.
47. See the notes on his interviews with Gaitskell on 11 and 27 September 1962, in file 3, documents 14 and 15, Hetherington papers, LSE.
48. Memorandum by Peter Tennant, 'Denmark and the Free Trade Area and Common Market', 21 March 1957 (MSS 200/F/3/02/2/10, Modern Records Centre, University of Warwick), written after a talk with Carsten of the Danish Industrial Federation on 15 March.
49. Speech at 'Common Market – In or Out', a conference organized by Britain in Europe and Federal Trust, 7–8 November 1962, Federal Union papers, file 31/2, LSE.
50. Robert J. Lieber, *British Politics and European Unity* (Berkeley, CA: University of California Press, 1970) p. 125.
51. Debate over the Brussels negotiations at the NFU Annual General Meeting, January 1963. See *British Farmer*, 270 (26 January 1963) 2.
52. Economist Intelligence Unit, *Commonwealth and Europe* (London: EIU, 1960).
53. Speech at 'Common Market – In or Out', a conference organized by Britain in Europe and Federal Trust, 7–8 November 1962, Federal Union papers, file 31/2, LSE.
54. See, for example, 'The Great Debate', *The Times*, 26 September 1962, p. 11; Walker, op. cit., note 41 above, p. 130.
55. PRO, CAB 128/29, CC (56) 66, 18 September 1956.
56. George Wilkes, 'Britain and the European Community, 1956–63', forthcoming PhD thesis, University of Cambridge. Macmillan's September 1956 rhetoric about Commonwealth–European ties is referred to above. Elizabeth J. Kane ('Tilting To Europe? British Responses to Developments in European Integration, 1955–58', unpublished DPhil thesis, University of Oxford, 1996, chapters 2 and 3) has shown on the other hand that there was much disillusionment with the Commonwealth within the British government in late 1956.

57. James Ellison, 'Harold Macmillan's Fear of "Little Europe": Britain, the Six and the European free trade area', Leicester University Discussion Papers on Britain and Europe, BE95/5, 1995, pp. 18–19.
58. Kane, op. cit., note 56 above.
59. Newspaper reports, September 1956; William Clark, *From Three Worlds: Memoirs* (London: Sidgwick & Jackson, 1986) pp. 193–4.
60. Ibid., pp. 193–4.
61. Cabinet Conclusions for the meetings between 14 September 1956 and 8 January 1957, PRO, CC(56)65–68, 83, 85, CC(57)3, CAB 128/29.
62. See Eccles's paper EA (58)41 and comments by R. W. B. Clarke, 14 May 1958, in PRO, T234/376.
63. Economist Intelligence Unit, op. cit., note 52 above.
64. Branston to M. Fraser, 20 February 1957, CRD, file 2/42/7, Conservative Party Archives, Bodleian Library, Oxford.
65. Kaiser, op. cit., note 13 above, pp. 145–6, 149–51. Aside from the implications of the assertions of Nora Beloff above, David Butler and Antony King, *The British General Election of 1964* (London: Macmillan Press – now Palgrave, 1965) p. 79, also mention the importance of electoral considerations to Conservative party officials, without clarifying whether this was after negotiations were opened or before.
66. Macmillan, op. cit., note 7 above, pp. 7–9.
67. Cabinet Conclusions for the meeting of 13 July 1960, PRO, CC(60)41, CAB 128/34. See also Home, *The Way the Wind Blows* (London: Collins, 1976) p. 176.
68. Ibid.
69. Joe Garner, *The Commonwealth Office, 1925–1968* (London: Heinemann, 1978) pp. 358, 397–401.
70. Cabinet Conclusions for the meeting of 27 July 1961, PRO, CC(61)44, CAB 128/35; Kaiser, op. cit., note 13 above, p. 139.
71. Ibid.
72. See, for example, the testimony of a member of Britain's negotiating team in Sir Christopher Audland, 'The Heath Negotiations', unpublished paper for Chatham House conference, 1993.
73. Oliver Bange, *The EEC Crisis of 1963: Kennedy, Macmillan, de Gaulle and Adenauer in Conflict* (London: Macmillan Press – now Palgrave, 1998).
74. Jeremy Moon, *European Integration in British Politics* (Aldershot: Dartmouth, 1985) pp. 208ff, and Hugo Young, *This Blessed Plot: Britain and Europe from Churchill to Blair* (London: Macmillan Press – now Palgrave, 1998) p. 139.
75. Minutes of the meeting of the Chairman's Committee, 17 July 1962, CRD papers, file 2/52/8, Conservative Party Archives, Bodleian Library, Oxford.
76. Ibid.

I would like to thank the keepers of the House of Lords Records Office and Lisl Biggs-Davison; the Modern Records Centre, University of Warwick; the Conservative Party Archives, Bodleian Library; the archives at the University of Birmingham; the archives at the London School of Economics; and the archives at Trinity College, Cambridge.

6

'Commonwealth or Europe?': Macmillan's Dilemma, 1961–63

Alex May

Speaking at the West Point Military Academy on 5 December 1962, Dean Acheson famously asserted:

> Great Britain has lost an empire and has not yet found a role. The attempt to play a separate power role – that is, a role apart from Europe, a role based on a 'special relationship' with the United States, a role based on being the head of a 'Commonwealth' which has no political structure, or unity, or strength, and enjoys a fragile and precarious economic relationship by means of the sterling area and preferences in the British market – this role is about played out.[1]

Acheson was a distinguished elder statesman: a former Secretary of State under President Truman, and now a senior adviser to President Kennedy; one of the most influential architects of Western international organization in the early years of the Cold War; and a long-established advocate of European integration, including Britain. Coming as they did at a particularly sensitive point in the negotiations between Britain and the six original members of the European Communities on the likely terms for British membership of the Communities, his remarks caused a furore. The Institute of Directors, under the presidency of Lord Chandos (Oliver Lyttelton, the former Conservative cabinet minister) challenged Macmillan to rebut what it described as 'a calculated insult to the British nation', and 'a bitter attack on the present policies of the British Government'.[2] Macmillan duly responded. In his view, 'Mr. Acheson has fallen into an error which has been made by quite a lot of people in the course of the last 400 years, including Philip of Spain, Louis XIV, Napoleon, the Kaiser and Hitler. He seems wholly to misunderstand the role of the

Commonwealth'.[3] Dean Rusk, the American Secretary of State, issued a statement emphasizing that Acheson had been speaking purely as a private citizen. President Kennedy issued another, regretting the attention given to Acheson's remarks, and denying any rift in Anglo–American relations.[4]

Yet Acheson's remarks struck a chord with many, both at the time and since, who believed that, in the decades following the Second World War, Britain (or at least the British political elite) suffered from a sort of post-imperial hangover, its judgement clouded by memories of its imperial past, an attempt to cling onto whatever of the past remained, and a consequent inability to see where its true interests lay – which were, self-evidently, in increasing cooperation and integration with its European neighbours. Jean Monnet, arguably the single most influential figure in the early history of European integration, described this as 'the price of victory – the illusion that you could maintain what you had, without change'.[5] His colleague and compatriot, Robert Marjolin, Vice-President of the first European Commission and former Secretary-General of the OEEC, identified the Commonwealth ('still an emotionally powerful reality') as the foremost obstacle to British integration in Europe, and wrote of 'a long evolution that was to lead Britain gradually to realise that her role as a great world sea power, whose interests were utterly distinct from those of the neighbouring continent, was ended and that her future lay in joining the Six [original members of the European Communities]'.[6]

What might be described as the Acheson thesis (though, of course, he was by no means the first to articulate the idea) has, to a greater or lesser degree, permeated much of the historical writing on Britain's foreign policy in the immediate postwar decades, to the extent that it can almost be described as an orthodoxy. Thus Peter Teed, the author of a widely-used schoolbook on British history, first published in 1976, wrote that after 1956 Britain faced a stark choice 'between Europe on the one hand, and the Commonwealth on the other'.[7] David Sanders, in a book borrowing its title from Acheson's claim, has argued that, once the mists of history and sentiment surrounding the Empire/Commonwealth began to lift, it was inevitable that Britain would assume the role of an integral part of Europe which was dictated by geography and economic interest: Britain's entry into the European Communities was thus 'the clear counterpart to the retreat from Empire and the abandonment of Britain's world role', and 'whatever the express calculations of the decision makers themselves, merely the response of a political system trying to catch up with economic realities'.[8] More recently, Wolfram Kaiser has

asserted that by 1960–61 the Commonwealth was 'no longer an asset…
but already a liability', and that the Macmillan government was motivated to seek admission to the European Communities in the latter year
partly by the belief that 'leadership of the EEC would…replace leadership of the Commonwealth as the main source of legitimation for
Britain's claim to a special role alongside the two superpowers'.[9]

The Acheson thesis is clearly open to a number of different interpretations, and begs a number of important questions. To what extent
were integration with Europe and continued cooperation with its Commonwealth partners in reality mutually exclusive 'alternatives' for
Britain? Equally importantly, to what extent were they *perceived* as alternatives? Was this dichotomy present throughout the postwar period, or
was it a product of particular, temporally specific, circumstances? To
what extent did the different levels or elements of the British political
system – ministers, parliamentarians, officials, political activists, pressure groups, the media, 'public opinion', etc. – view this 'choice' in different ways? And what effects did the existence of this 'choice' have on
Britain's relations with its Commonwealth and European partners, and
on perceptions of Britain's role in international relations? This chapter
will seek to provide answers to some of these questions by examining
the interaction of Britain's Commonwealth and European policies,
specifically in the period immediately before and during Britain's first
application to join the European Communities (1961–63).

The 'three circles'

In an often-quoted remark, Churchill observed (at the Conservative
Party conference in October 1948) that Britain stood at the 'point of
junction' of three international alignments, or 'circles': the Commonwealth, the North Atlantic and 'United Europe'.[10] The weight attached
to these circles by British policy-makers had varied enormously over
time. During its Victorian heyday, Britain's concerns had been almost
exclusively imperial, epitomized by Lord Salisbury's policy of 'splendid
isolation'. The increasing division of Europe, as well as its own isolation, forced Britain in the early 1900s into a reluctant (and initially
half-hearted) 'continental commitment', by means of a series of
alliances with other European powers.[11] In the aftermath of the First
World War, British policy-makers attempted to construct an Atlantic
alliance, and to mobilize the Commonwealth alliance, in order once
again to keep out of European entanglements. Only in the late 1930s
did the unwisdom of this policy become apparent. Thereafter, British

policy-makers were forced to recognize the 'continental commitment' as a political, ideological and strategic necessity, first in response to Hitler's barbaric drive for world power, and secondly in response to what some contemporaries perceived as an equally barbaric menace from Soviet Russia. At the same time, Britain was, at last, able to seal an alliance with a non-isolationist United States, although by no means on the same favourable terms as had been anticipated before the war.

By the late 1940s, then, Britain was a 'continental' and an 'Atlantic' power, in a sense which would not have been true before 1939. But its policy-makers still saw it, above all, as a 'world' power, with responsibilities and spheres of influences more extensive than those of any other power, the United States included. These responsibilities and spheres of influence were very largely, although not exclusively, based on the continued existence of the Empire and on the existence of the Commonwealth, which British policy-makers still saw as an, albeit decentralized and flexible, imperial system. After all, it was not Britain but the Commonwealth which had 'stood alone' through the dark days of 1940.[12] Britain's Commonwealth orientation goes a long way towards explaining its 'missed opportunities' in Europe in the late 1940s and early 1950s. Thus Churchill, whose speech at Zurich University on 19 September 1946 was a milestone in European integration, predicated his call for a 'United States of Europe' on a belief that Britain and the Commonwealth would remain a separate entity, influencing Europe but not becoming a part of it: 'I never thought that Britain or the British Commonwealth should, whether individually or collectively, become an integral part of a European Federation, and have never given the slightest support to the idea', he explained to his Cabinet colleagues shortly after taking power in October 1951.[13]

Nevertheless, changes in the British–Commonwealth relationship between the late 1940s and the early 1960s profoundly altered both the psychological and the political and strategic value of the Commonwealth for Britain. First, there was the Canadian Citizenship Act of 1946, followed by the British Nationality Act of 1948, which replaced the previous notion of a common Commonwealth citizenship (based on common allegiance to the British crown) by a system of local citizenship, with the privileges afforded citizens of other Commonwealth states to be determined on an ad hoc and reciprocal basis.[14] Secondly, the presence of the Prime Ministers of India, Pakistan and Ceylon at the Commonwealth Prime Ministers' meeting of October 1948, and the decision to allow India to maintain its Commonwealth membership as a republic at the Prime Ministers' meeting of April 1949 (by means of its recognition of George VI as 'the symbol of the free association of its independent member nations, and as such the Head of the Commonwealth') not only transformed the previously 'British' into a 'multiracial' Commonwealth, but paved the way for the inclusion of Ghana (1957), Malaya (1957), Nigeria (1960), Cyprus (1960), Sierra Leone (1961), Tanganyika (1961, joined with Zanzibar in 1964 to form Tanzania), Jamaica (1962), Trinidad and Tobago (1962), Uganda (1962), Kenya (1963), and further former colonies, so that by 2000 the Commonwealth comprised 54 member countries, more than two-thirds of them with no constitutional connection to the British crown, and one of them (Mozambique) with no formal connection to the former British Empire.[15] Thirdly, the year 1949 also saw the first and most significant step towards the regionalization of Commonwealth defence policies, when Canada and the UK (but no other Commonwealth states) signed the Washington Treaty, establishing NATO. Australia and New Zealand (but not, to its chagrin, the UK) were signatories to the Pacific Security Agreement (the ANZUS Pact) in 1951; and the UK, Australia, New Zealand and Pakistan (but not India and Ceylon) to the Manila Pact (inaugurating SEATO) in 1954. In all three organizations it was the US, and not the UK, which was the leading partner. India, meanwhile, held fast to Nehru's principle of non-alignment, to which increasing numbers of former colonial territories were attracted.[16]

Even before the Second World War, in the days of the 'British' Commonwealth, it was clear that Britain could not automatically assume that its own policies would be accepted and supported by its Commonwealth partners: this was conspicuously the case in relation to the Chanak incident in 1922, the Treaty of Lausanne of 1924 and the Treaty of Locarno of 1925. Nevertheless, the limits of British influence in the Commonwealth were cruelly exposed by the Suez crisis of 1956. The fact that Canada and India were among the most vociferous leaders of the international opposition to the Anglo-French action prompted many Conservatives (formerly its most vociferous proponents) to turn their backs on the Commonwealth. Richard Crossman was not alone in thinking that 'the light that blazed on this Damascus road [to Europe] was ... the baleful glare of the Suez fiasco'.[17] One historian of the Commonwealth has described the Suez crisis as 'a psychological watershed', which 'led to a hastening of the removal of the vestiges of Britain's imperial statehood, a diminishing pride in the Commonwealth among Britain's relative "attentive publics", and a willingness to reduce or shed the role of principal in Commonwealth affairs'.[18] Britain found itself increasingly on the receiving end of criticism from its Commonwealth partners in the late 1950s, as it attempted to extricate itself from the quagmire represented by the Central African Federation. Finally, in May 1961, there was the further humiliation for the Conservative govern-ment of seeing South Africa drummed out of the Commonwealth, despite all Britain's attempts to prevent such an outcome. 'The wind of change has blown us away', Macmillan commented to the High Commissioner in South Africa afterwards.[19]

Over the same period, changes on the continent of Europe signifi-cantly eroded the position of leadership which many thought to have been Britain's in the late 1940s, and threatened to relegate it to the position of a spectator, while western Europe transformed itself and experienced unparalleled economic growth. Britain belatedly con-cluded an association with the European Coal and Steel Community in 1954, but the attitude of its policy-makers towards the Messina resolu-tion and the negotiations which resulted in the Treaties of Rome was that there was 'not the slightest possibility of the...common market coming into existence' without Britain, and that 'the only troublesome point [is] whether we should strive to kill it or let it collapse of its own weight'.[20] The common market did not collapse, and Britain's attempts to divert the initiative towards a wider free trade area came to nothing.[21] After 1958, Western Europe was divided into two economic blocs, EFTA and the EEC, with Britain confined to the weaker of the two. Growth-rates in Britain and the EFTA countries lagged signifi-cantly behind those in the EEC. The economic attractions of joining 'the Six' were complemented by increasingly urgent political impera-tives, in particular the need to respond to Washington's signals that it favoured European integration, and was prepared to transfer its patron-age from London to Brussels to encourage this trend.[22] Indeed, the European Economic Association Committee of the Cabinet reported in May 1960 not only that membership of the European Communities was 'from a straight economic standpoint...almost certainly...the solution which would be most advantageous to the United Kingdom', but that, if Britain did not join:

The Community may well emerge as a Power comparable in size and influence to the United States and the USSR. The pull of this new power bloc would be bound to dilute our influence with the rest of the world, including the Commonwealth. We should find ourselves replaced as the second member of the North Atlantic Alliance and our relative influence with the United States in all fields would diminish...The independence which we have sought to preserve by remaining aloof from European integration would be of doubtful value, since our diminished status would suggest only a minor role for us in international affairs.[23]

Increasingly, membership of the EEC seemed the only alternative both to economic decline and to political isolation.

Britain and the Commonwealth: self-interest and sentiment

By 1960–61 the Commonwealth was clearly no longer the expression of British power that it had been before the war or even before the Suez crisis. Nevertheless, it remained a highly significant vehicle of British influence. Military and diplomatic ties with the independent Commonwealth states, as well as substantial areas of direct imperial rule, underpinned Britain's global reach, enabling it to continue playing the role of a great power in Africa, the Caribbean, South-East Asia, the Persian Gulf and elsewhere. The 'emergencies' in Kuwait (1961), Aden (1963–67), Borneo (1963–66), East Africa (1964), Oman (1970–75) and Belize (1972–94), and the war over the Falkland Islands (1982), were, of course, yet to come. That Britain still desired to play the role of a world power, and that both its imperial legacy and its Commonwealth connections were expected to enable it to do so, is made clear by a senior officials' report on policy for the next ten years, in 1960:

> Despite the contraction of our former strength and resources the United Kingdom still has many of the responsibilities of a world Power; and our influence need not shrink in proportion to our material strength ... Our leadership of the Commonwealth, the progressive fulfilment of our Colonial responsibilities, our special relationship with the United States, our European associations, the legacy of our Imperial past, the maturity of our political experience outside Europe, our national quality of rising to an emergency and our reliability in the defence of freedom and justice: all these can continue to justify for the United Kingdom a leading position among the Powers and a higher place in their counsels than our material assets alone would strictly warrant.[24]

More tangibly, Britain still derived substantial economic benefits from the Commonwealth connection. The system of Commonwealth preferences, inaugurated by the Ottawa agreements of 1932, provided Britain with relatively secure markets for its industrial goods, while the import of low-tariff or tariff-free Commonwealth food and raw materials similarly softened the impact of its declining competitiveness by enabling it to keep down its manufacturing costs. Furthermore, Britain's balance of trade with its Commonwealth partners was extremely favourable. Britain's position as banker of the sterling area (roughly coterminous with the Commonwealth, excluding Canada but including Eire and the Scandinavian countries) also significantly bolstered Britain's economic position in the immediate postwar years, and was expected by many (including the Radcliffe Committee of 1959) to continue to do so. By means of this position, Britain had been enabled to circumvent many of the difficulties of trading with the dollar area. Moreover, Britain's position as the leading supplier of capital to the sterling area gave it 'enormous leverage in adjusting the external policies of other member states to Britain's economic and currency needs'.[25]

By the late 1950s strains were already apparent in both the Commonwealth preference and (more particularly) the sterling area systems. The disparity between Britain's sterling reserves and its sterling liabilities became increasingly obvious following the return to convertibility in 1958, leading eventually to the sterling crises of the 1960s and devaluation in 1967. The Commonwealth preference system (already undermined by tariff reductions through GATT) came under mounting pressure, both from British manufacturers wishing to exclude the manufactured goods in particular of low-cost economies such as India and Hong Kong, and from manufacturers in other Commonwealth countries wishing to end tariff preferences for British manufactured goods. By 1961, preferences for British goods entering India, Pakistan and the African states other than Sierra Leone were insignificant.[26] Increasingly, there was a realization also that the system of support for British agriculture which was a necessary concomitant of the preference system represented a vast drain on the Treasury's resources. In 1956 renegotiation of preferences between Britain and Australia was seen by many in British government circles as a distinctly one-sided affair, and a foretaste of similar renegotiations to come. In the same year, Sir Frank Lee, Permanent Under-Secretary at the Board of Trade, argued that 'there is little dynamic life left in the Commonwealth Preference System'.[27] Britain's trade with its Commonwealth partners grew throughout the 1950s (and 1960s) markedly less rapidly than its trade with the developed economies of Europe. Nevertheless, material self-interest still bound Britain tightly to the Commonwealth. In 1960 the Commonwealth took some 40.2 per cent of British exports (almost three times as much as 'the Six'), while providing some

34.6 per cent of its imports.[28] It was only in the late 1970s (after Britain had secured entry into the European Community) that Britain's trade with the six original members of the EEC overtook its trade with the Commonwealth.[29]

Popular attitudes in Britain towards the Commonwealth are necessarily unquantifiable. It was only in reaction to events that opinion crystallized, and an event such as the Suez crisis had so many peculiar aspects that it serves as a poor guide. Indeed, the 1961–63 application to join the European Communities provided the first real test of Commonwealth sentiment in Britain in the postwar period. Undoubtedly the cultural and sentimental ties linking Britain with the Commonwealth and especially with the 'old Dominions' were still a factor of political significance. Whatever the reality, British people still thought of themselves as being at the centre of a global association, not as occupying a small island off the mainland of continental Europe. In January 1955, asked 'Would you like to see the Commonwealth break up or stay as it is?', 82 per cent of Gallup poll respondents said that they would like to see it stay as it was, and only 5 per cent said that they would like to see it break up.[30] In 1960 T. E. Utley and John Udal believed that few of their countrymen 'would…dare to suggest publicly that the Commonwealth has outlived its usefulness'.[31] Nevertheless, whether this sort of low-level sense of pride in the remains of the imperial connection could translate itself into positive support for the new Commonwealth as it evolved after 1949 is open to question. Enthusiasts for the Commonwealth (such as those associated with the *Round Table* journal, or the Royal Commonwealth Society) frequently lamented the lack of popular interest in things Commonwealth. Similar laments had been the staple fare of imperialists even in the heyday of Empire, though *The Economist* (often an acute observer of the trends of opinion) detected as early as 1952 'a widespread lack of genuine interest in the Commonwealth idea'.[32]

Whatever the real extent of popular support for the Commonwealth, Britain's political and economic ties with the Commonwealth were often cited as the main reason why Britain could not involve itself fully in the process of European integration in the late 1950s. Thus Macmillan (as Chancellor of the Exchequer), proposing a free trade area in the Commons in November 1956, asserted that 'I do not believe that this House would ever agree to our entering arrangements which, as a matter of principle, would prevent our treating the great range of imports from the Commonwealth at least as favourably as those from the European countries'.[33] The following year (as Prime Minister) he went further, stating that 'if there should at any time be a conflict between the calls upon us, there is no doubt where we stand; the Commonwealth comes first in our hearts and in our minds'.[34] These words would come back to haunt Macmillan as he tried to lead Britain into Europe in the years 1961–63.

Negotiations with the Commonwealth

Initially, Macmillan's government hoped to negotiate some form of arrangement with the EEC which would leave Commonwealth preference intact, and which might even extend Commonwealth access to European markets. In this, the government was perhaps encouraged by the proceedings of a Council of Europe working party, which reported in favour of an association between 'the Six' and the Commonwealth as a whole.[35] Nevertheless, informal discussions between representatives of the UK and of 'the Six' made clear that such an association was not on offer, and that the conditions for British entry included full acceptance of the Treaties of Rome. In June 1961 Olivier Wormser, a senior (and in English eyes Anglophobe) official at the Quai d'Orsay in Paris, emphasized that any proposal to retain the Commonwealth preference system would 'not provide a useful basis for discussion'; if Britain joined the EEC, it would, at the end of any transitional arrangements, have to impose the common external tariff on 'all imports from non-member countries, including the Commonwealth'.[36] Thereafter, the question at issue was whether the detrimental effects of British entry on Commonwealth trade could somehow be kept to a minimum.

Commonwealth protocol demanded that action by any member-state which was likely to have a detrimental effect on the interests of other member-states should be preceded by consultation and, if possible, agreement. Aware of this, but also of the fact that a full-dress meeting of Commonwealth Prime Ministers might saddle his government with unfulfillable promises, Macmillan dispatched five Europhile cabinet ministers to consult with Commonwealth governments before formally announcing Britain's application at the end of July 1961. Miriam Camps has suggested that Macmillan hoped thereby to obtain some expression of approval for his government's proposed course of action.[37] If so, he was to be disappointed.

Only the government of the Malayan Federation, whose major exports were unlikely to be affected by EEC tariffs, appeared relatively unconcerned. The Indian government spoke of possible 'serious damage' to its exports (as did the government of Pakistan), and warned that

British membership 'might weaken existing Commonwealth links'. The government of New Zealand – whose exports were likely to be the worst affected – spoke of the 'grave consequences' for New Zealand of British entry. Duncan Sandys, the Minister responsible for consultations in Wellington, was forced to promise 'special arrangements' for New Zealand. Even so, New Zealand's representatives 'made it clear that they could not at present see any effective way of protecting New Zealand's vital interests other than by maintenance of unrestricted duty-free entry'. In 1960 50.7 per cent of New Zealand's exports went to the UK, compared to 23.9 per cent of Australia's and 15.8 per cent of Canada's.[38] Nevertheless, New Zealand at least expressed a willingness to understand Britain's position. This was not the case with Canada and Australia, both of whose governments were in part dependent on the support of rural constituencies. The Australian government, while recognizing that it was not appropriate openly to criticize British plans, 'made it clear that the absence of objection should in the circumstances not be interpreted as implying approval'.[39]

The hostility of Commonwealth governments appears to have altered very little, if at all, during the 18 months which separated Macmillan's announcement of Britain's application in July 1961 and the final breakdown of negotiations in January 1963. A meeting of Commonwealth finance ministers at Accra in September 1961 again made clear the predominant attitude of Britain's partners:

> Representatives of the United Kingdom reviewed the various reasons that had led them to make the application. All other Commonwealth representatives expressed grave apprehension and concern regarding the possible results of the initiative taken by the United Kingdom ... Because of the inseparable nature of economic and political relations within the Commonwealth, and because of the political and institutional objectives of the European Economic Community and the terms of the Rome Treaty, it was feared by the other Commonwealth countries that United Kingdom membership in the European Economic Community would fundamentally alter the relationship between the United Kingdom and Commonwealth countries, indeed this relationship might be so imperilled as to weaken the Commonwealth as a whole and thus reduce its effectiveness as a world instrument for understanding, prosperity and peace.[40]

Under pressure from his Commonwealth partners, from the Opposition and from sceptics in his own party, Macmillan was finally forced to concede a Commonwealth Prime Ministers' meeting in London, in September 1962. The atmosphere was tense and again dominated by concern at the erosion of the Commonwealth relationship. Macmillan later judged the meeting to have been 'a clear success for the British Government', in that the negotiations were not stopped dead in their tracks, and Commonwealth criticism of Britain's actions was successfully directed towards discussion of particular problems.[41] Nevertheless none of Britain's partners appears to have been satisfied by the progress of negotiations; indeed, the final communiqué noted 'the extent to which their interests had not so far been met'.[42]

The depth and persistence of Commonwealth concern at the prospect of British membership of the EEC is clear. Inevitably, the Commonwealth and Europe began to take on the aspect of 'alternatives', for all Macmillan's and Heath's attempts to paper over the cracks. Not only was Commonwealth concern an important factor in itself, it also fed directly into the debate in Britain, fuelling the hostility of the anti-Common Market lobby, and fouling the government's attempts to win control of public opinion's undecided middle ground. It also made the Brussels negotiations much more difficult, forcing Britain to make greater demands than it might otherwise have done, and reinforcing the doubts of those Europeans who thought Britain insufficiently 'communautaire' to take part in the project of an increasingly integral Europe. Heath asserted in June 1962, to Gough Whitlam, that 'if we had not had the Commonwealth but only our own domestic interests to think of, then negotiations would probably have taken little more than a few weeks'.[43]

Party politics and public opinion

From the moment it declared its intention to open negotiations with 'the Six', the British government adopted an essentially tentative and defensive line in promoting the merits of British membership of the Communities. Indeed, Macmillan's announcement in the Commons at the end of July 1961 stressed that the government had not come to a decision one way or another, and that negotiations were being undertaken primarily to see if arrangements acceptable to Britain's Commonwealth and EFTA partners, and to British agriculture, could be found.[44] This emphasis on the potential obstacles to British membership continued to characterize public debate throughout the next 18 months, making it difficult for supporters of British entry to construct a positive case, and making it correspondingly easy for opponents to find grounds on which to criticize the policy of the government. Thus Macmillan's approach – entirely necessary in order to carry his party with him – gave what would prove to be highly embarrassing hostages to fortune.

Of the three potential obstacles dominating the debate (the Commonwealth, EFTA and British agriculture), it was the Commonwealth which excited the most passion and which attracted the most attention.[45] Initially, the government's approach was to play down the possible effects of British entry on the Commonwealth. Indeed, in his speech announcing Britain's application, Macmillan stated that he 'did not think that Britain's contribution to the Commonwealth will be reduced if Europe unites. On the contrary, I think its value will be enhanced'.[46] Against a background of increasingly manifest disquiet among Britain's Commonwealth partners, the government adopted a different approach, focusing on economic questions, and attempting (as at Brussels) to break the Commonwealth problem down into its constituent elements, in particular by advocating a country-by-country and product-by-product approach.[47] More generally, government spokesmen emphasized that a more prosperous Britain would provide better markets for Commonwealth products; that Commonwealth countries would in any case have to find new markets for any increased production; and that by joining the EEC Britain would be able to swing it away from autarchism towards trade liberalization. On the political ramifications, the government maintained a discreet silence, except to suggest that, by standing out, Britain (and with Britain the Commonwealth) would lose influence with the United States, and that, by joining in, Britain would be able to prevent Europe becoming a federal super-state.[48]

Similar arguments were put forward by promotional and pressure groups favouring British entry, such as the European Movement, the United Europe Association, Britain in Europe and the Common Market Campaign. Again the emphasis was primarily defensive, especially where the Commonwealth was concerned.[49] Even Federal Union – theoretically committed to a federal Europe as the first step towards a federation of the world – played down the potential conflict between Commonwealth and Europe.[50] A major weakness of the pro-market groups was that they were forced into this position by Macmillan's choice of tactics, and therefore found it difficult to argue the positive advantages of membership for Britain. Moreover, the impression of constant retreat was exacerbated by the pro-market groups' tendency to come up with solutions to the Commonwealth problem which, as soon as they were published, were rendered out-of-date by developments (usually involving British concessions) at Brussels.[51]

If, on the whole, proponents of British entry tended to 'fudge' the Commonwealth issue, their opponents veered in the opposite direction, positing a simple Commonwealth–Europe dichotomy in the hope of making as much political capital out of the issue as possible.

The Labour Party contained a small but active group of committed pro-marketeers, and an equally small but active group of committed anti-marketeers. The majority of the party, including its leader Hugh Gaitskell, initially adopted a 'wait and see' attitude, expressing a willingness to support British entry should certain conditions be met. First and foremost among these conditions was that the EEC should provide 'strong and binding safeguards for the trade and other interests of our friends and partners in the Commonwealth'.[52] Concern for Commonwealth interests, and vigilance lest the government should sell the pass in its negotiations at Brussels, remained constant themes of Labour Party literature throughout the period of the application. Two of the six issues of *Talking Points*, the party's briefing on Europe, were devoted entirely to Commonwealth issues, and others linked Commonwealth interests to those of British agriculture and (perhaps more potently) those of British consumers. Supporters of entry were forced to compete on the ground chosen by opponents. Thus Roy Jenkins, at the 1962 Labour Party conference, devoted more than half his speech to rebutting objections made on Commonwealth issues. By this time Gaitskell and the majority of his party had concluded that acceptable conditions of entry would not be offered, and thereafter they came out firmly in opposition to British entry. The inadequacy of the terms negotiated at Brussels for Commonwealth trade was said by Gaitskell to be the decisive consideration, a conclusion he reached after the meeting of Commonwealth socialist leaders in London immediately prior to the Commonwealth Prime Ministers' Meeting.[53] Echoing Macmillan, Wolfram Kaiser has argued that Gaitskell's shift towards outright opposition to entry into Europe on the terms then likely was motivated primarily by a desire to appease the left wing in his party.[54] While there is undoubtedly some truth in this assertion, the fact that Gaitskell saw that there was political capital to be made out of opposing the government indicated the extent to which supporters of the application had failed to get their own message across.

The likely effect on the Commonwealth was again the most prominently stated reason for backbench and grassroots Conservative opposition to Macmillan's policy.[55] Conservative rebels formed the core of the Anti-Common Market League, which attracted some 30 000 members by January 1963, and far outpaced the pro-Europe pressure groups in terms of fundraising and propaganda. 'Does Europe mean more to you than the British Commonwealth?' was the first question in a *Common Market Quiz* distributed by the ACML to more than a million homes, indicating the ease with which the League could pose Europe and the Commonwealth as 'alternatives'.[56] Most members of the League were probably satisfied merely with the retention of the status quo, but some argued for the development of the Commonwealth as an economic bloc to rival the EEC. Ronald Russell MP, vice-chair of the Conservative Commonwealth Relations Committee, put forward in an ACML pamphlet a proposal for Britain to withdraw from GATT in order to offer an extension of preference to its Commonwealth partners.[57] The ACML cause attracted a number of eminent economists. Professor C. E. Carrington argued cogently that the government's policy was 'a plan for the liquidation of the Commonwealth by easy stages'.[58] Sir Roy Harrod, a former adviser to Churchill and Macmillan, drew attention to the detrimental effects on poorer countries of restricting their export markets for manufactures as well as primary goods, 'the over-riding issue remaining whether Britain is to divert her custom from the developing countries of the overseas world to the rich countries of Europe'.[59]

Other anti-market groups gave different emphases to their campaigns. The left-wing Forward Britain Movement portrayed the EEC as a capitalist conspiracy. The (Liberal) Keep Britain Out group portrayed it as a menace to free trade. Nevertheless both united with the ACML in emphasizing the dangers to the Commonwealth (and Britain's Commonwealth connections) of British entry into Europe. The (Conservative/Liberal) Cheap Food League campaigned specifically on the question of arrangements for Commonwealth agricultural imports. The Commonwealth Industries Association lost no opportunity to present the case for Commonwealth preference, holding some 300 public meetings by January 1963, and funding a campaign specifically targeted at members of the Conservative Party. The National Farmers' Union was another anti-market lobby which made much of the Commonwealth issue, linking the best interests of British and Commonwealth farmers together, and directly with those of British consumers.[60]

A perhaps surprising absence from the debate was any clear articulation of Commonwealth concern through the medium of the established Commonwealth-minded pressure groups based in Britain. Few of those active in the ACML or other anti-market groups appear to have had convincing track records of involvement with Commonwealth issues before the application, while many of the most prominent supporters of the

Commonwealth declined to jump on the anti-market bandwagon. The New Commonwealth group published articles from both sides of the debate in its eponymous journal. The Round Table went further, welcoming Britain's application. In the Round Table's view, the Commonwealth and the EEC were fundamentally different types of association, operating in different spheres. The system of Commonwealth preferences was breaking down anyway, and it was one of the fundamental understandings underlying the Commonwealth relationship that each member had the right to determine its own economic interest.[61] The Royal Commonwealth Society maintained a studious silence on the EEC application throughout the period of the negotiations. When, after they broke down, the editor of the Society's *Commonwealth Journal*, Patrick Lacey, published a notice expressing relief, he was censured by the Society's Council.[62]

The Beaverbrook papers (*The Daily Express, The Sunday Express* and *The Evening Standard*) made great play of the historical and sentimental ties binding Britain to the Commonwealth, and of the ties of interest linking British consumers and Commonwealth producers. *The Daily Express* anticipated Margaret Thatcher by more than 25 years with its headline 'No, No, No' of 18 September 1962 (opposing the government's concessions on Commonwealth interests). With 4½ million readers, the *Express* was a formidable potential and actual opponent of the government. Nevertheless the other mass-circulation papers supported the application. This was true even of the left-leaning *Daily Herald* and *Daily Mirror*, although some fudging of the issue was evident after the Commonwealth Prime Ministers' Meeting of September 1962 and the Labour Party conference of October 1962. *The Times, The Daily Telegraph* and *The Guardian* all initially supported the application, to varying degrees, some even arguing that British entry to the EEC would be in the long-term interests of the Commonwealth, providing more prosperous markets and a greater political influence. *The Guardian* lurched towards opposition to the application in the autumn of 1962, ostensibly because of the poor deal negotiated for the Commonwealth. Both *The Times* and *The Daily Telegraph* adopted more critical attitudes, though neither came out in outright opposition to the application.[63]

For most of the period of the application, the evidence of Gallup polls would suggest that the Commonwealth was highly regarded, that Britain should decline to join the EEC if the price was long-term damage to the Commonwealth relationship, but that this was thought to be unlikely to happen. The importance of Commonwealth sentiment was highlighted by the response to a question in September 1961, 'Which of these three – Europe, the Commonwealth, or America – is the most important to Britain?'. Forty-eight per cent replied 'The Commonwealth', 19 per cent 'America', and 18 per cent 'Europe', with 15 per cent 'don't knows'. The same month, asked how important an obstacle unsatisfactory arrangements for the Commonwealth would be to Britain joining the EEC, 49 per cent replied 'very important', and a further 29 per cent 'important'. Six months later, when asked if any difficulties were so overriding that they should prevent Britain from joining, in the absence of a satisfactory solution, 25 per cent said 'none', 24 per cent didn't know, and 39 per cent said 'the Commonwealth'. That a majority of respondents believed that the Commonwealth would not prove a major obstacle is shown by the result of a poll as late as October 1962, when only 13 per cent thought that the effect of British entry would be the collapse of the Commonwealth, while 10 per cent thought that British entry would be good for the Commonwealth. Attitudes to the EEC were measured monthly and sometimes weekly by Gallup, from the launching of the British application, in response to the question, 'If the British Government were to decide that Britain's interest would best be served by joining the European Common Market, would you approve or disapprove?' A steady 30–40 per cent had no opinion throughout the period of the application. Of the remainder, support for membership consistently outpaced opposition to it by a factor of about 2 to 1 until September/ October 1962, when it slipped rapidly. From November 1962 the 'disapproves' outnumbered the 'approves', although by a very small margin.[64] Opinion polls also suggest that the Labour Party forged ahead of the Conservative Party following Gaitskell's conference speech of October 1962.[65]

Negotiations with Europe

The persistent and well-known misgivings of Britain's Commonwealth partners, and the increasingly strident opposition of the Labour Party and the ACML, undoubtedly made the task faced by Edward Heath and the British negotiating team at Brussels more problematic than it might otherwise have been. On the one hand, it was all the more difficult to make concessions and compromises. On the other, the governments of 'the Six' – and in particular the government of France – were all the more inclined to disbelieve in Britain's purported change of heart, and to doubt whether Macmillan's government could carry its policy through. Other factors added to the British negotiators' troubles. In particular, the Common Agricultural Policy and the arrangements for Associated Overseas Territories were still a matter for negotiation within the EEC. The method adopted by 'the Six' for conducting the negotiations (the six EEC members meeting to hammer out agreed positions before meeting with the UK's representatives) made it very difficult for the UK to modify any arrangements which had already been made. Finally, de Gaulle's patent hostility to British entry pressed on the negotiators from the European side, and hung over the conduct of the talks like a Damocles' sword.

Richard Bailey has commented that 'Britain brought to the conference table too many of its own and its associates' problems to have any hope of satisfying everybody'.[66] The difficulty here was exacerbated by the manner in which the Conservative government presented its approach to the negotiations – that is, as an attempt to see whether Britain's own conditions for entry could be met.

The British team set out optimistic that the EEC would offer terms which would, at least, maintain intra-Commonwealth trade at existing levels. As Heath pointedly remarked at the outset, 'it is a striking fact, and very relevant to the Commonwealth problem, that in no case was a tariff imposed on trade where one had not been in force before the Treaty [of Rome] was signed'.[67] Nevertheless, the Commission soon made clear that there were 'limits within which the negotiations could take place', and that negotiations 'must essentially concern transitional arrangements only'.[68] 'Morocco' protocols – that is, bilateral arrangements which would have maintained existing tariffs between Britain and the Commonwealth – were ruled out from the start. 'Associated status', giving preferential access to the wider European market, in return for certain guarantees of European economic and political leverage, was offered to the Caribbean and African states (except Rhodesia), but was for the most part rejected as a new form of European 'imperialism'.[69]

For the purposes of negotiation, Commonwealth exports were divided into five broad categories: raw materials, high-wage-cost manufactures, low-wage-cost manufactures, temperate agriculture and tropical agriculture. As negotiations proceeded, these broad categories were further broken down, on a country-by-country and product-by-product basis.

Raw materials posed few problems, as most were subject to low- or zero-rated common tariffs. High-wage-cost manufactures (i.e. manufactures from Canada, Australia and New Zealand) posed obvious problems of competition. Britain's request for continued duty-free entry was rejected. Apart from a few items of little importance, on which it was agreed to reduce the common tariff to zero, all such products were, under the terms of an agreement reached by May 1962, to be subjected to a *décalage* – a graduated imposition of the common external tariff between the date of British entry and 1 January 1970.

Low-wage-cost manufactures (i.e. manufactures from the 'new' Commonwealth) posed even greater problems. On the one hand, the threat to European industries was obvious. On the other, the EEC's protectionism (which resulted in consistently favourable balances of trade with the Indian subcontinent and elsewhere) clearly worked against the interests of developing countries. Here, again, the British team was unable to gain substantial concessions. Tariffs on handloom products and a few other items were to be reduced to zero, but for the most part all that was offered was a *décalage*, together with an undertaking to negotiate general trade agreements of an unspecified nature. A British request to delay implementation of any tariffs until such agreements were reached was not favourably received by the Six. Moreover, cotton textiles and jute products – mainstays of the Indian and Pakistani export sectors – were to be subjected to the full tariff by the beginning of 1967; and no agreement on Hong Kong's exports was reached, despite a British offer to apply tariffs on the same timetable as applied to India and Pakistan.

Britain's request for a zero tariff on tea was accepted by 'the Six', but its requests for changes to the tariffs on other tropical agricultural products were rejected. In the case of the Caribbean and African countries, 'associated status' was the main concession on offer from the EEC. The alternative was a *décalage* and a vague commitment to future trade agreements.

Temperate agriculture was without doubt the most difficult problem facing the negotiators. Here the largest quantity of exports was involved, the most vulnerable economies (especially New Zealand's) were threatened, but also the most vital economic interests of 'the Six' (especially France) were at stake. Agreement on many aspects of the problem had not been reached by the time of the breakdown of negotiations – partly because of the long delay in formulating the CAP – but the lines of negotiations were nevertheless clear. Again Britain requested continued duty-free access, or at least guaranteed quotas, but again the EEC demanded a *décalage* and offered only a commitment to seek worldwide price-stabilization agreements. The Commission recognized the special problem of New Zealand products, but no agreement had been reached on how the problem might be ameliorated by the time of de Gaulle's veto in January 1963.[70]

The sticking-point

Pride, Anglophobia and French chauvinism have often been put forward as explanations of de Gaulle's actions in January 1963. But most historians would now agree that at least two, more substantial, reasons underlay de Gaulle's decision to act as he did. First, and not without reason, he believed that British membership would create a formidable obstacle to the further development of intergovernmental cooperation, to the goal of economic union (as opposed to a free trade area), and (in particular) to the CAP, which he saw as essential to France's national interests.[71] Secondly, and again perhaps correctly, de Gaulle feared that Britain would act as a Trojan horse for American strategic interests, and that his own plans for a European 'third force' would be fatally undermined. De Gaulle's veto came less than a month after Macmillan's meeting with Kennedy at Nassau, when Macmillan persuaded the President to provide Britain with Polaris missiles, on condition that they would be firmly integrated within NATO.[72] There was a further factor: the Commonwealth. Within Britain itself, the likely effects on the Commonwealth dominated public debate on the merits of British entry (no doubt contributing to de Gaulle's belief that Britain clearly did not 'prefer the European Community to every other connection'), while in Brussels problems related to the Commonwealth constituted the largest group of questions exercising the minds of Britain's negotiators and their European counterparts. Significantly, de Gaulle himself asserted that 'the main problem' with Britain's application 'was the Commonwealth'.

> It would not be possible to make exceptions in favour of the Commonwealth beyond a certain point consistent with the economic structure of the Community. On the other hand it would not be possible for us [the British] to carry the Commonwealth with us unless we obtained terms which they would consider satisfactory.[73]

The official British interpretation of de Gaulle's veto was that the French President had become uncomfortably aware of how near the negotiations were to completion. As Heath put it, the 'plain fact is that the time had come when the negotiations were, for some, too near to success. It is clear to the world that they have been halted, not for any technical or economic reasons, but on purely political grounds and on the insistence of a single Government'.[74] Undoubtedly there is a large measure of truth in this view. Nevertheless, as Miriam Camps pointed out, 'the problems outstanding were ... potentially rather more troublesome than some of the statements made by Mr. Macmillan and Mr. Heath seemed to suggest'.[75] Moreover, to the extent that an agreement was close, that agreement was based largely on a British willingness to compromise. Even had the negotiations proceeded to a conclusion, the government would almost certainly have faced an uphill struggle persuading its Commonwealth partners and the British public (including many Conservative supporters) that it really had succeeded in safeguarding the vital interests of the Commonwealth, as it set out to do. Many contemporaries were deeply unconvinced. In the opinion of the authors of a Bow Group paper, for instance, 'had the Government been prepared to sign the Rome Treaty on the terms negotiated, this would have been inconsistent with [its earlier] pledges'.[76]

Following de Gaulle's veto, there was a small flurry of schemes for Commonwealth economic integration as an alternative to British integration with the EEC.[77] These held a brief attraction for the Labour Party under Harold Wilson, but in power, after October 1964, Wilson soon realized their impracticability.[78] In May 1967, after a particularly bumpy ride for the British economy, there was little opposition when Wilson launched the second British application for entry to the European Community (as the EEC, the ECSC and Euratom had become). In the exploratory talks which followed, Britain raised the questions only of (mainly Caribbean, Mauritian and Fijian) sugar, and New Zealand lamb and dairy products. A veto from de Gaulle again put pay to the negotiations, and it was left to Edward Heath (following de Gaulle's resignation, and his replacement by Georges Pompidou) to lead Britain into Europe (with temporary safeguards for Commonwealth sugar and New Zealand dairy products) in January 1973. The government White Paper recommending entry made a point of observing that the Commonwealth no longer represented a viable economic framework for Britain:

> Nor does the Commonwealth by itself offer us, or indeed wish to offer us, alternative and comparable opportunities to membership of the European Community. The member countries of the Commonwealth are widely scattered in different regions of the world and differ widely in their political ideas and economic development...They have developed and are still developing with other countries trade and investment arrangements which accord with the requirements of their basic geographical and economic circumstances.[79]

The 1961–63 application had a profound effect on the attitudes of other Commonwealth countries to Britain. Sir Alexander Bustamente,

Prime Minister of Jamaica, observed at the time of the 1962 Prime Ministers' Meeting that 'They're bound to join, whatever we say'.[80] The sense of a rupture in the relationship, particularly in the 'old' Commonwealth, was almost palpable. J. D. B. Miller reckoned that the period of the first British application was when New Zealand finally 'lost its innocence'.[81] All countries in the Commonwealth expected a second British application, and embarked on programmes of trade diversification. By 1971 only 7.6 per cent of Canadian and 10.3 per cent of Australian exports went to the UK (though New Zealand remained a special case, with 32.1 per cent of its exports going to the UK).[82] Many Commonwealth countries also entered into direct negotiations with the EEC. In 1966 Nigeria negotiated a special treaty of association with the EEC, which discriminated in favour of the EEC against Britain. Its lead was followed by Kenya, Uganda and Tanzania, through the Arusha agreement.[83]

While the immediate effect of the 1961–63 application was to bring to the fore evidence of a widespread feeling of attachment to the Commonwealth in Britain, its longer-term effect appears to have been to increase a feeling of detachment. It was noticeable throughout the period of the application that Commonwealth countries were keen to put forward their own interests, but were highly critical of Britain for attempting to do the same, and this without offering Britain any really constructive alternative. At one point Macmillan was driven to confide to his diary that 'the thought that [the] UK might declare herself independent seems so novel as to be quite alarming'.[84] The application process inevitably cast the Commonwealth as an obstacle standing in the way of Britain pursuing its own interest: a matter of duties, obligations and responsibilities, the result (and possibly the relic) of a once-great past. In 1964 'A Conservative' (widely thought, denied at the time, but later confirmed to be Enoch Powell) sparked a lively debate by describing the Commonwealth as a 'gigantic farce': 'They give nothing; they get any advantage that may be going'.[85] Britain's unease with the Commonwealth was increased in the later 1960s by severe criticism of Britain's handling of the Rhodesian problem and of its increasingly restrictive policies on Commonwealth immigration, and by the rise in many of the newer Commonwealth countries of military governments or one-party states (thus undermining a previously cherished British conceit that the Commonwealth was bound together by shared liberal traditions imparted by Britain). Richard Crossman was not alone in believing that the Commonwealth was 'fading out'.[86] Asked, in January 1971, 'How concerned would you personally be if the Commonwealth were to break up?', 40 per cent of Gallup poll respondents answered 'not very', and a further 13 per cent didn't know.[87]

The establishment of the Commonwealth Secretariat in 1965 and the Commonwealth Foundation in 1966 opened a new stage of development for the Commonwealth. Under successive Secretary-Generals, the Commonwealth extended enormously the institutional machinery for intergovernmental cooperation, enabling it to play an important and constructive role in conflict resolution (not least in southern Africa) and in the promotion of development issues. At the same time, the Commonwealth provided the framework for a unique development of international non-governmental organizations. The Commonwealth which emerged by the end of the twentieth century was clearly multipolar, and was regarded in many of its member countries as dynamic, adaptable and forward-looking.[88] Much of this passed Britain by. The Wilson government's grudging acquiescence in the creation of the Commonwealth Secretariat (which took over roles previously performed by the British government) had more to do with a desire to distance Britain from the Commonwealth than one to equip the Commonwealth with the means of its development.[89] Thereafter, British attitudes remained firmly in the mould of seeing the Commonwealth as a relic of the imperial past rather than as a reflection of the interdependence of the future. Thus David Adamson could suggest in 1989 that the Commonwealth was 'in a state of decline which would be regarded as terminal if it were not for the fact that in British institutional life no one ever pulls the plug' – entirely ignoring the fact that there were (then) 49 other members of the association.[90] Ironically, it was just such emphases on the outdatedness of the Commonwealth which indicated that Britain itself was stuck in the past.

Conclusions

Clearly there is some truth in what was described at the beginning of this chapter as the 'Acheson thesis'. Britain's turn towards Europe necessarily involved a reassessment of its Commonwealth connection, and eventually involved a downgrading of that connection. Nevertheless, the thesis needs qualification on at least three important points. First, it was only in 1961–63 that the dimensions of the potential conflict between Britain's Commonwealth commitments and its European aspirations became clear. In those years, despite the best hopes and intentions of the Macmillan government, the Commonwealth and Europe rapidly established themselves as competing commitments in British foreign policy. This was due in various measure to the previous complacency of British governments and the British public (Acheson's point), the way the application was handled by Macmillan's government, the intransigence of European (and particularly French) negotiators, the exaggerated stances taken by other Commonwealth countries, and the way the debate about the application was framed in Britain itself. Indeed, Britain's application for EEC membership was as much a cause as a consequence of any reappraisal of Britain's Commonwealth relationships. Secondly, it is by no means clear that the issue of whether Britain 'preferred' Europe to the Commonwealth was ever explicitly resolved. Macmillan's government was spared the embarrassment of fighting for the terms it had agreed and looked likely to agree at Brussels. Various indications would suggest that 1961–63 was too early for many segments of British opinion to face any 'choice' between the Commonwealth and Europe in favour of the latter. Thereafter the question went almost by default. Thirdly, the circumstances and presentation of the 1961–63 application crucially affected the way in which the rival claims of the Commonwealth and Europe were perceived. The 'choice' faced by Britain was not so much a choice between Europe and the Commonwealth as it existed and continued to develop after 1949, as a choice between Europe and the fading relics and conceits of an imperial system which was already in decline. That in Britain the two were so frequently conflated is perhaps an indication that Britain was at this time as little Commonwealth-minded as it was Europe-minded.

Notes

1. Douglas Brinkley, Dean Acheson, *The Cold War Years, 1953–71* (New Haven, CT: Yale University Press, 1992) p. 176. The full text of Acheson's speech was printed in *The Times* of 11 December 1962. The earliest reports in the British press had Acheson say that Britain's 'attempt to play a separate power role ... is about *to be* played out' – a slip that in itself reveals much about the state of British feelings.
2. *The Times*, 7 December 1962.
3. Ibid., 8 December 1962.
4. Ibid., 8 and 9 December 1962.
5. Michael Charlton, *The Price of Victory* (London: BBC Books, 1983) p. 307.
6. Robert Marjolin, *Architect of European Unity: Memoirs, 1911–1986*, trans. William Hall (London: Weidenfeld & Nicolson, 1989) pp. 332–3. The French original bore the less egocentric title *Le Travail d'une vie: mémoires, 1911–1986* (Paris: Laffond, 1986).

7. Peter Teed, *The Move to Europe: Britain, 1880–1972* (London: Hutchinson, 1976) p. 376.

8. David Sanders, *Losing an Empire, Finding a Role: British Foreign Policy since 1945* (London: Macmillan Press – now Palgrave, 1990) pp. 8 and 156.

9. Wolfram Kaiser, *Using Europe, Abusing the Europeans: Britain and European Integration, 1945–63* (London: Macmillan, 1996) pp. 122 and 129–30.

10. Anne Deighton, 'Britain and the Three Interlocking Circles', in Antonio Varsori (ed.), *Europe, 1945–1990s: The End of an Era?* (London: Macmillan, 1995) pp. 155–6. Churchill's point was echoed by Anthony Eden, who spoke of 'three unities' or a 'three-legged stool', and by Ernest Bevin, who spoke of 'three main pillars of our policy'.

11. (Sir) Michael Howard, *The Continental Commitment* (London: Temple Smith, 1962).

12. John Darwin, *Britain and Decolonisation* (London: Macmillan, 1988) pp. 122–5 and *passim*; and 'Britain's Withdrawal from East of Suez', in Carl Bridge (ed.), *Munich to Vietnam* (Melbourne: Melbourne University Press, 1991).

13. Winston Churchill, 'United Europe', 29 November 1951, Public Record Office, Kew, London (PRO), CAB 129/48, c(51)32, reproduced in Alex May, *Britain and Europe Since 1945* (London: Longman, 1999) p. 100. Churchill's Zurich speech is reproduced in Robert Rhodes James (ed.), *Winston S. Churchill: His Complete Speeches, 1897–1963*, Vol. VII, *1943–49* (London: Chelsea House Publishers, 1974) pp. 7379–82.

14. Nicholas Mansergh, *The Commonwealth Experience*, Vol. 2, *From British to Multiracial Commonwealth* (two-volume edition, London: Macmillan Press – now Palgrave, 1982) pp. 136–7; for the significance of the alteration in the basis of citizenship, see 'The British Subject', *The Round Table*, 38/151 (June 1948) 655–63.

15. Mansergh, op. cit., note 14 above, pp. 145–62; R. J. Moore, *Making the New Commonwealth* (Oxford: Oxford University Press, 1987).

16. Mansergh, op. cit., note 14 above, pp. 167–70; John Baylis, *The Diplomacy of Pragmatism: Britain and the Formation of NATO* (London: Macmillan Press – now Palgrave, 1993); W. David McIntyre, *Background to the ANZUS Pact* (London: Macmillan Press – now Palgrave, 1995); George Modelski, *SEATO: Six Studies* (Melbourne, Cheshire Press, 1962); Vijay Gupta, *India and Non-Alignment* (New Delhi: New Literature, 1983).

17. Richard Crossman, 'Britain and Europe: A Personal History', *The Round Table*, 61/244 (October 1971) 590.

18. Peter Lyon, 'The Commonwealth and the Suez Crisis', in Wm. Roger Louis and Roger Owen (eds), *Suez 1956: The Crisis and its Consequences* (Oxford: Oxford University Press, 1989) p. 272.

19. Harold Macmillan, *Pointing the Way, 1956–61* (London: Macmillan Press – now Palgrave, 1972) p. 302.

20. Foreign Office minute of 16 January 1956, quoted in Richard T. Griffiths and Stuart Ward, 'The End of a Thousand Years of History: The Origins of Britain's Decision to Join the European Community, 1955–61', in Richard T. Griffiths and Stuart Ward (eds), *Courting the Common Market: The First Attempt to Enlarge the European Community* (London: Lothian Foundation Press, 1996) p. 10.

21. The conventional view is that the Free Trade Area proposal ('Plan G') was little more than a spoiling tactic. For a contrary view, that it represented a

genuine attempt to associate with the 'Six', see Elizabeth J. Kane, 'Tilting to Europe? British Responses to Developments in European Integration, 1955–58', unpublished DPhil thesis, University of Oxford, 1996.

22. Sean Greenwood, *Britain and European Co-operation Since 1945* (Oxford: Blackwell, 1992) pp. 80–1; see also Kaiser, op. cit., note 9 above, who argues that 'the British government primarily moved nearer to Europe so that the Americans would not move further away from them', and that, by this standard, even though it 'failed', the first British application must be judged a success (pp. 130 and 199–203).

23. Report of the European Economic Association Committee, 25 May 1960, PRO, CAB 134/1820, EQ(60)27.

24. 'Future Policy Study, 1960–70', Report of Officials' Committee (Chairman: Sir Norman Brook), 24 February 1960, PRO, CAB 129/100, C(60)35.

25. Darwin, op. cit., note 12 above, p. 236. See also Scott Newton, 'Britain, the Sterling Area, and European Integration', *Journal of Imperial and Commonwealth History*, 13/3 (1985) 163–82.

26. Central Office of Information, *Commonwealth Preference* (London: HMSO, 1969).

27. Sir Frank Lee, Memorandum, 8 June 1956, PRO, CAB 134/1231, EP(56)52.

28. John Darwin, *The End of the British Empire* (Oxford: Blackwell, 1991) p. 50.

29. Catherine R. Schenk, 'Britain and the Common Market', in Richard Coopey and Nicholas Woodward (eds), *Britain in the 1970s* (London: UCL Press, 1996) p. 150 and *passim*.

30. George H. Gallup (ed.), *The Gallup International Public Opinion Polls: Great Britain, 1937–1975* (New York: Random House, 1976), vol. 1, p. 341. Polling on the Commonwealth was virtually non-existent before 1961, and this was the only question which attempted directly to gauge opinion on the value of the Commonwealth before the launch of the EEC application.

31. T. E. Utley and John Udal (eds), *Wind of Change* (London: Conservative Political Centre, 1960) p. 9.

32. *The Economist*, 29 November 1952.

33. *Hansard* (Commons), vol. 561, 26 November 1956, cols 37–8. Using virtually the same words, the government White Paper on the Free Trade Area proposal pledged that 'Her Majesty's Government could not contemplate entering arrangements which would in principle make it impossible for the United Kingdom to treat imports from the Commonwealth at least as favourably as those from Europe': *A European Free Trade Area: United Kingdom Memorandum to the Organisation for European Economic Co-operation*, Cmnd. 72 (London: HMSO, 1957) p. 3.

34. *The Times*, 8 July 1957; cf. Duncan Sandys, *The Modern Commonwealth* (London: HMSO, 1962) p. 20, 'if we are faced with the necessity of choosing between the Commonwealth and Europe, we should unquestionably choose the Commonwealth'.

35. *The Commonwealth and Europe: Study Prepared by a Working Party of Members of the Secretariat under the Direction of the Deputy Secretary-General* (Strasbourg: Council of Europe, 1961).

36. Heath to Macmillan, 14 June 1961, PRO, PREM 11/3556. See here Griffiths and Ward, op. cit., note 20 above, pp. 27–30, and Stuart Ward, 'Anglo–Commonwealth Relations and EEC Membership: The Problem of the Old

Dominions', in George Wilkes (ed.), *Britain's Failure to Enter the European Community, 1961–63* (Ilford: Frank Cass, 1997) pp. 95–6.

37. Miriam Camps, *Britain and the European Community, 1955–63* (Oxford: Oxford University Press, 1964) p. 343.

38. *Yearbook of International Trade Statistics, 1961* (New York: United Nations Department of Economic and Social Affairs, 1963), pp. 60, 134 and 463. The figures for India and Pakistan were 24.3 per cent and 14.2 per cent respectively (ibid., pp. 322 and 495).

39. *Commonwealth Consultations on Britain's Relations with the European Economic Community*, Cmnd. 1449 (London: HMSO, July 1961). For the background to these consultations, see Camps, op. cit., note 37 above, pp. 338–51; Ward, op. cit., note 36 above, pp. 96–8; and John O'Brien, 'Canadian and Australian Responses to Britain's First Application to Join the EEC, 1960–63', in Andrea Bosco and Alex May (eds), *The Round Table, The Empire/Commonwealth and British Foreign Policy* (London: Lothian Foundation Press, 1997) pp. 551–66.

40. Communiqué of the Commonwealth Economic Consultative Council Meeting, Accra, 12–14 September 1961, reprinted in Nicholas Mansergh (ed.), *Documents and Speeches on Commonwealth Affairs, 1952–1962* (London: Oxford University Press for Royal Institute of International Affairs, 1963) pp. 650–1.

41. Harold Macmillan, *At the End of the Day, 1961–63* (London: Macmillan Press – now Palgrave, 1973) p. 141.

42. *Commonwealth Prime Ministers' Meeting, 1962: Final Communiqué*, Cmnd. 1836 (London: HMSO, Oct. 1962); see also *The Times*, 12 to 20 September 1962, and Camps, op. cit., note 37 above, pp. 434–4.

43. Heath to Whitlam, 12 June 1962, PRO, DO 159/60.

44. *Hansard* (Commons), 5th Series, vol. 645, 31 July 1962, cols 928–31.

45. See Jeremy Moon, *European Integration in British Politics, 1950–63: A Study of Issue Change* (Aldershot: Gower, 1985) pp. 155–212.

46. *Hansard* (Commons), 5th Series, vol. 645, 31 July 1962, cols 928–31.

47. Most notably through the circulation of Edward Heath's speech at Paris in October 1961, reproduced as Cmnd. 1565, *The United Kingdom and the European Economic Community* (London: HMSO, Nov. 1961).

48. See especially Harold Macmillan, *Britain, the Commonwealth and Europe* (London: Conservative and Unionist Party, 1962).

49. Moon, op. cit., note 45 above, pp. 194–8.

50. See, for example, John Leech, *Europe and the Commonwealth* (London: Federal Union, 1962). This followed on from a massive study of *The Commonwealth and Europe*, published by the Economist Intelligence Unit, London, on Federal Union's behalf in 1960, which had also sought to reconcile Commonwealth interests with an active British role in European integration. For Federal Union's activities, see Richard Mayne, John Pinder and John C. de V. Roberts, *Federal Union: the Pioneers* (London: Macmillan Press – now Palgrave, 1990) pp. 159–74.

51. See, for example, Leech, op. cit., note 50 above, p. 23, suggesting that Britain could negotiate a 'Rome Treaty on purely functional lines' linking the Commonwealth with the EEC.

52. *Labour and the Common Market: A Statement by the National Executive Committee* (London: Labour Party, 1962) p. 1.

53. Philip Williams, *Hugh Gaitskell* (London: Jonathan Cape, 1979) p. 722; Brian Brivati, *Hugh Gaitskell* (London: Richard Cohen Books) pp. 410–11; Douglas Jay, *Change and Fortune* (London: Hutchinson, 1980) p. 282.

54. Macmillan, op. cit., note 41 above, p. 130; Kaiser, op. cit., note 9 above, pp. 144ff.

55. Moon, op. cit., note 45 above, pp. 161–71; Ronald Butt, 'The Common Market and Conservative Party Politics, 1961–62', *Government and Opposition*, 2/3 (1967) 372–86.

56. Lord Windlesham, *Communication and Political Power* (London: Jonathan Cape, 1966) p. 274. The ACML also distributed some 600 000 copies of a leaflet entitled *Commonwealth or Common Market*.

57. Ronald Russell, 'The Value of Commonwealth Preference', in R. H. Corbet (ed.), *Britain, not Europe: Commonwealth before Common Market* (London: Anti-Common Market League, 1962) pp. 45–8.

58. C. E. Carrington, 'Commonwealth or Common Market?', *The Statist*, 15 December 1961. See also his 'Commonwealth Endangered by Britain's Entry into Common Market', *East Africa and Rhodesia*, 12 July 1962, and 'Between the Commonwealth and Europe', *International Affairs*, 38 (October 1962) 449–59.

59. Sir Roy Harrod, 'Britain, the Free World and the Six', *The Times*, 2 January 1962.

60. Much of this is covered in Moon, op. cit., note 45 above, pp. 194–8.

61. 'Britain in Europe', *The Round Table*, 52/208 (Sept. 1962) 326.

62. T. R. Reese, *The History of the Royal Commonwealth Society, 1868–1968* (London: Oxford University Press, 1968) p. 251.

63. Moon, op. cit., note 45 above, pp. 198–204.

64. Gallup Poll, 'British Attitudes to the EEC, 1960–63', *Journal of Common Market Studies*, 5/1 (1966) 49–61; Henry Durant, 'Public Opinion and the EEC', *Journal of Common Market Studies*, 6/3 (1968) 231–49; Roger Jowell and Gerald Hoinville, *Britain into Europe: Public Opinion and the EEC, 1961–75* (London: Croom Helm, 1976).

65. David and Gareth Butler (eds), *British Political Facts, 1900–1994* (London: Macmillan, 1994) p. 251; Brivati, op. cit., note 53 above, p. 418.

66. Richard Bailey, *The European Connection: Implications of EEC Membership* (Oxford: Pergamon, 1983) p. 19.

67. Edward Heath's speech at Paris opening the negotiations, 10 October 1961, reproduced as Cmnd. 1565, *The United Kingdom and the European Economic Community* (London: HMSO, Nov. 1961) para. 30.

68. Quoted in Leonard Beaton et al., *No Tame or Minor Role* (London: Bow Group, 1963) pp. 10–11.

69. Ali A. Mazrui, 'African Attitudes to the European Economic Community', *International Affairs*, 39 (1963) 24–36.

70. For the negotiations, see Camps, op. cit., note 37 above, pp. 367–413 and 455–68, and Commission of the EEC, *Report to the European Parliament on the State of the Negotiations with the United Kingdom* (Brussels: EEC Commission, 26 Feb. 1963) pp. 30–67.

71. Gerard Bossuat, 'The Choice of "La Petite Europe" by France (1957–63): An Ambition for France and for Europe', in Griffiths and Ward, op. cit., note 20 above, pp. 59–82; Maurice Vaïsse, 'De Gaulle and the British "Application" to Join the Common Market', in Wilkes, op. cit., note 36 above, pp. 51–69.

72. Camps, op. cit., note 37 above, pp. 502–4; Greenwood, op. cit., note 22 above, pp. 86–90; Kaiser, op. cit., note 9 above, pp. 191ff.
73. Sir Pierson Dixon's report of a meeting with de Gaulle, 22 May 1962, quoted in Deighton, op. cit., note 10 above, p. 46.
74. Quoted in Camps, op. cit., note 37 above, p. 492.
75. Camps, op. cit., note 37 above, p. 493.
76. Beaton et al., op. cit., note 68 above, p. 22.
77. See, for example, Michael Barrett Brown, *After Imperialism* (London: Heinemann, 1963), Guy Arnold, *Towards Peace and a Multiracial Commonwealth* (London: Chapman & Hall, 1964), H. Victor Wiseman, *Britain and the Commonwealth* (London: Allen & Unwin, 1965).
78. Michael P. O'Neill, 'The Changing Concept of the Commonwealth, 1964–70', unpublished PhD thesis, Manchester, 1977, pp. 122–5 and *passim*; Ben Pimlott, *Harold Wilson* (London: Harper & Collins, 1992) p. 433.
79. *The United Kingdom and the European Communities*, Cmnd. 4715 (London: HMSO, 1971) para. 37.
80. *The Guardian*, 12 September 1962.
81. J. D. B. Miller, *Survey of Commonwealth Affairs: Problems of Expansion and Attrition, 1953–1969* (London: Oxford University Press for Royal Institute of International Affairs, 1974).
82. *Yearbook of International Trade Statistics, 1970–71* (New York: United Nations Department of Economic and Social Affairs, 1973), pp. 24, 99 and 554. The figures for India and Pakistan were now 10.2 per cent and 9.8 per cent respectively (ibid., pp. 323 and 592).
83. Central Office of Information, op. cit., note 26 above.
84. Macmillan, op. cit., note 41 above, p. 132.
85. *The Times*, 2 April 1964.
86. Richard Crossman, *The Diaries of a Cabinet Minister*, vol. 2, *1966–68* (London: Hamilton, 1976) p. 30.
87. George H. Gallup (ed.), *The Gallup International Public Opinion Polls: Great Britain, 1937–1975* (New York: Random House, 1976), vol. 2, p. 1122.
88. W. David McIntyre, *The Significance of the Commonwealth, 1965–90* (London: Macmillan, 1991); *Commonwealth 2000: The Royal Commonwealth Society's Millennium Book* (London: Agenda Publishing, 1999).
89. W. David McIntyre, 'Britain and the Creation of the Commonwealth Secretariat', *Journal of Imperial and Commonwealth History*, 28/1 (2000), pp. 135–58. See also Peter Lyon, 'The Round Table since 1965', in Bosco and May, op. cit., note 39 above, pp. 568–9.
90. David Adamson, *The Last Empire: Britain and the Commonwealth* (London: I. B. Tauris, 1989) p. 1.

7
Commonwealth International Financial Arrangements and Britain's First Application to Join the EEC

Michael David Kandiah and Gillian Staerck

If the United Kingdom had joined the European Economic Community following its first application in 1961 it was highly probable that many Commonwealth countries would have experienced, in the short term at least, a disruption in their international financial arrangements: in the way they paid for their trade with other countries, and particularly in the way they accessed capital on the world markets. However, this issue was wilfully ignored by the British government, which chose to concentrate on issues relating to Commonwealth preferences and tariffs. It is not surprising, therefore, that this issue has scarcely been discussed in the academic literature on the British application to join the EEC.[1]

This chapter will explain why Britain remained important to the way in which many Commonwealth countries conducted their international finances and commerce. It will show also why there was some apprehension about the impact of Britain's EEC entry in this particular regard. By focusing on the responses and actions of the principal policy-makers in the government and in the Bank of England – the UK's central bank – the chapter will detail how the United Kingdom dealt with such Commonwealth concerns, explore why this question did not figure more largely in the discussions between the Commonwealth and the UK, and suggest the reasons why it ultimately had such little impact on the British policy-making process.

Thus, it will be argued, the discussion of the issues raised has wider implications for an understanding of the British/Commonwealth relationship at different levels at the time of the first UK application to join the EEC.

Commonwealth financial and commercial arrangements

In 1961 all Commonwealth countries – with the sole exception of Canada – operated within the sterling area.[2] Through it they maintained the value of their currencies and conducted their international trading arrangements. However, the sterling area was an informal organization, with no real statutory status in any of the participating countries. The legal basis of membership of the sterling area, such as it was, was vested in UK exchange control regulations, with member countries listed as 'scheduled territories' (and generally referred to as the Rest of the Sterling Area, or RSA). What was called the 'sterling bloc' had come into existence during the interwar years, following Britain's abandonment of the gold standard, as a way to facilitate trade within the British Empire and with certain countries whose economies were closely linked with the UK. The 'sterling area' was born in 1940, when wartime emergency led to the suspension of the convertibility of the pound and was accompanied by the introduction of rigorous exchange controls and the pooling of gold and US dollar earnings of member countries of the sterling bloc. In the immediate post-Second World War period the continued operations of the sterling area were made necessary as a result of the severe dislocation in world trade brought about by the war, and because of the so-called 'dollar shortage' in the latter half of the 1940s. By mutual agreement RSA countries rationed the spending of those currencies that might be in short supply. Principally this meant that sterling area countries discriminated against the dollar.[3] Consequently, the pound sterling was the method whereby most Commonwealth countries paid for their international trade and conducted commerce within the area.[4] As international commercial and financial linkages were restored after the Second World War, the relevance of the sterling area declined, principally because the dollar shortage was eliminated by the late 1950s (indeed by then there were surplus American dollars available, all largely resident in London). Moreover, in December 1958 most of the world's principal currencies became externally convertible. Consequently, it was clear to all that the need for Commonwealth RSA countries to hold sterling would be progressively reduced and, as sterling area relationships with the UK were in the process of reverting to ordinary (non-preferential) currency and commercial associations, that the sterling area would eventually be wound up. Thus the need for most member countries to hold the pound sterling to finance their international trade was in the process of diminishing and would further diminish over time.[5]

Nevertheless, at the time of the UK's first EEC application sterling area relationships continued to be of some importance to Commonwealth countries, for several reasons. The broad centralization of foreign exchange reserves (through individual countries' holding of sterling balances at London) represented the shared economic interest of Commonwealth countries not merely with Britain, which, it should be remembered, was one of the world's principal economic powers, but also collectively between member countries. Even though the centralization of reserves became increasingly less important as the need to ration the spending of scarce dollars and other hard currencies diminished, from about the mid-1950s onwards there was growing awareness within the RSA of the interdependence of commerce between sterling area countries. There was a regular exchange of statistical data between RSA countries, and Commonwealth officials met annually to discuss financial matters and issues which would need to be considered by their respective finance ministers.[6]

Commonwealth countries had an interest in preserving, for the time being at least, their financial arrangements with the UK for two further reasons. First, the pound sterling was a reserve currency and, although the dollar shortage no longer existed, sterling continued to provide a link with the dollar (through a central gold and dollar pool held in London). Importantly, from the point of view of Commonwealth RSA countries, the international purchasing power of their currencies was still pegged to the value of the pound. As a result of the 1944 Bretton Woods Agreement, it was maintained at a general parity of $4.80 to £1, and this provided stability to their international currency movements and trade. Secondly, some Commonwealth countries still believed that the operations of the sterling area could work to their advantage. Principally this was because they felt that it promoted the movement of capital within the RSA in general and the Commonwealth in particular and, much more significantly, it facilitated capital flows from the UK to the RSA.[7] The latter was particularly important because the London market was virtually reserved for Commonwealth countries as far as official borrowings were concerned.[8]

These inflows of both private and government capital into Commonwealth countries have been estimated to have been considerable. According to a 1960 *Economist* survey, between 1954 and 1958 the UK exported at least £1500 million capital to sterling area Commonwealth countries. The survey also showed that virtually all Commonwealth countries used their sterling area relationships with Britain to raise loans and access capital. Moreover, in some regions, such as East Africa, 'the UK was overwhelmingly the main source of private capital and the only source of public capital'. Nevertheless, the survey pointed out that many Commonwealth countries had begun to look beyond London to satisfy their borrowing needs: to the USA and the Federal Republic of Germany, and to institutions such as the International Bank for Reconstruction and Development (or World Bank). Indeed, it was clear that over time it was highly probable that America would replace Britain as the principal source of capital in some areas of the Commonwealth. In part this was because the rate of return on investments in these countries did not make them attractive to London's private capital markets. Partly this was also because official American money was more forthcoming, for strategic Cold War reasons. Nevertheless, the *Economist* survey concluded that London's role as international banker would, for the foreseeable future at least, remain important to the Commonwealth.[9]

However, in this particular regard the 1957 Treaty of Rome, to which the UK would have to accede if it were to join the European Common Market, posed significant problems, because, depending on how the treaty was interpreted, it was possible that Britain would have to abolish controls on capital movements between the UK and the Community and concomitantly impose controls on extra-European capital movements. Moreover, even if external controls were not imposed, or if they were gradually imposed, the opening up of British capital, foreign exchange and financial markets to the Six inevitably would have affected sterling's status as an international and a reserve currency. Either way, this would have had an impact upon the operations of the sterling area and thus the financial arrangements of most Commonwealth countries. Additionally, the Treaty of Rome would have legally obliged the UK to act in concert with other EEC countries on many aspects of international finance, superseding the informal arrangements it then had with RSA countries.

The Commonwealth vs. Europe

While engaged in fighting the Second World War the United Kingdom could not accumulate reserves of gold and currency – indeed it had to sell off its external assets to offset American lend-lease aid[10] – and, instead, it went into debt with other countries, in particular individual sterling area Commonwealth countries.[11] The exigencies of war allowed it to obtain this credit from RSA countries without either their formal permission or their approval. The sums Britain owed were referred to as 'sterling balances' and by the end of the war the value of these sterling balances was enormous, being about seven times the size of the reserves of gold and dollars the UK had left in its possession. The need to build reserves by dollar currency earnings and to gain easy access to necessary raw materials meant that, in the immediate postwar period, Britain took a renewed interest in those territories which were still under its direct control in Africa, the Far East and the Middle East.[12] As Cain and Hopkins have suggested, these regions were holders of large sterling balances which 'could be manipulated more freely than elsewhere', and sterling area relationships ensured that their currency earnings 'contributed to the reserves held in London and hence to support the pound'.[13] The UK also succeeded in reaching agreements with most sterling area countries to 'block' a portion of their balances – that is, they agreed not to demand settlement of these liabilities for a fixed period, usually one or two years. The 1949 devaluation of sterling saw most RSA countries attempt to defend the value of sterling to the considerable benefit of the British economy.

There were other ways the United Kingdom benefited in the early postwar years from its ability to control its financial relationships with the Commonwealth and the remnants of the British Empire via the sterling area. As the Bank of England explained to the UK government:

> ...the Colonies have lent us over the period the money needed to pay off the NSA [non-sterling area] (and to some extent the RSA). This has been a major contribution to the UK's economic position in the post-war years, and without it...the whole sterling system and with it our own currency, sterling, must have crumbled. Of course, during the period we have made grants and loans to and invested in the Colonies but that in no way detracts from a contribution which could have been made *only* within the framework of the Sterling Area and system.[14]

Therefore, during the early post-Second World War years sterling area relationships were important to the rebuilding of the international financial strength of Britain, and its informal arrangements underpinned the pound sterling's position as an international currency. In 1950 sterling cleared nearly half of the world's trade.[15]

However, in the subsequent period the financial linkages between the UK and the Commonwealth began to be undermined by a number of factors. First, stresses began to emerge in consequence of the development of differences between the individual and collective interests of the Commonwealth and those of the UK. As the 1950s progressed, nationalist pressures became irresistible and decolonization gathered momentum, with more and more colonies gaining independence. Even though all were to stay within the Commonwealth and sterling area system, formal independence inevitably led to alterations in bilateral monetary relations with the UK, and the need to run currency and trading regimes which were dictated by the requirements of their indigenous economies meant growing divergences with the former colonial power.[16] Additionally, the maintenance of the system of imperial preference, however informally practised between Britain and the Commonwealth and the colonies, had helped sustain sterling area relationships, but this was becoming increasingly difficult to apply in a world in which the USA was keen to promote freer trade and disband discriminatory blocs. In 1952 the UK approached Commonwealth countries to support it in a bid to remove the No New Preference rule from forthcoming GATT negotiations, but it was rebuffed by nearly all of them. This was principally because Commonwealth countries indicated to Britain that they had no wish to reduce or jeopardize their non-sterling area trade, particularly with the USA. Later in 1952 the UK met with another rebuff when it attempted to promote what was called the 'collective approach', which would have allowed for a return to convertibility for the pound sterling and other Western European currencies through a system of flexible exchange rates. The problem for the Commonwealth was that the proposed system would have left their currencies pegged at a fixed rate to a floating pound. This would have been very good for sterling and for British exports but not so good for their own currencies and exports. Additionally, they feared that the move would antagonize the Americans, and that they would be excluded from expanding their commercial relations with the USA.[17] Indeed, the only way the system of imperial preference and the sterling area could realistically have been strengthened was if the Commonwealth was willing and able to form a closed economic bloc under British aegis, excluding American trade and finance. However, this option was neither realistic nor possible for either the UK or for the Commonwealth to contemplate.[18] Additionally, for non-white members of the Commonwealth, the explicit strengthening of economic ties to the UK after years of nationalist struggle would have been impossible. Certainly both India and Pakistan had indicated to Britain that they were not prepared to allow it any overt economic privileges.

Following the resolution of the 1956 Suez crisis there was a reappraisal of Britain's general international position by the Bank of England.

According to Lord Cobbold, the Bank's Governor, the UK was 'over-stretched by our banking liabilities to overseas holders of sterling, due partly to paying for the war and partly to the swollen balances of certain colonies, which derive in turn both from their earned surpluses and from the development programmes we have felt bound to support'. With regard to financial arrangements with the Commonwealth, he thought that, '[a]s our own position becomes more in question and as certain colonies move towards self government, the pressures from this source, both on our domestic economy and on our exchange reserves, tend to become heavier…and there is plenty more to come'.[19] In short, British policy-makers came to perceive sterling area responsibilities as posing, and continuing to pose, unnecessary financial and economic difficulties for Britain.

In the early 1960s some RSA countries – most vocally the Australians – had begun to suggest that there was a substantially increased need for a more formal consultative machinery between sterling area countries. This need had developed as a result of the creation of independent states from former UK colonies whose economies had previously been coordinated by London. Post-independence, given that their trade and financial arrangements were often still closely linked to RSA countries, how they conducted themselves economically and financially was of some concern. Frequently their balance of payments and economic problems were affecting the others, and it would have been useful for Commonwealth countries if there had been a method to discuss and act on such matters. Nevertheless, the British government was to resist consistently the creation of a more rigorous system, for a number of reasons. First, the UK's international financial arrangements were considerably more advanced than those of the Commonwealth, and had close links with the USA and Europe. Although its Commonwealth economic connections were still strong, and its trade with them still accounted for a substantial proportion of its external commerce (nearly 50 per cent), most British policy-makers believed that the UK would be limiting its economic freedom, particularly with regard to expanding trade and financial links with Europe and the USA, by agreeing to a formal system. Secondly, an institutionalized structure inevitably would have involved Britain in regularization of these informal arrangements. This would have been unacceptable to British policy-makers because they had no wish to extend the scope of their responsibilities to the Commonwealth or in any way be held accountable to them. Moreover, the Bank of England believed that a more formalized arrangement might mean that Commonwealth countries would feel that they should be consulted about the mechanisms being employed to maintain the value of the pound, and this the Bank had no intention of encouraging. A Bank memorandum which considered the future of sterling area relationships if the UK joined the EEC commented: 'the link between RSA currencies and sterling has been informal, with the UK retaining the right to change the sterling parity without prior consultation and the RSA countries being free to follow or not as they please'.[20] This situation was one which policy-makers in London liked, and had no desire to change, because they anticipated the eventual decay of sterling area relationships and the shrinkage of Britain's trade with the Commonwealth.

By the early 1960s most policy-makers came to believe that Britain's economy would have to expand faster than it was then doing, and that its 'modernization' and expansion could be facilitated by EEC membership. Although UK growth rates during the 1950s were respectable in historical terms (between 2 and 3 per cent), they did not match those of EEC countries since the formation of the Community in 1957 – particularly those of France and West Germany (6 per cent and upwards).[21] Cooperation between Britain and Western European countries on financial matters had begun in the late 1940s with the establishment of the Organization for European Economic Cooperation, and deepened following the establishment of the European Payments Union in 1950. Once a member of the EPU system, British policy-makers found that they had to pay close attention to European countries. The UK discovered that it could use the EPU to run up large debts (or balances), which was extremely useful, as it could not always count upon gaining credit from the International Monetary Fund. For these and other reasons, particularly from the mid-1950s onwards, the Bank of England generally found that it was in the UK's interest to act in concert with, in particular, the Banque de France (the French central bank) and the West German central bank. This was clearly apparent, for example, in 1958 during Operation Unicorn, which brought about the end of EPU, the birth of the European Monetary Agreement and the return to currency convertibility.[22] It was well-recognized in policy-making circles that the goal of currency convertibility could not have been achieved without the consent of Western European countries. This played a part in the shift in British elite thinking on cooperation with Europe.[23]

Additionally, since the end of the Second World War, the pound sterling was consistently revealed to be vulnerable to currency speculators, partly because of the need to maintain it as a reserve currency within the narrow limits set by the Bretton Woods Agreement. The weakness of sterling led the German central bank to intervene on the money markets in 1957 and in 1961. Indeed, in 1961 other European central banks helped to support sterling by agreeing not to make demands upon it and by allowing the UK special arrangements whereby it could sell European currencies against sterling. These actions helped shore up UK reserves, and suggested to some British policy-makers the clear advantages of closer financial linkages to Europe. This was even though the Australian government had sold to the UK convertible currencies (worth $145 million) which it had drawn from the IMF.[24] While this had been useful, the support of the European banks had been considerably more crucial to the stabilization of the pound sterling on the international money markets. Cooperation on currency matters with Western Europe was also fortified through formal participation in the Bank of International Settlements, based in Basle, Switzerland. At the time of the first application in 1961 it was noted by the Australian government that 'in practice' the UK had been 'working more closely with its European partners' than with Commonwealth countries in consequence of BIS membership and that 'the United Kingdom Government already accords its European partners *preferential* treatment over its Sterling Area partners' because of the dollar guarantees to their holdings of liquid sterling balances.[25]

Therefore, by the time of the 1961 British application to join the Common Market, the financial linkages between the UK and the Commonwealth had weakened considerably, and the weakening showed little sign of being reversible.

The Commonwealth response

Nevertheless, British policy-makers had realized that EEC membership would have an impact upon UK–Commonwealth relations at all levels, and for this reason Britain's decision to explore the conditions for entry into the EEC was officially announced to them on 26 July 1961, five days before the official statement to the House of Commons on 31 July. The government had also previously made some intimation of its intentions with regard to EEC membership to the various Commonwealth governments, and Commonwealth Secretary Duncan Sandys and four other ministers travelled to Commonwealth capitals during the summer of 1961 to explain the British government's reasons for seeking admission to the Common Market. Regarding UK–Commonwealth financial relationships, the official line which Sandys conveyed to Commonwealth governments was that 'to join would be good for the pound' and that 'by going into the Common Market, the UK could expect to be in a better position to invest in the Commonwealth'.[26] Britain told them that sterling area relationships would change, but not to their detriment or significantly, and that, potentially, both the UK and Commonwealth would benefit through EEC entry as London would be able to draw upon a larger pool of capital to export than hitherto had been available.

Of all the Commonwealth countries, the Australians were the most apprehensive. Their government had begun to consider the situation well in advance of the official notification by the British government because they had, for some time, found that the UK had become less than frank in communicating with Commonwealth countries on matters relating to sterling and the sterling area.[27] The Australian Treasury circulated a carefully considered memorandum to all cabinet ministers, dated 6 July 1961 and entitled 'Possible UK entry into the EEC: Implications for Sterling Area Arrangements'. It concluded that the impact on sterling area relationships would be profound – certainly not beneficial or even neutral, as the UK appeared to be suggesting. Much would depend on the way in which the Common Market countries might choose to interpret the Treaty of Rome during the forthcoming Brussels negotiations, and upon the willingness of Britain to defend Commonwealth sterling area privileges at the bargaining table. Additionally, the memorandum felt that it was regrettable that the British government had not consulted Commonwealth countries more openly regarding this decision, given the potential disruption to their international financial arrangements.

The memorandum urged the Australian government to seek assurance and clarification from the British government in two key areas. First, it exhorted the government to seek unequivocal assurances from the UK that, if it were to join the EEC, it would not agree to impose restrictions on the export of capital to Commonwealth countries; moreover, that if the then privileged position of Commonwealth private and official borrowers in British financial markets were to be revoked, some provision would be made for the maintenance of UK overseas investment that went to the Commonwealth. Securing these assurances was particularly important for Australia, and the Australian Treasury thought that its government should point out to Britain that 'a drying up of capital from UK to Australia, both official and private, could precipitate acute balance of payments difficulties for Australia'. Secondly, the Australian Treasury thought that the UK should make clear the future of informal cooperation with the Commonwealth, which had been the cornerstone of sterling area relationships, and that it should outline the extent to which it, once in the Common Market, would be forced to follow the EEC line on currency matters. For instance, if balance of payments difficulties resulted in the devaluation of the pound on EEC insistence, sterling area countries would be heavily penalized as they would suffer an automatic drop in their international purchasing power. The UK should be asked how it proposed to prevent this. Additionally, if in the event of balance of payments difficulties the EEC insisted that the UK restrict trade and payments to non-EEC members, it seemed clear that the UK would be required to comply, even though the action would be against the interests of Commonwealth countries. According to the Australian Treasury, these issues had been previously broached to the United Kingdom: however, inquiries had generally been dismissed as 'not important'. Nevertheless, these issues were, in fact, 'not only important for Australia, but also for the United Kingdom and other members of the Commonwealth and the Sterling Area', and therefore Britain should have been examining implications for sterling area arrangements 'with those whose interests would be most affected'. This, the Australian Treasury found, was something the UK government appeared to wish to circumvent.[28]

Following the official announcement of Britain's intention to join the Common Market, the Australian Treasurer, Harold Holt, sent to the Chancellor of the Exchequer, Selwyn Lloyd, a long memorandum, dated 14 August 1961 and prepared by the Australian Treasury. The memorandum, which was constructed along the lines of the 6 July memorandum sent to Australian cabinet ministers, detailed their grave reservations and identified a whole series of articles in the Treaty of Rome as being potentially problematical for Australian and Commonwealth financial arrangements with Britain.[29] The memorandum asked how the British government intended to deal with the issue of interpretation of these articles during the negotiations, and asked for an explication of UK government policy. This was necessary because, it was pointed out, the UK government had already confirmed that, if Britain were to follow the strictures of the Treaty of Rome, it might well be forced to undertake certain obligations to the EEC in the capital field, including a commitment not to re-impose restrictions without approval and not to discriminate against residents of the EEC. Furthermore, they also had conceded that it would be quite compatible with the Treaty of Rome for the UK to be asked to restrict the export of capital to non-members of the EEC.

At the September 1961 Commonwealth finance ministers' meeting in Accra, Selwyn Lloyd personally handed to Holt a response which purported to elucidate the British government's position. Lloyd's letter stated that the UK had no wish to let anything disrupt sterling area relationships as they were then current, and said that he did not believe that acceding to the Treaty of Rome would force the UK to behave less favourably towards the Commonwealth. He did not attempt to answer any of the questions raised in the Australian note and concluded by saying 'you will have the assurance that if we enter the Community we shall have a powerful voice to raise against the emergence in it of policies which would be unwelcome to the Sterling Area. In this context such an issue as the flow of capital to Australia and other Sterling Area countries will be of great concern to us'.[30] Holt, reporting back to the Australian cabinet, said that he found Lloyd's response to be not particularly reassuring because it was 'extremely guarded and non-committal, especially where the questions sought to elicit direct statements on United Kingdom intentions for the future'.[31]

Frustration lay behind the Australian government's subsequent stated desire to have an official presence to defend its interests at the Brussels negotiations which were scheduled to start in late 1961, and it kept up pressure on the UK government to clarify its policy. The Australians also suggested to the British government that it should attempt to negotiate with the EEC for 'a special protocol that would recognise [the UK's] special position as a supplier of capital to the sterling area', and for a recognition of 'the preferred access of Commonwealth countries to the London market'.[32]

However, the UK government refused to be drawn into discussing such details. The British Treasury felt that 'we should be wise to avoid any definite comment on what we will or will not do', and suggested that Lloyd should write 'a soothing letter about the value of the Australians to the sterling area and the sterling area to Australia and our objects and intentions of continuance of the present sterling area arrangements with her and others'. The UK government, after several requests for clarification, sought to assure the Australians that 'the provisions of the Treaty of Rome in regard to capital movements [were] really not as far-reaching as the Australians appear to think', and that these 'arrangements mean comparatively little change in our broad arrangements'.[33] Inquiries along the Australian lines were also received from New Zealand, which raised around 85 per cent of its international loans in the London money markets and depended even more than the Australians upon sterling area relationships to facilitate its international trade. Bluntly put, potentially the New Zealand economy would collapse if its established international financial arrangements were dramatically altered. These inquiries were met with a response similar to that given to the Australians.[34]

British evasiveness

Such official evasiveness may have stemmed from the fact that at the Brussels negotiations the UK was seeking entry on terms which were most favourable to it. The Macmillan government had previously given assurances at home that entry would only occur under the right conditions, and the demands for the clear explication of UK government policy which had come from the Australians and New Zealanders were mirrored in Britain by both pro- and anti-Europeans.[35] It may have been felt that making firm statements of policy either domestically or to the Commonwealth would make bargaining with the Six at Brussels more difficult. However, the British government was not merely being vague about its sterling area financial policy, it was deliberately avoiding any real discussion of it.

British negotiators in Brussels had been encouraged to think by no less a person than Jean Monnet – one of the founders of the movement for European unity – that, if interpreted correctly, there were no explicit provisions in the Treaty of Rome actually preventing the UK from continuing to operate the sterling area.[36] Nevertheless, they were also finding that France appeared to be reluctant to support sterling and was contemplating using the possibility of future sterling crises as an excuse to scupper the Brussels negotiations. The French Foreign Minister, Couve de Murville, had let it be known that in his opinion the sterling area questions and the weakness of sterling would pose problems for the Common Market.[37] British officials in Brussels reported to their home government that they thought the French line would be to argue that:

> It was one thing to undertake a liability to support the currencies of the original Six, which were purely domestic currencies, and another to support an international currency whose fortunes were to some extent at the mercies of countries outside the EEC. Therefore it was thought that the French objective would be to limit this liability to support sterling under Article 108, unless it was designed as a wrecking exercise, in which case they might make unacceptable demands for a Community voice in the management of Sterling.[38]

The British government did not wish for this to happen, because what they hoped for was a '[g]reater commitment on the part of the Six to the support of sterling' – which previous experience had shown to be extremely important – and the eventual establishment of London as the financial centre of Europe, harvesting the surplus capital of Common Market countries.[39] The latter was a prize which, it was hoped, would be realized in the long run. The former, however, was a necessity in the short run: 'How far in[to] the negotiations do we reveal whatever are the limitations of our position', the Bank of England wondered.[40] Additionally, the problems of the sterling area highlighted the extent to which Britain was still an extra-European power with extra-European problems. By not bringing to the attention of the EEC negotiators the issues surrounding sterling, Commonwealth finance and the sterling area, British policy-makers were hoping not to throw any light on the problems which potentially might follow British entry. They hoped that a satisfactory solution to the issues might be found at a later stage, when the UK was actually a member of the EEC. It was possible that the UK would then be in a strong position to present Commonwealth preference in London capital markets as a *fait accompli* and bring into the orbit of the Common Market the sterling area in the way the French had done with the franc area.[41] Edward Heath, who was one of the key British negotiators, and Lord Perth, Minister of State at the Colonial Office, were of the opinion that the issues of sterling area relationships and Commonwealth finance were best left ignored.[42]

Another factor which certainly contributed to this situation was the lack of collective Commonwealth pressure which could have compelled the UK to act differently. There were only two countries, Australia and New Zealand, which were demanding a clear British response on this matter and they were never really able to get the broader Commonwealth to join with them in their protests to London. Even at the 1961 Accra finance ministers' meeting neither of the two was able to put it firmly on the agenda. It was apparent to the UK that these two particular countries were pressing their concerns because the financial impact of Britain's EEC entry was likely to fall hardest on them. This was because under then current arrangements both countries enjoyed the highest credit ratings in the London markets and both had extensively used their privileged access to British capital to build up their already sophisticated economies and establish their versions of a welfare state. Since the initial phase of white settlement of both countries, the bulk of the overseas capital which had underwritten their economic development had come from the UK. In the case of Australia, the flow of capital from the USA and Western Europe in the late 1950s and the early 1960s had been increasing somewhat, but well over half the total continued to come from the UK. Moreover, the economies of Australia and New Zealand were more sophisticated than those of the rest of the Commonwealth (excluding Canada) and more aligned to the UK's. Most newly-decolonized Commonwealth countries (who formed the bulk of the Commonwealth), however, had different economic structures, and their need to access London's financial markets was much more limited. Consequently they would be affected differently. For this reason India and Pakistan had indicated to the Bank of England that if Britain were to join the EEC, and if their access to UK capital markets were immediately restricted, they expected that their balance of payments would be affected adversely in the short run; however, they thought that they would benefit in the long run, especially if the UK were to negotiate favourable Commonwealth tariff terms with the Common Market.[43] Additionally, according to British negotiators at the Brussels negotiations, France would not conclude British entry arrangements until the French Associated Overseas Territories achieved new trading arrangements with the Six. Consequently, taking a lead from the French, it is possible that the UK felt encouraged to focus on tariffs and other economic issues.[44]

Another fact which undermined the Australian case, as presented in the August 1961 memorandum to Britain by Holt, was that its arguments had been based on a belief that the UK would be willing to discriminate in perpetuity in favour of sterling area Commonwealth countries. This was a fallacious assumption because, as the Bank of England observed, the Australians did not 'realise, or perhaps do not wish to realise, that the discriminatory aspects of the Sterling Area arrangements will eventually disappear whether we become members of the EEC or not'.[45] Additionally, according to the Bank, the emphasis of the management of British international financial policy had been shifting 'steadily away from the balance of payments of the Sterling Area as a whole to the balance of payments of the UK alone'. Moreover, they believed that both the UK and individual Commonwealth countries had begun to take a global view of their trading and financial arrangements rather than a purely sterling area one.[46]

Consequently British policy-makers were willing to take the gamble that, as sterling area relationships had become increasingly moribund and as RSA countries held sterling because they needed to, and not because there was any compulsion for them to do so, the majority of sterling area countries would not abandon holding sterling precipitously if the UK did enter the Common Market. The Bank of England observed that 'if the Rest of the Sterling Area...lost the privileges it now enjoyed...some members might attempt to move out of sterling on a large scale', but they believed that it was 'unlikely that such a move would be rapid or massive' and that in all probability any movement would be 'spread over several years'.[47] After all, what alternatives did sterling area countries really have? Providing the movement away from sterling was gradual, the British economy could absorb the shocks.

To an extent the British government's resistance to doing anything to clarify its position was a strategy that paid off. It was clear that the Australians were forced to accept the UK position when in November 1962 the Australian Prime Minister championed, in his House of Commons, Britain's decision to join the EEC, saying that overall this would be better for the Commonwealth.[48]

However, this does not mean that the anxieties voiced by his government were invalid. There can be little doubt that the British government behaved shiftily in how it dealt with the questions put to it by its Australian counterpart. The Bank of England had from the beginning been willing to accept as correct – if only in private – the Australian point that the Treaty of Rome could be interpreted in a way which could be detrimental to Commonwealth financial arrangements, and that this would need to be addressed at some point. However, it did not press its government on this matter because it did not think that the situation would be as bad as the Australians had been suggesting. Regarding major alterations to sterling area relationships, the Bank said that it found it 'hard to believe that the Six would argue that because we have no Exchange Control against the Sterling Area we should move, immediately on becoming members, to the same basis with other members of the EEC since...the Sterling Area is a Monetary Area in the same sense as the French Franc Monetary Area'.[49] Nevertheless, by November 1962 the Bank acknowledged that the situation whereby the Commonwealth had received virtually no proper information concerning the government's policy regarding sterling area financial arrangements had gone on for too long, and that this represented a serious policy gap at the heart of the negotiations. While the Bank recognized that the Brussels negotiations had by necessity thus far 'been concerned with subjects for which legal instruments to effect our accession will be required', it thought that 'it would be timely to start conversations with the Six (either individually or collectively) with a view to discovering what steps they see ahead in the monetary field in the event of our accession'.[50]

But this was not official government policy and the issue was left unexplored because French President de Gaulle vetoed British entry in January 1963.

Conclusions

That Commonwealth financial and sterling area relationships with the UK would have been disturbed by EEC entry, there can be no doubt. When Harold Wilson's Labour government reviewed this matter during the 1967 application, it too found that much depended on how the Common Market negotiators would choose to interpret the Treaty of Rome. Even during this, the second application, it was not clear to what extent the UK would be required to restrict Commonwealth access to its financial markets if it joined the EEC and how seriously the interests of the Commonwealth would be compromised.[51] However, these questions were made virtually irrelevant by the time of Britain's entry into the European Community in 1973 because the pound had been devalued in 1967, the Bretton Woods system had come to an end with the oil shocks in the early 1970s, the sterling area had become defunct, and Commonwealth countries' access to UK capital markets had come to be on the same footing as the rest of the world.

The reason why it was potentially a serious issue at the time of the 1961 application to join the Common Market was that the UK position in the world was in a state of transition. It was still a major international power with global responsibilities. The sterling area and the financial linkages the UK continued to have with the Commonwealth were representations of this. However, at the same time, the UK began to perceive that the international capitalist structure had fundamentally altered since the Second World War, and that it was now existing in a bipolar world with the United States of America as the dominant economic and military power in the West. The UK no longer needed an empire to sustain it and it would have to reorientate itself away from countries that were principally producers of primary products – that is to say, loosen the links with the Commonwealth.[52] If the British economy were to grow faster, if its currency were to be stabilized and strengthened, and if it were going to maintain itself in the front rank of nations, it would have to link its economy more closely with other sophisticated, first world economies that could help shore up the international position of sterling and provide it with access to new and substantial sources of capital. While UK policy-makers may have recognized that the Commonwealth would be disadvantaged if Britain joined the Common Market, the reasons why they had decided to pursue EEC entry were more important to them.

Additionally, the problems surrounding the issue of Commonwealth financial relationships show that there was a growing divergence between Britain's interests and those of the Commonwealth, and that these divergences were likely to continue rather than diminish. The growth of a largely non-white Commonwealth whose economies were no longer formally tied to London could only accelerate this process. This was a fact that was tacitly recognized by many Commonwealth Prime Ministers who did not believe that an alternative to EEC entry for Britain 'could be found in a self-contained bloc'.[53]

Nevertheless, at the time of the 1961 EEC bid, Britain was important to the Commonwealth, as was the Commonwealth to Britain. For Britain, being at the head of the Commonwealth gave it international prestige and was a symbol of its global reach. As US Secretary of State Dean Rusk told a UK delegation in 1964, the United States government valued its relationship with the UK because 'Britain was the senior member of the Commonwealth', and because it still had 'traditional ties and major interests in many parts of the world'.[54] Its commercial linkages with the Commonwealth were then still extensive and commercially important. Indeed when considering the prospect of joining the EEC the British government had to admit that 'the Commonwealth markets give us an enormous advantage' and that 'British exporters would be less anxious to join Europe if they knew that it would affect their Commonwealth trade'.[55] Even so British policy-makers believed that the UK had to join, and this was the reason why they did not allow the issue of sterling area financial arrangements to develop during the discussion with the Europeans, and chose to behave with some duplicity towards the Commonwealth.

Notes

1. In, for instance, George Wilkes (ed.), *Britain's Failure to Enter the European Community, 1961–63: The Enlargement Negotiations and Crises in European, Atlantic and Commonwealth Relations* (London: Frank Cass, 1997), sterling area arrangements are only mentioned three times.
2. The sterling area also included certain non-Commonwealth countries, such as the Scandinavian bloc and Iceland. There were other countries that conducted a large proportion of their international payments using sterling, such as Egypt and the Sudan, but who were not part of the sterling area group.

3. Additionally, economy measures were also enforced against Swiss and Belgian francs and German marks until the formation of the European Payments Union in 1950.

4. K. M. Wright, 'Dollar Pooling in the Sterling Area, 1939–52', *American Economic Review*, 44 (1954) 559–76.

5. Catherine R. Schenk, *Britain and the Sterling Area: From Devaluation to Convertibility in the 1950s* (London: Routledge, 1994) and L. S. Pressnell, *External Economic Policy Since the War*, Vol. 1, *The Post-War Financial Settlement* (London: HMSO, 1986).

6. National Archives of Australia, Canberra (AA), A4940/1 C3368, Pt. 2, Memorandum, 'Financial Implications of United Kingdom Entry into the European Economic Community', 14 August 1961.

7. *The Commonwealth and Europe*, prepared by the Economist Intelligence Unit (London: Economist Intelligence Unit, 1960) p. 25. Also see Bank of England papers (Bank), OV47/64, 'Position of sterling and the future of the sterling area & Possible plans for pooled reserves or a common currency', prepared by Guy de Moubray, 27 May 1963.

8. Under UNISCAN (United Kingdom/Scandinavia) arrangements Norway and Denmark were granted access to the London market for both official and private borrowings but did not appear to have availed themselves of these facilities to any substantial extent.

9. *The Commonwealth and Europe*, op. cit., note 7 above, pp. 29–35.

10. Alan P. Dobson, *US Wartime Aid to Britain, 1940–1946* (London: Croom Helm, 1986).

11. The non-sterling area countries the UK incurred sterling liabilities to included Egypt, Sudan and many dollar area countries (including, obviously, the USA).

12. See L. J. Butler, *Industrialisation and the British Colonial State: West Africa, 1939–51* (London: Frank Cass, 1997); A. J. Stockwell, 'British Imperial Policy and Decolonization in Malaya, 1942–52', *Journal of Imperial and Commonwealth History*, 13/1 (1984) 66–87; and Wm Roger Louis, *The British Empire In the Middle East, 1945–51: Arab Nationalism, the United States and Postwar Imperialism* (Oxford: Clarendon, 1984).

13. P. J. Cain and A. G. Hopkins, *British Imperialism: Crisis and Deconstruction, 1914–1990* (London: Longman, 1993).

14. Bank, G1/99, Raw to Makins and Chancellor of the Exchequer, 15 November 1957.

15. Judd Polk, *Sterling: Its Meaning In World Finance* (New York: Harper, 1956).

16. Public Record Office, Kew, London (PRO), CAB 134/786/CCM(54)1, 'The Future of Commonwealth Membership, Report of the Official Committee', 21 January 1954, recognized the difficulties that independence would cause the Commonwealth.

17. PRO, T236/3085, various minutes and letters relating to the October 1952 Commonwealth Economic Conference (Officials Meetings). Also see PRO, T236/3094, Minutes of the December 1952 Sixth Meeting of Ministers, Commonwealth Economic Conference.

18. Catherine Schenk, 'The Sterling Area and British Policy Alternatives in the 1950s', *Contemporary Record*, 6/2 (Autumn 1992) 274–80.

19. Bank, G1/99, Cobbold to Macmillan, 20 December 1956.

20. Bank, OV47/47, Draft Memorandum (concerning the probable effects on sterling and on sterling area of UK membership of the EEC), 19 September 1961.
21. For the concerns of government policy-makers, see Harold Macmillan's diaries, *Pointing the Way, 1959–61* (London: Macmillan Press – now Palgrave, 1972) *passim*. For the performance of the UK's economy compared to those of Western Europe see Angus Maddison, *Phases of Capitalist Development* (Oxford: Oxford University Press, 1982).
22. John Fforde, *The Bank of England and Public Policy, 1941–1958* (Cambridge: Cambridge University Press, 1992) pp. 585–605.
23. Sylvia Schwaag, 'Monetary Co-operation and Exchange Rate Management in the 1950s: Britain, Germany and France in the Return to Currency Convertibility', unpublished PhD thesis, University of London, 1997, has compellingly argued that Fforde's argument that the three central banks drove the convertibility process is incorrect. Nevertheless, it is perfectly clear that the three banks did indeed cooperate extensively during the process, even if they were principally seeking to implement their respective governments' policies rather than pursuing their own.
24. AA, A571/161 61/1966, Pt. 1, 'Possible United Kingdom Entry into the European Economic Community: Implications for Sterling Area Arrangements', 6 July 1961.
25. AA, A4940/1 C3368, Pt. 1, 'Implications of UK Entry into the EEC: Financial Aspects', prepared by Australian Commonwealth Treasury, 26 June 1961.
26. Bank, OV47/46, CRO to all, 1 August 1961, Tel. W419.
27. AA, A4940/1 C3368, Pt. 1, Memorandum, 'Implication of UK Entry into the EEC: Financial Aspects', 26 June 1961.
28. AA, A571/161, 61/1966, Pt. 1, 'Possible UK Entry into the EEC: Implications for the Flow of Capital from the UK to Australia', Commonwealth Treasury Paper, 6 July 1961, prepared for visit of UK Commonwealth Secretary, Duncan Sandys.
29. Bank, OV47/46 Holt to Lloyd, 14 August 1961 and copy in AA, A4940/1 C3368, Pt. 2. The Articles in the Treaty of Rome which were in question were: Articles 67–73 (relating to capital), Article 103 (policy trends), Articles 104–109 (balance of payments), Articles 30–37 (elimination of quantitative restrictions between member states), Articles 123–128 (the European Social Fund) and Articles 129–130 (the European Investment Bank).
30. AA, A572/262, 62/2966, Pt. 1, copy of letter, Lloyd to Holt, September 1961.
31. AA, A4940/1 C 3368, Pt. 3/366, Holt to the Cabinet, 'Implications of United Kingdom Entry into the European Economic Community', 4 October 1961.
32. AA, A571/161, 61/1966, Moore to Daniel, 9 October 1961.
33. Bank, OV46/47, Copeman (UK Treasury) to Luce (Bank of England), undated but filed at 14 August 1961.
34. Bank, OV47/48, Memorandum, 'New Zealand', 28 September 1961.
35. See Michael David Kandiah, 'British Domestic Politics, the Conservative Party and Foreign Policy Making', in Wolfram Kaiser and Gillian Staerck (eds), *British Foreign Policy, 1955–64: Contracting Options* (London: Macmillan Press – now Palgrave, 2000).
36. PRO, DO 165/50, Notes of a Meeting between Sandys, Heath, Shuckburgh and Bottomley, 7 June 1961.

37. Wilkes, op. cit., note 1 above, p. 223.
38. PRO, DO 159/10, Extract from Conversation with de Grooters, 5 July 1962, No. 102.
39. Bank, OV47/61, Draft Synopsis, 'London – The Financial Centre of the Common Market', 29 November 1962.
40. Bank, OV47/49, Memorandum on 'Common Market Negotiations', 31 October 1961.
41. PRO, DO 165/69, Treasury Brief, 'Effect of UK Membership of the Common Market on the Sterling Area', 23 June 1961.
42. PRO, DO 165/51, Record of Conversation between Jean Monnet, Edward Heath and Lord Perth, 8 August 1961.
43. Bank, OV47/48, Memorandum, 'Consultations with Commonwealth Officials', September 1961.
44. Wilkes, op. cit., note 1 above, p. 222.
45. Bank, OV47/49, Memorandum, 'Financial Aspects of UK membership of EEC', prepared by Guy de Moubray, 23 October 1961.
46. Bank, OV47/49, Memorandum, 'Developments Likely to Affect Sterling and the Sterling Area Even if the UK had Not Applied for Membership of EEC', November 1961.
47. Bank, OV47/49, Notes of Meeting of 6 October 1961 to discuss 'The Future of Sterling' paper.
48. Bank, OV47/61, 'Economic and Monetary Policy of the EEC', 2 November 1962.
49. Bank, OV47/49, Memorandum, 'Common Market Negotiations', 31 October 1961.
50. Bank, OV47/61, draft paper for CMN(O) Committee, 'EEC Commission – Action Programme Monetary Policy and Capital Movements', 26 November 1962.
51. See PRO, CAB129/129, Memorandum, 'The Value of the Commonwealth', 7 April 1967, section entitled 'Economic Relations Within the Commonwealth'.
52. Bank, OV46/47, Review of Trade Problems by John McEwen (Australian Minister for Trade), 5 August 1961.
53. PRO, PREM11/3133, Treasury paper of 20 May 1960.
54. Quoted in Michael David Kandiah and Gillian Staerck, '"Reliable Allies": Anglo–American Relations', in Kaiser and Staerck, op. cit., note 35 above, p. 148.
55. PRO, PREM11/3133, Bishop to Macmillan, 26 May 1960, 'The European Economic Problem'.

We would like to thank Stuart Ward for providing us with material from the Australian National Archives and also the late Edmund Dell, who offered us valuable comments on an early draft of this chapter.

8
The Labour Government, Commonwealth Policy, and the Second Application to Join the EEC, 1964–67

Philip R. Alexander

In examining the issues which confronted members of the Labour government and their officials as they deliberated whether to join the European Economic Community in the 1960s, it is both useful and appropriate to employ lines of analysis similar to those of contemporaries themselves. Above all, their understanding of Commonwealth policy and of the EEC's impact upon it derived from comparison with Britain's first application under Macmillan. Decisions were thus reached in view of how far circumstances in the Commonwealth, in the EEC and in Britain itself had changed, and how far they had remained the same since the failure of Britain's bid for membership in January 1963. This contrast is therefore the method I aim to use in exploring the interaction between the Commonwealth and European integration as dimensions of British policy from Wilson's accession in 1964 up to the collapse of Britain's second candidature in late 1967.

Much material on the subject has recently become available at the Public Record Office in London. It is this which I have used most extensively in attempting to provide a fresh analysis of the topic. Given that these files have only just been released, little secondary literature has been written on the subject. The best general studies were written not long after the events themselves, in particular Kitzinger's *The Second Try* for the EEC aspect, and Miller's *Survey of Commonwealth Affairs* for the Commonwealth angle.[1] However, the period was rich in memoirs and diaries, and upon these a wide range of biographies were based. I have referred to all these published works where useful.

I have divided the chapter into four sections. The first deals with events within the EEC subsequent to Labour's election victory in 1964, their implications for the Commonwealth, and in particular for the likely terms on which Britain might enter the Community. The second looks at the circumstances within British politics which led to the Labour Party's decision to apply for membership in 1967. It will try to explain what was undoubtedly a striking transformation for the Party which had maintained constant criticism of the first application, not least out of concern for its impact on the Commonwealth. The third section explores developments more broadly across the Commonwealth, and their likely effects on British policy-makers. Finally, there are some general conclusions outlining trends across the period on a wide scale, drawing parallels between the political experiences in Britain, the Commonwealth and the EEC.

Events within the EEC

Since the end of the first application in 1963, the six existing members of the EEC had continued to proceed towards the completion of the internal Common Market in July 1967. This process entailed both the progressive lowering of commercial barriers among the member states, and the harmonizing of tariffs between the Community and the rest of the world. Many had predicted that this would induce a fall in world exports to the EEC. Indeed such an economic exclusion had been cited during debates on the first application both as justification for Britain's entry, to prevent isolation, and at the same time, by defenders of the Commonwealth, most notably Hugh Gaitskell, as a reason to remain outside the Community, to avoid a damaging fall in Commonwealth exports to Britain. In fact, some liberalization of tariffs towards the rest of the world had accompanied the integration process. In some cases, especially with France and Italy which had previously adhered to a more protectionist tradition, adoption of the EEC's Common External Tariff (or CET) resulted in a reduction in barriers to British goods.[2] This was why French foreign minister Couve de Murville recorded in his memoirs, 'it appeared more and more that the drama of Europe's economic division was turning into a myth'.[3] The significance of this for British policy was not entirely clear. Certainly, contrary to expectations, exports from both Britain and the Commonwealth to the EEC rose in volume at an increasing rate during the 1960s.[4] This strengthened the hand of those who supported joining the EEC, as it indicated that the trauma for Commonwealth exporters would not be as great as once thought. However, opponents of membership, such as Douglas Jay, pointed out it also made entry itself less urgent, since the CET no longer seemed such a formidable obstacle to British exporters.[5]

Furthermore, the development of the Community since 1963 had not been at all straightforward. From July 1965 to January 1966, the French government sustained a boycott of all EEC institutions as part of an ongoing battle with its fellow members and the European Commission over various aspects of the Community and its future objectives. Once again, the results of this had been ambivalent for Britain and the Commonwealth. One of the primary aims of Charles de Gaulle during the dispute had been to curb the power of the Commission itself. Clearly he still harboured a view of the Community as a confederation based on political union, as the French had proposed in the Fouchet Plan, which had eventually been rejected by the other members in 1962.[6] To the extent that de Gaulle had succeeded in blocking further moves towards a Community based on supranational principles, he actually assuaged the concerns of some Labour politicians who, like Gaitskell himself, were unnerved at the prospect of conceding British sovereignty to European institutions, which might restrict policy towards the Commonwealth in particular. Harold Wilson above all recognized that British conceptions of the ideal institutional nature of the EEC were not dissimilar to those of de Gaulle. Hence he told the General when they met in January 1965 that he fully agreed with the French President's preference for 'l'Europe des Patries' over 'l'Europe de la Commission'.[7] Moreover, French obstinacy discouraged Walter Hallstein from seeking to renew his presidency of the Commission for a further five years in 1967. His successor, the Belgian Jean Rey, was regarded in Whitehall as more pragmatic and 'outward-looking' than the German European ideologue.[8] Finally, there were some at the Foreign Office who were tempted to see the episode as a defeat for the French at the hands of the other five members of the EEC. This opened up the possibility that, should Britain apply to join, de Gaulle might no longer find it practical to veto the application.[9]

Over time, however, it became apparent in London that other concessions made to the French by the so-called Luxembourg Compromise were not so favourable for British adherence, particularly in view of the likely impact upon the Commonwealth. First, in the talks over new conditions for the Common Agricultural Policy (CAP), the French had extracted terms which reinforced the Policy's support for French agriculture, including high common pricing and levies on non-EEC agricultural imports. This coincided with the French system of labour-intensive and self-sufficient farming, but in the process widened the gap with

Britain. The British system was based upon a far smaller proportion of the population employed in agriculture, with much of the country's needs supplied by cheap foodstuffs from Commonwealth countries, above all New Zealand, Australia and Canada. However, as Chancellor Erhard of West Germany warned Wilson when he visited London in May 1966, despite manifest, uneconomic over-pricing, the new CAP had proved so difficult to agree that it was unlikely that the EEC members would want to re-open the wound by discussing changes to it in the wake of a British application.[10] Secondly, when the Association Agreements with former colonies of the EEC member states (the Associated Overseas Territories, or AOTs) had been formalized under the Yaoundé Convention in 1965, the French had again pressured their partners into agreeing highly preferential terms of aid and trade for the Francophone signatories. Britain was the only country which had a larger number of former colonies than France. Its membership of the Community could well lead to a host of new AOTs, which would inevitably dilute the benefits to the Francophone states. Michael Stewart, then Foreign Secretary, in one of his first papers considering EEC membership, recognized that the more power the French attained within the Community, the harder it would become to obtain satisfactory terms of association for African and Caribbean Commonwealth states.[11] Finally, the problems of agriculture and the AOTs imposed a sense of urgency on the British. Both the CAP and the Yaoundé Convention were to be renewed in 1969, so that if the government did intend to take Britain into the Community, it would be preferable to do so before that date, to prevent further developments worsening possible terms of entry.[12]

The attitude of the French themselves was the final, crucial factor within the EEC which influenced British policy. From 1964, de Gaulle's anti-American stance became increasingly strident. He began to wind down the French commitment to NATO, criticized US intervention in Vietnam, and welcomed the Communist Chinese foreign minister to Paris at a time when Washington still refused to recognize the regime in Peking. The French also obstructed progress at the Kennedy Round of the GATT negotiations, and at the United Nations Conference on Trade and Development (UNCTAD), both of which drew criticism from Commonwealth countries at the Trade Ministers' Meeting in June 1966.[13]

The most serious challenge for Britain, however, lay in French financial policy. In February 1965, at one of his characteristic press conferences, de Gaulle launched into a polemic against the excessive power of the dollar, and called for a collective effort on the part of the EEC to promote gold as the new international reserve, describing it as the currency 'which has no nationality'.[14] When visiting London in July 1966, the French Prime Minister Georges Pompidou took up this issue directly with the British. He expressed concern that the maintenance of the overseas sterling area and sterling balances could introduce a decidedly non-European element into the EEC. He encouraged Britain to abandon these burdens, and join the French in pursuing a truly European solution to the problem of the dollar shortage. The best demonstration of the Labour government's commitment to Europe would be for them to devalue their currency, as France had done before joining the EEC in 1958. To reinforce the point, he subsequently made an extremely unwelcome statement to the French press about the weakness of sterling, which further fuelled speculation against the pound.[15] In December 1966, Michel Debré, the French Minister for Economic Affairs, met James Callaghan, then Chancellor of the Exchequer, and his Permanent Under-Secretary Sir William Armstrong. Debré reiterated French calls for Britain to participate in the scheme devised by French economic adviser Jacques Rueff. This involved doubling the value of gold in European markets, in order to force the United States to end the fixed parity of $35 to an ounce of gold.[16] Finally, in January 1967, the leading Gaullist politician Maurice Schuman made a statement explicitly linking French acceptance of a possible EEC membership application to British cooperation in the Rueff Plan.[17]

Yet the British government could not cooperate in such plans, precisely because its ministers were keenly aware that gold categorically did have a nationality: the Commonwealth Office estimated that 70 per cent of gold in the non-communist world was supplied by South Africa.[18] At this time, the well-established policy of containing the power of Pretoria in the southern African region had never been more urgent, as the politics of race in Rhodesia threatened to tear the Commonwealth apart. Indeed, almost immediately after the Labour Party won office in 1964, South Africa became the focus of an awkward tension between Britain's Commonwealth policy and its financial difficulties. The Cabinet decided to overturn Conservative policy by complying with UN sanctions on sales of arms to South Africa, despite the vast balance of payments deficit. However, they then also reversed the line taken at the Labour Party Conference in 1963 by agreeing to fulfil the existing contract to supply Buccaneer military aircraft to the South African regime. This contradiction was to resurface in the severe economic climate which followed devaluation in November 1967.[19] In the meantime, in a Cabinet memorandum on the implications of United Nations sanctions against Southern Rhodesia, Commonwealth Secretary Herbert Bowden warned that Britain could ill afford to indulge in economic warfare with South Africa.[20] The increase in the value of gold projected by the Rueff Plan would have handed South Africa an even greater opportunity for political and economic blackmail which could hardly have appealed to the Wilson government.

In the end, de Gaulle used Britain's financial position to justify what was effectively his second veto, in another press conference on 27 November 1967. His argument, vindicated by the devaluation of the pound earlier that month, asserted that the British sought only a remedy for their economic ills. They would not find it in joining the EEC. The Community's existing members had strengthened their position by economic and monetary solidarity, but Britain, as it functioned at that time, could not follow suit. The overseas sterling balances would remain a drag on the economy, and above all, as the British provisioned themselves with cheap Commonwealth imports, London would never agree to conform to the CAP: 'The levies required by its financial regulation would be crushing'. With this judgement, the French President condemned British claims to have turned away from the Commonwealth, towards Europe.[21]

Circumstances in Britain

In considering the role of Commonwealth concerns in British politics at the time of the second application, it is important to remember three factors which worked to reduce the extent to which such issues were discussed. The first was that no full Commonwealth Prime Ministers' Meeting was called to debate the issue, so precluding the focus for objections which the meeting in 1962 had provided. In part this was a consequence of the lessons learned from the first application. Secondly, negotiations between Britain and the Six never actually began. Thus no specific terms of entry were agreed which could have provoked complaints from the Commonwealth and its sympathizers in Britain. Linked to this, the third factor was what one of de Gaulle's biographers called the 'negative drip-treatment to the British bid' by the Quai d'Orsay, fully in evidence in Foreign Office correspondence, especially that from Sir Patrick Reilly, the ambassador in Paris.[22] This made it improbable from the outset that the application would succeed. Hence Richard Crossman apparently told Richard Marsh in October 1966 that 'the General will save us from our folly'. For the same reason even the application's staunchest critic in the Cabinet, Douglas Jay, decided the matter was not worth resigning over in May 1967.[23]

With these provisos in mind, the debates on EEC membership which took place formed essentially a part of wider issues. At heart the problem facing the Labour government with a greater degree of severity than most postwar British governments was the choice between the conflicting needs of an active foreign policy and a sound financial policy. One can identify several strands of response to this dilemma. The first, which gained ascendancy in the Foreign Office, was to turn to the EEC as a way of reinforcing Britain's international position. The Commonwealth preference area was declining in significance due to the tariff concessions made at the Kennedy Round and UNCTAD.[24] It was hoped that membership of the EEC might bring about increased trade with Europe to compensate for Britain's declining share in Commonwealth markets. Above all, senior officials at the Foreign Office hoped to use entry to reverse the inward-looking tendencies of the existing six members, and in particular to contain the isolationist stance of de Gaulle.

This was the view forcefully expressed by Sir Con O'Neill, who returned to the Foreign Office as Deputy Under-Secretary after having served as the British Representative to the EEC at Brussels. O'Neill's valedictory despatch from Brussels was essentially a lengthy polemic against de Gaulle, filled with complaints which Jay himself would have echoed. He lambasted the General's destructive attitude to NATO, but most important from the point of view of the Commonwealth, he blamed the French for the thoroughly inward-looking and protectionist agricultural and commercial policies pursued by the EEC. In particular, he mentioned French refusal to sign commodities agreements on cereals, coffee and bananas, all of which had hit exporters in various regions of the Commonwealth. The French had also demanded the right to exclude Dutch finished textiles made from Indian raw textile exports. Finally, he pointed out that it was France alone which had forced Nigeria to offer preferences to EEC exporters, instead of subscribing to the usual terms of the Yaoundé Convention. It was this offer which had most embarrassed Britain in the context of Commonwealth commercial policy.[25]

From this critique, it is easy to see how Michael Stewart developed the opinion which he first began to express in memoranda to Wilson on adherence to the Rome Treaties, from mid-1965 onwards. Stewart acknowledged in his memoirs that when he commenced work as Foreign Secretary in 1965, his priorities lay with the Commonwealth, which for him represented 'an excellent opportunity to promote understanding between black and white, new and old nations', but that later, he remembered 'being persuaded to take a more favourable view of the E.E.C. than I had held at first'.[26] The expressions which recur often in the records are those mentioning the benefits of joining 'the right kind of Community', and suggesting that it could be influenced from within to make it more 'outward-looking'. In the end, this latter phrase was to turn up in Wilson's own speech announcing his plan to tour the capitals of the EEC with George Brown, on 10 November 1966.[27]

In practice, this was only the middle path between the two irreconcilable positions held by other Cabinet members. On the one hand, there were Douglas Jay and Herbert Bowden. These two were asked by Wilson in August 1967 to step down as President of the Board of Trade and Commonwealth Secretary respectively because of their opposition to EEC membership. In Douglas Jay's view, membership of the EEC was not compatible with the Labour government's handling of foreign affairs or financial difficulties. Adherence to the CAP would terminate the policy of cheap food from the Commonwealth and force up food prices, which in turn would fuel demand for wage increases. Added to this, the CET would have to be applied to a number of raw materials which were also admitted duty-free from Commonwealth countries. The combined result would be a significant new burden to production costs. This meant poor prospects for long-term industrial competitiveness, which could prevent Britain from ever breaking out of recurring balance of payments crises.[28]

These objections were supported by the Cabinet and Treasury economic advisers, including Nicky Kaldor, Robert Neild and above all Thomas Balogh. Twice these officials infuriated the pro-Europeans by warning of the dire financial consequences of membership. The first occasion was at the Chequers meeting on the subject on 22 October 1966. This report was followed by a second prepared for the full Cabinet meetings of 27 April to 1 May 1967, out of which came the decision to apply.[29] Balogh also submitted a number of strongly-worded memoranda to Wilson directly, complaining that the Foreign Office had disregarded economic issues in their assessment of EEC membership. He also suggested that Britain's flirtations with European integration were a primary cause of centrifugal tendencies within the Commonwealth, asserting that 'the accelerating tendency for Commonwealth and EFTA members to run for cover by seeking closer relations with EEC is the *result of the continuous declarations made by British Ministers in favour of an immediate entry by Britain*'. Wilson's Private Secretary, Michael Palliser, was sceptical of this, noting in the margin 'would that it were only that'.[30]

Nevertheless, even if Balogh's polemical style tended to undermine his case, it was significant that his objections worked not only on the economic, but also on the political plane. In this way, he reinforced the arguments of Douglas Jay and even the more mild-mannered Herbert Bowden. All of them warned that the constraints, economic and political, which would be imposed by joining a Community dominated by France would preclude Britain any foreign policy outside of Europe, above all in the vital Middle and Far Eastern regions. This was why Jay cast doubt on the Foreign Office argument that membership would enable Britain to change the EEC from within, since the basis of any active foreign policy had to be a healthy economy. It was also why Balogh, like Wilson himself, expressed satisfaction at what he saw as de Gaulle's success in blocking any further appropriation of national sovereignty by the European Commission – the manoeuvre offered reassurance to Britain as much as to France.[31]

On the other hand, to some of the advocates of EEC membership, and even some of those uncommitted on the matter, Britain on the contrary had to shed itself of the burden of Commonwealth commitments in respect of trade and especially defence. These were the luxuries of past prestige which Britain could no longer afford. This was the opinion later reached by Denis Healey, architect of the Defence Expenditure reviews which were to terminate Britain's role East of Suez, and by Richard Crossman. The latter compared what he called 'breaking the status barrier' to breaking the sound barrier – it seemed to hurt people's ears.[32] The two most important and 'pro-European' proponents of such a comprehensive change of foreign policy were Roy Jenkins and George Brown. Jenkins believed Britain's overseas undertakings, including the sterling area, were an obstacle which would discourage the EEC from welcoming Britain. Wilson appointed Brown as Foreign Secretary in August 1966 ostensibly to lead the approach to Europe. In his memoirs, pugnacious as ever, Brown described the Commonwealth as a costly irrelevance. Where he differed from the others was in his grandiose vision that EEC membership was actually a way to restore Britain's world role, as leader of a united Europe.[33]

Among such diverse and strongly held opinions, it is difficult to place the views of Wilson himself. One recent study of Wilson's foreign policy has suggested that Michael Stewart exerted the greatest influence on the Prime Minister's ideas. Stewart's quiet and dependable rationality made him a more reliable ally than the impulsive George Brown. Certainly, there is some evidence for this. In Cabinet and in his memoirs, Wilson supported Stewart's line that membership of the EEC would reinforce Britain's existing foreign policy.[34] Equally, the plan for a tour of European capitals which he persuaded the Cabinet to adopt in October 1966 had originally been proposed by Stewart nearly a year previously. Finally, like Stewart, he wrote in his rather unrevealing memoirs that he took longer than many of his colleagues to accept the necessity of a withdrawal from 'East of Suez', and reach a pro-European stance.[35]

There are a number of events which may well have subdued his initial enthusiasm for the Commonwealth. In fact, a financial crisis faced the government immediately after the election victory in October 1964, resulting from the £800 million balance of payments deficit bequeathed by the Conservatives. To tackle this, the Cabinet imposed a 15 per cent surcharge on all manufactured imports. Regardless of Commonwealth preference, this had to be levied equally on all such products to prevent a diplomatic dispute with any of Britain's other trading partners. The Commonwealth leaders themselves appear to have learned a valuable lesson from all this, demonstrated at the Commonwealth Prime Minister's Meeting of June 1965. On this occasion, Wilson sought to launch the concept of closer Commonwealth economic cooperation. However, the individual interests of so many countries had not been overcome, and Wilson was forced to conclude that 'there is, in fact, nothing under the sun more *laissez-faire* than Commonwealth trade'.[36] Perhaps the most disheartening signs followed the Unilateral (sometimes referred to as the Illegal) Declaration of Independence by Ian Smith's regime in Rhodesia on 11 November 1965. Its apparent determination to sustain the rule of a tiny white minority (5 per cent of the total population) nearly destroyed the Commonwealth at the Prime Ministers' Meetings of January and September 1966, the latter described by Wilson as 'the worst ever held up to that time'.[37]

If Wilson lost faith in the Commonwealth, it is still unclear whether he was wholly converted to the idea of EEC membership. In July 1966, during his talk with Pompidou, he seemed more inclined to criticize European assurances than to convince the French that Britain's 'conversion' to Europe was genuine, which had been the agreed Cabinet stance since February of that year. Indeed he cast doubt on whether transitional arrangements would be of any help to Britain or the Commonwealth, asking 'whether slow strangulation was really preferable to sudden death'.[38] After the decision to undertake a 'probe' to the European capitals had been announced to Parliament in November 1966, Wilson sent a private telegram to President Johnson. In this, he asserted that 'I have never been one of the little band of so-called

"Europeans".' He may have thought it necessary to reassure Johnson he would not align himself with de Gaulle, but given how unlikely such a direction was, there seems little need for this degree of candour, if it was not the whole truth.[39]

Furthermore, the clues in the archival material are corroborated by the recollections of some of Wilson's associates. Callaghan observed that, on the economic front, 'neither the PM nor myself had any doubt that joining would have a serious adverse effect on our balance of payments'.[40] Government economic adviser Alec Cairncross recorded at several points in his diaries the continued ambivalence of the Prime Minister towards EEC membership. Indeed, it seems as if many of the senior officials at Whitehall were despairing of the situation: 'Back from Geneva/EFTA with Derek Mitchell [then Private Secretary at the DEA]. He told me yesterday that for the first time Burke Trend [then Cabinet Secretary] had confessed to him that he really didn't know where the PM stood on Europe. There was "layer upon layer upon layer".' This was in November 1966, once again after Wilson had persuaded the Cabinet to authorize a 'probe' to Europe.[41]

It is therefore possible that the crisis of July 1966 was the most significant event for Harold Wilson, but not purely for policy reasons. In that month, the Labour government faced a run on the gold reserves which dipped the balance of payments far into the red, and forced a round of massive government cuts. One of the largest economies was in overseas expenditure on aid and defence. It was this which precipitated the full withdrawal from East of Suez, although the policy itself was never actually announced in public until 1968.[42] The implications of this were not confined to economic and foreign policies. As a result of the cuts, Brown threatened resignation since much of the National Plan he had spent over a year devising at the DEA had to be suspended. In transferring him to the Foreign Office and allowing him a free rein to push a British application to the EEC, Wilson avoided the damaging loss of his second-in-command.[43] Yet the official opinions available both to Wilson and to Brown indicated that the French veto remained, and would not be lifted in the foreseeable future. The two of them were told by the General himself when they visited Paris in March 1967 that he doubted Britain would enter the EEC in his lifetime. Alec Cairncross concluded in his diary in May, after the application had been announced, 'It looks as if G. Brown would now bang his head a second time against a closed door'. Even the Prime Minister's Principal Private Secretary, Michael Palliser, an ardent 'pro-Marketeer' and son-in-law of Paul-Henri Spaak, had little faith in the application's success.[44]

In explaining this enigma, parallels with the first application and with Commonwealth policy are both helpful. Wolfram Kaiser has argued that Macmillan did not believe the first application would succeed, but pursued it anyway to maintain Conservative unity.[45] In fact, the evidence drawn on above for such an interpretation is more extensive and more compelling for the second application than for the first. As to Commonwealth policy, a recent study of the crisis over arms sales to South Africa in late 1967 reached similar conclusions. Despite the troubled economic climate which prevailed in the months immediately after devaluation, neither financial concerns nor even the issue of an ethical foreign policy dominated Wilson's thinking. Rather, he was exercised by the needs of Cabinet and Party management.[46] It may be, therefore, that Wilson did not in fact overcome his misgivings about the impact of the EEC on the Commonwealth and above all on Britain's balance of payments. Instead, he gave priority to the unity of the Cabinet and the Parliamentary Labour Party by allowing the application to proceed, all the while aware that it was likely to fail.

Developments in the Commonwealth

I have already touched upon many of the vital elements of the Commonwealth context, but it might be helpful here to consider them in a more consolidated fashion. The central, almost terminal, occurrence in the Commonwealth was the prolonged crisis which followed the Rhodesian UDI. From December 1965, both Ghana and Tanzania broke off diplomatic relations with Britain. These were re-established following the failure of Wilson's talks to Smith on board HMS *Tiger* in December 1966 and the subsequent statement by the British government which confirmed there would be no independence for Rhodesia before majority rule, the promise demanded by many of the African Commonwealth members. By the time of the application to the EEC in May 1967, the immediate crisis had therefore been averted, and a long attritional battle involving sanctions had begun. Nevertheless, the overall effect was doubtless to dampen the relations of many of the newer Commonwealth countries with Britain. As a result, the prospect of EEC membership for Britain did not excite great concern in the African Commonwealth.

In fact, some damage had already been done to Commonwealth relations in the very first month of the Labour government by the 15 per cent import surcharge on most manufactured goods. As explained earlier, the surcharge applied equally to Commonwealth countries, although its impact was mitigated by the fact that many Commonwealth countries, especially the underdeveloped ones, supplied raw materials exempt from the charge. Wilson also explained in a personal telegram to Commonwealth Prime Ministers that only by righting Britain's economic situation could his government contribute greater aid for Commonwealth development.[47] Most Commonwealth replies were sympathetic, though the resentment caused among some members, and above all among EFTA countries, led to an early end of the surcharge. Yet Britain's financial difficulties did not recede, and consequently the next three years saw fierce cuts in overseas spending instead of the promised increase in aid, the largest being that of July 1966. Britain's usefulness to the Commonwealth diminished accordingly.

For the developing states among the Commonwealth, the most important considerations were the opportunities offered by the international conferences on trade and tariffs. The most important of these was the so-called 'Kennedy Round', completed after three years' intermittent negotiation in May 1967, but the UNCTAD launched in 1965 also opened up the hope of tariff concessions by the developed countries towards their poorer trading partners. At the same time, by granting tariff cuts to all developing countries, Britain struck a further blow at the principle of Commonwealth preference. This did not raise objections from Commonwealth countries, as they were in turn being presented with concessions by states which had previously exercised a high level of protectionism, but it did inevitably erode the commercial element of the Commonwealth relationship.[48] Both these conferences, however, had been delayed by the inactivity of the theoretically united EEC delegation, as the French walk-out induced paralysis for more than six months. In the end, the talks accomplished less than had originally been envisaged, and Commonwealth countries took note. Expectations of the concessions which Britain might be able to negotiate for them following entry to the EEC were lowered accordingly.[49]

The final factor which had changed the Commonwealth was quite simply the first application itself. The possibility of British adherence to the EEC was acknowledged by the policy-makers of Commonwealth countries, who then sought to come to their own arrangements with the EEC. During the negotiations of 1961 to 1963, many African members of the Commonwealth had protested that the concept of Associate status was demeaning and 'neo-colonial'. Nkrumah had been the main source of such complaints. He believed that association to the EEC would become a source of division among the African states, and he therefore saw the concept as a threat to his own Pan-Africanist ideals. By 1965, however, he had fallen from power in Ghana. Moreover, the existing six members of the EEC had responded to this line of criticism when the terms of association were redrafted as the Yaoundé Convention in July 1963. As British officials were aware, the new terms represented association more as an agreement between equals, and did not include some of the institutional aspects which African heads of state had felt to contain imperialist overtones.[50] The value of these changes was demonstrated by Nigeria's Association Agreement referred to earlier, but there were many states waiting to follow the example set by Lagos. Kenya, Tanzania and Uganda began joint negotiations for association in 1964, temporarily suspended as the French boycott began to bite in 1965.[51] Once the benefits of association were understood, the floodgates were opened. When the Commonwealth Relations Office in February 1966 canvassed its representatives overseas on the likely reactions to an EEC membership application, it became apparent that Ghana, Sierra Leone, Zambia, Malawi and the Gambia had all considered applying for association irrespective of British membership. As a result of both the Rhodesian crisis and the lead taken by Nigeria, response from African countries when Britain did apply to the EEC was muted, most intending to seek AOT status.[52] The case of the newly or soon to be independent High Commission Territories of Lesotho, Botswana and Swaziland represented an exception. All three were part of a customs union with the Republic of South Africa, and therefore it was thought they would require a less direct form of arrangement with the EEC. The most suitable solution seemed to be along the lines of the special protocol accorded to Morocco, whereby goods from those countries would retain the same terms of entry into the UK as previously, but would not then have free access into the rest of the Community. This was a return to the formula agreed in 1962.[53]

These were the trends prevailing before the general election of 1966 and the Labour government's reconsideration of its policy towards the EEC. There were a number of matters to consider in various Commonwealth countries specifically in the event of an application. The South Asian countries, Pakistan, India and Sri Lanka, had all derived benefit from the worldwide agreements in the GATT which reduced tariffs for tea, textiles and other major exports, and it was hoped to extend such agreements by reviving the offer for comprehensive trade arrangements made by the EEC during the earlier negotiations in 1962. There was an awareness in the subcontinent, given Britain's own restrictions on low-cost textiles mentioned above, that concessions for these exports would be limited. Essentially, concerns in the region were predominantly economic.[54]

The same was true in Canada. The Liberal government under Pearson which had replaced Diefenbaker's Conservatives did not share their predecessors' anxieties over Canada's dependence on the United States. Thus in 1964 Pearson was already negotiating a free trade agreement with the US for motor cars, which was to be the first of many. Consequently, transatlantic links were less important, and although Trade Minister Winters expressed reservations about damage to certain sectors of Canadian agriculture, multilateral agreements, particularly that on cereals, looked set to soften the blow of the CET.[55]

The Caribbean Commonwealth, again, maintained a purely economic view of the situation. Prime Minister Williams of Trinidad had been one of the few to express enthusiasm for the British application at the crucial Commonwealth Prime Ministers' Meeting in September 1962. Williams remained keen to explore the possibilities, especially if AOT status could enhance commercial relations with the French and Dutch Caribbean states. Together with Sangster and Lightbourne of Jamaica, he led a group of states and dependencies in pressing two salient points on Britain. The first was to ensure, when applying, that applications by Caribbean states for AOT status would be accepted. The second was to pledge the continuation of the Commonwealth Sugar Agreement, undisturbed, until 1974, as originally intended, as part of any transitional arrangements. This demand was echoed by Fiji and Mauritius, two other states which earned over 50 per cent of their national income from sugar exports.[56] In the event, the Commission's Preliminary Opinion acknowledged both these requests, but General de Gaulle's veto intruded before they could be tested in negotiation.[57]

Conversely, the issue was viewed as a political one in the Mediterranean Commonwealth states, Cyprus and Malta, since both were already considering associate membership of the EEC under Article 238. The Cypriot government had shown some initial reservations about possible competition between its principal exports, namely citrus fruits, and those of Italy. Quickly, such matters were overshadowed by the possibility that EEC association might form part of a remedy to the nationality problem, as both Greece and Turkey had previously become Article 238 associates. In the case of Malta, there was little which could worsen relations with Britain anyway, as the Maltese government made it perfectly clear that the Defence Expenditure Review might mean ruin for their economy. In January 1967, the Prime Minister, Borg Olivier, threatened to revoke all agreements with Britain, as he felt the scale of the cuts was a breach of faith by the British government anyway.

He did not carry out his threats, but if he had a European grievance against Britain at all, it remained low on his list.[58]

It should perhaps, then, be no surprise that the most serious difficulties arose among the Pacific members of the Commonwealth, where the Defence Review bit deeply, and at the same time combined with the economic implications of the CAP and CET. It was evident no concessions would be likely for Hong Kong, but again, this had been accepted during the first application. Economically, Malaysia and Singapore would be little affected. The principal Malaysian exports of tin and rubber had always been exempt from the CET. Singapore toyed with the idea of applying for AOT status to enhance its role as international entrepôt. Eventually, though, Lee Kuan Yew rejected the idea. He disliked the 'colonial flavour' of the term, and recognized the unwillingness of the EEC to agree to such an arrangement anyway, given the distinct differences between Singapore's own economy and those of the other associated territories.[59] In neither case were these details at the heart of the commentary on the possibility of EEC membership. When Herbert Bowden toured the Far East in February and March 1967, both governments impressed upon him their unceasing watchfulness against the communist threat. The dangers might have seemed to recede with Suharto's seizure of power from Sukarno in Indonesia the previous year, but the Vietnam war was escalating. British entry into the EEC might coincide with the military withdrawals from the Pacific, thus appearing to mark an overall British retreat from the region. If this were the case, the subversive elements could well take heart and resume their campaign. Lee of Singapore was especially apprehensive lest the communists should be assisted by the economic damage wrought to Singapore. A decline in exports to Britain due to EEC membership would be compounded by the disappearance of British naval facilities and personnel, which contributed a substantial proportion of the island's earnings.[60]

New Zealand was the country for which the economic effects of the CAP were expected to be the most deleterious. Nearly half its exports were to the UK, and most of these were temperate foodstuffs in which the EEC was striving for, or had already reached, self-sufficiency. These included 83 per cent of its lamb, facing a 20 per cent levy where it had previously enjoyed 12 per cent preference, and above all, 86 per cent of its butter and 78 per cent of its cheese, both of which appeared set to double in price for the British consumer.[61] In practice, however, the New Zealanders were not as alarmed as British officials expected. As with some of the African members of the Commonwealth, they had approached the European Commission directly, and been offered guarantees that they were recognized as a 'special case'.[62] They put their faith in Britain's pledges of seeking 'adequate safeguards', not merely transitional, but permanent. These looked more credible after the signing of a renewed Anglo-New Zealand trade agreement in November 1966 due to run until 1972.[63]

The will of London to uphold such promises was not in the end to be tested, but the Wellington government might have been less confident had they seen some of the information being received in London from Brussels. In June 1966, Dr Sicco Mansholt, the agriculture commissioner, explained to George Thomson that it was in New Zealand's interests that there should not be too much competition in dairy products resulting in a fall in price. Yet he 'seemed slow to understand' that the CAP as it stood entailed a fixed price at a level which would not only jeopardize Britain's delicate balance of payments, but would also deprive New Zealand exporters of any competitive advantage. According to British estimates, the EEC was already 102 per cent self-sufficient in dairy produce (hence a net exporter), which indicated that New Zealand products could be excluded altogether. Nor were the Italians any more understanding. Their Foreign Minister claimed in August 1966 that the New Zealand problem no longer remained, as Italy had become a substantial importer of butter. In fact, the quantities involved were a mere 100 tons per annum, compared to 170 000 tons imported by the UK. When taken alongside the well-known French opposition to any lowering of the CAP prices fixed to benefit their own farmers, it was little wonder that the Commission's Opinion of September 1967 barely mentioned the New Zealand issue at all: word reached the DEA that Mansholt's officials had simply refused to agree to any other suggestion than that 'New Zealand would have to look for other markets'.[64]

Yet in many ways, and in contrast to the first application, Australia represented the thorniest problem of all. This was because, for a variety of political reasons, its ministers were not so willing to take British guarantees at face value. Paradoxically, the Australians combined some of the sternest criticism of Britain's approach to Europe with an unfriendly attitude on a number of problems confronting London at the time. Wilson was reminded by an official that the then Prime Minister, Harold Holt, had referred to himself as 'all the way with L.B.J.'. Holt's displeasure over the East of Suez withdrawals was the consequence of this stance. Holt could hardly have been reassured by the mauling he received from the British press after expressing his misgivings at Britain's refusal to commit forces alongside the Americans in Vietnam.

Most worrying of all for Wilson were the views of the Australian Cabinet on Rhodesia. The CRO in July 1966 warned Michael Palliser, then at the Foreign Office but soon to be Wilson's Principal Private Secretary, that Holt and certain members of his Cabinet had alluded to the sympathy felt by the Australian public for the position of Ian Smith and the white minority in Rhodesia.[65]

Despite such unhelpful poses by his own Prime Minister, the Australian trade minister John McEwen still objected strongly to Britain's EEC entry on economic grounds. He was widely credited as the man who had engineered Australia's rapid industrialization and growth to support a rise in population. Partly in response to the first application, and partly due to the regional reorientation of Australian politics, the early 1960s witnessed a shift in exports away from Britain and towards the Far East. In consequence, Japan became Australia's best customer. To this end, after his initial irritation at slow progress in the Kennedy Round, McEwen suggested bargaining away British preferences in return for concessions in the Japanese market.[66] In private, he told British ministers that Australian export diversification, coupled with the multilateral agreements on cereals, would tide Australia over the shock of British entry. But his public pronouncements were a different matter entirely. He fulminated against the rising tide of regionalism, declaring after the delays to the Kennedy Round in 1966 that 'although countries inside the EEC might see scope for better opportunities, countries outside would see only high tariff walls'.[67] The reasons for this dichotomy were well known in Whitehall. McEwen had expected to be Sir Robert Menzies' successor after the latter's retirement in 1964, but had instead found himself and his Country Party the junior partners in a coalition government. Nor had he ever enjoyed close relations with Holt when the two had served under Menzies. Holt had been Treasurer and their departments were often in conflict. Hence McEwen was always willing to use the EEC – a subject on which he was considered an expert following his experience of the first application – as a chance to upstage Holt. Moreover, his own party drew much of its support from the farmers of South Australia (McEwen himself had once been a dairy farmer), and these were the group most likely to suffer as a result of Britain's acceptance of the CAP. He was therefore being fairly honest when he told Herbert Bowden in 1967 that, 'even if she [Australia] were large enough to stand the knock of our entry in financial terms, she could not do so in human terms, through standing by and seeing her sugar growers, butter producers and fruit farmers ruined'.[68] In many ways, Australia was in a similar position to Britain, undergoing a profound economic and strategic transformation. This presented McEwen and his rather traditional constituency with a complex challenge.

Conclusions

It is to these parallel trends occurring worldwide during the period that I now turn in trying to draw together the threads of material. On one of the memoranda advocating a new approach to Europe sent to Harold Wilson by George Brown and Michael Stewart in January 1966, the Prime Minister noted 'I'm getting at odds with First Secretary and Foreign Secretary'.[69] In response, his Principal Private Secretary, Oliver Wright, composed for him a long paper on why he thought the Prime Minister might be taking a different view from that of the Foreign Office. Wilson described it as 'a fascinating, frank look at the whole thing – ahead of the way I had been thinking, and certainly ahead of establishment thinking'. In this submission, Wright argued that world politics were going through a number of dramatic alterations. The reasons were the nascent détente between the USA and the USSR, brought about by nuclear stalemate, and the rise of China as a third great power, confusing the existing balance. 'Because the giants won't fight', Wright explained, 'the tiddlers have felt free to pursue their own interests and create their own troubles'. The result was a considerable degree of introversion and regionalism, what he called a 'narcissistic phase', of which the EEC was just one example. From Britain's point of view, the rise of China, when observed alongside the success of Franco–German reconciliation and the improbability of a Soviet invasion of Western Europe, required a shift of priorities. The most important struggles Britain would face into the next decade were not those between individual European states, but on a larger scale, conflict between regions and races, fuelled by a return to isolationism which de Gaulle was demonstrating so obstinately at the Kennedy Round and in NATO. Thus increasingly, the most important affairs were passing out of the hands of the Foreign Office and into those of the Commonwealth Office. The Foreign Office's 'obsession' with the EEC had emerged in response to this trend. Yet in practice, it was misplaced and out of date, above all in its demonizing of de Gaulle, 'who has a clearer idea of the way the world is moving'. It was imperative that the Rhodesian problem be solved, and the Commonwealth sustained, as in the event of a 'dismemberment of the Commonwealth ... I think that public opinion in this country would undergo a revulsion from responsibilities and would seek refuge in a form of Euro-chauvinism. I doubt whether that is what even the Foreign Office would want'. Wright concluded, 'The time for joining Europe and influencing it is past. The time may come again in the future. But certainly the time is not the present'.[70]

In many ways, Wright's observations are upheld by a study of the situation in the Commonwealth at this time. The emergence of the EEC had itself heralded an era of regionalism, as much in evidence in the Commonwealth as anywhere else. In some cases, political issues unrelated to Europe drew Commonwealth countries into a narrower regional outlook. Examples of this were the African reaction to the Rhodesian crisis, and the Australian government's emerging emphasis on resolving the Vietnam War, the Malaysian–Indonesian confrontation and even the Indo-Pakistani conflict over Kashmir. Lester Pearson also recognized the regionalization of commitments, and offered Canadian sponsorship of the Caribbean Commonwealth, both politically (mainly at the UN) and economically.[71] In part, the EEC encouraged economic regionalism indirectly, by offering an example for others to follow. Hence a series of customs unions and free trade areas blossomed in the mid-1960s. The trade agreements between Canada and the US have already been mentioned. A free trade area was also created between Australia and New Zealand, and between the United Kingdom and Eire, both in 1965. An organization for cooperation in the Asian and Pacific region (ASPAC, the forerunner of ASEAN) included Malaysia, Australia and New Zealand among its members. Many members of the Caribbean Commonwealth were contemplating adherence to a Latin American free trade area, or the Organization of American States.[72] There was also a customs union in East Africa, as well as the older economic union (a special case in the eyes of the Commonwealth and the EEC) between South Africa and the former High Commission Territories. Equally, in some cases the EEC was a direct cause of cooperation among Commonwealth states. The three East African States negotiated collectively with the European Commission for associate status in 1965, and Kingston hosted a meeting of the Caribbean and Latin American Commonwealth states and dependencies in May 1967 to discuss a joint approach to Britain's application and the process of associating to the EEC under Part 4 of the Rome Treaty.[73]

Consequently, Britain was not alone, nor even necessarily making the running among Commonwealth countries, in facing the challenge of the EEC. Other members of the Commonwealth, collectively or on an individual basis, made their own approaches. Even New Zealand, regarded as the most complex Commonwealth obstacle to membership, had embarked upon talks with the European Commission. This was effectively a continuation of the decentralizing of power within the Commonwealth, which began with decolonization itself, but by no means finished with the end of empire. Two of the most symbolic developments of the period were the creation of a Commonwealth Secretariat independent of the Whitehall apparatus in 1965, and the decision to hold Commonwealth Prime Ministers' Meetings outside of London. Hence the stormy crisis meeting over Rhodesia in 1966 was held at Lagos. Such a process of devolution did not signify the dissolution of the Commonwealth as a whole, but indeed its growing maturity. Its response to the challenge of the EEC, both in multilateral negotiations such as the Kennedy Round and when faced by Britain's own membership application, is a clear demonstration of this maturity. It is surely significant that both the Commonwealth Heads of Government Meeting in October 1997 and the European Union Ministers' Meeting in February 1998 were held not in London, but in Edinburgh.

Notes

1. U. Kitzinger, *The Second Try: Labour and the EEC* (Oxford: Oxford University Press, 1968); J. D. B. Miller, *Survey of Commonwealth Affairs, 1953 to 1969: Problems of Expansion and Attrition* (Oxford: Oxford University Press, 1974).
2. Public Record Office, Kew, London (PRO), CAB 133/269, p. 102: Board of Trade brief for Prime Minister's trip to Paris, 24 March 1965.
3. M. Couve de Murville, *Une politique étrangère, 1958–1969* (Evreux: Plon, 1971) p. 44. Translations from French are my own.
4. Miller, op. cit., note 1 above, p. 334.
5. D. Jay, *Change and Fortune: A Political Record* (London: Hutchinson, 1980) pp. 354–5.
6. See Couve de Murville, op. cit., note 3 above, chapter 9, for a record of these discussions.
7. PRO, PREM 13/306, p. 179: minutes of meeting between Wilson and de Gaulle, 29 January 1965.
8. PRO, EW 5/7, p. 117: Marjoribanks to O'Neill, 7 June 1967.
9. PRO, FO 371/188327: Robinson to Ashford, 10 March 1966.
10. PRO, CAB 133/339, p. 7: minutes of meeting between Erhard, Wilson and Brown, 23 May 1966.
11. PRO, PREM 13/904: memorandum by Foreign Secretary on possible adherence to the Treaty of Rome, 10 December 1965.
12. PRO, EW 5/7, p. 156: memorandum paper by First Secretary and Foreign Secretary, 17 August 1966.
13. PRO, EW 5/6: final communiqué of Commonwealth Trade Ministers' Meeting, 16 June 1966.
14. C. de Gaulle, *Discours et messages*, vol. 4, *Pour l'effort* (Evreux: Plon, 1970) p. 333.
15. PRO, CAB 133/338, pp. 15–19: minutes of a meeting between Pompidou and Wilson, 6 July 1966.

16. PRO, PREM 13/826: minutes of a meeting between Debré, Callaghan and Armstrong, 10 December 1966.
17. Kitzinger, op. cit., note 1 above, p. 135.
18. PRO, CAB 129/127, C(66)172: Commonwealth Secretary's memorandum on mandatory sanctions, 25 November 1966.
19. T. Bale, 'A "deplorable affair"? South African Arms and the Statecraft of British Social Democracy', *Labour History Review*, 62 (1997) 22–40.
20. PRO, CAB 129/127, C(66)172: Commonwealth Secretary's memorandum on mandatory sanctions, 25 November 1966.
21. C. de Gaulle, *Discours et messages*, vol. 5, *Vers le terme* (Evreux: Plon, 1970) p. 243.
22. D. Cook, *Charles de Gaulle: A Biography* (London: Secker & Warburg, 1984) p. 391. PRO, FO 371/188365 and 188366, 'Approach to Europe – Attitude of the French'.
23. R. Marsh, *Off the Rails: An Autobiography by Richard Marsh* (London: Weidenfeld & Nicolson, 1978) p. 96; Jay, op. cit., note 5 above, p. 389.
24. PRO, CAB 129/128, C(67)35: memorandum by President of the Board of Trade on the Kennedy Round, 21 March 1967.
25. PRO, PREM 13/306, pp. 8–12: O'Neill to Stewart, 3 May 1965.
26. M. Stewart, *Life and Labour: An Autobiography* (London: Sidgwick & Jackson, 1980) pp. 144–6.
27. PRO, PREM 13/904: Stewart to Wilson, 10 December 1965, and subsequent correspondence; H. Wilson, *The Labour Government, 1964 to 1970: A Personal Record* (London: Weidenfeld & Nicolson, 1971) p. 299.
28. PRO, CAB 128/42, CC 24(67)2: Cabinet conclusions, balance of payments impact of EEC membership, 29 April 1967.
29. PRO, CAB 130/298: minutes of meeting at Chequers, 22 October 1966; PRO, CAB 129/129, C(67)61: 'Europe: the balance of payments – report by economic advisers', 25 April 1967.
30. PRO, PREM 13/908: Balogh to Wilson, 15 and 20 October 1966 (emphasis in original).
31. PRO, CAB 129/129, C(67)63: Commonwealth Secretary's memorandum on Commonwealth interests affected by EEC membership; Jay, op. cit., note 5 above, pp. 427–8; PRO, PREM 13/904: Balogh to Wilson, 13 January 1966.
32. R. Crossman, *Diaries of a Cabinet Minister*, vol. 2, *1966–68* (London: Hamish Hamilton, 1976) p. 639.
33. Ibid., pp. 82–5; G. Brown, *In My Way: The Political Memoirs of Lord George-Brown* (London: Gollancz, 1971) p. 209.
34. C. Wrigley, 'Now You See it, Now You Don't: Harold Wilson and Labour's Foreign Policy, 1964 to 1970', in R. Coopey, S. Fielding and N. Tiratsoo (eds), *The Wilson Governments, 1964 to 1970* (London: Pinter, 1993) pp. 123–37; PRO, CAB 128/42, CC 14(67): Cabinet minutes, 21 March 1967; Wilson, op. cit., note 27 above, pp. 386–90.
35. PRO, PREM 13/904: Stewart to Wilson, 10 December 1965; Wilson, op. cit., note 27 above, p. 243.
36. Wilson, op. cit., note 27 above, p. 117.
37. Ibid, p. 277.
38. PRO, PREM 13/907, p. 9: minutes of a meeting between Wilson, Pompidou and Couve de Murville, 8 July 1966; on Cabinet stance, see PRO, CAB 128/41, CC 5(66)2: Cabinet conclusions, 3 February 1966.

39. PRO, PREM 13/910: Wilson to President Johnson, 11 November 1966.
40. J. Callaghan, *Time and Chance* (London: Collins, 1987) p. 210.
41. A. Cairncross, *The Wilson Years: A Treasury Diary 1964 to 1969* (London: The Historians' Press, 1997), entry for 29 November 1966, p. 173.
42. PRO, CAB 130/294: minutes of Working Party on Economies in Oversea Expenditure, 15–27 July 1966.
43. E. Roll, *Crowded Hours* (London: Faber & Faber, 1985) p. 173.
44. PRO, CAB 129/129, C(67)60: Cabinet memorandum by Prime Minister and Foreign Secretary, 24 April 1967; Cairncross, op. cit., note 41 above, entry for 17 May, p. 212; PRO, PREM 13/897: Palliser to Wright, 21 October 1966.
45. W. Kaiser, *Using Europe, Abusing the Europeans* (London: Macmillan Press – now Palgrave, 1997).
46. Bale, op. cit., note 19 above, pp. 22–40.
47. PRO, PREM 13/260, pp. 5ff: telegrams to Commonwealth Prime Ministers, and responses, December 1964.
48. PRO, CAB 129/128, C(67)35: memorandum by President of the Board of Trade on the Kennedy Round, 21 March 1967.
49. PRO, CAB 133/335: Board of Trade Steering Brief for Commonwealth Trade Ministers' Meeting, 10 June 1966.
50. PRO, FO 371/188329: draft memorandum, Shannon to C. O'Neill, 9 February 1966.
51. PRO, CAB 133/335: Commonwealth Relations Office brief on East African cooperation, 6 June 1966.
52. PRO, EW 5/6: Commonwealth reactions to an approach to Europe, February 1966 to April 1967.
53. PRO, CAB 129/129, C(67)63: Commonwealth Secretary's memorandum on Commonwealth interests affected by EEC membership.
54. PRO, EW 5/6: telegrams from Scott (Delhi) to CRO, 23 April 1966; Carter (Karachi) to CRO, 26 April 1966; Tomlinson (Colombo) to CRO, 26 April 1966.
55. PRO, CAB 133/266, p. 16: minutes of a meeting between Wilson and Pearson in Ottawa, 9 December 1964; PRO, EW 5/6: brief for First Secretary's meeting with Mr Winters, 9 June 1966.
56. PRO, EW 5/6: Hampshire (Port of Spain) to CRO, 14 April 1966; Britten (Kingston) to Keeble (CRO), 7 June 1966.
57. For copy of the European Commission's Opinion, see Kitzinger, op. cit., note 1 above, Doc. No. 27.
58. PRO, EW 5/6: Bishop (Nicosia) to CRO, 7 April 1966; PRO, CAB 128/42, CC 4(67)1: Cabinet conclusions, 31 January 1967.
59. PRO, EW 5/6: Walker (Kuala Lumpur) to CRO, 8 April 1966; Rob (Singapore) to CRO, 16 April 1966.
60. PRO, CAB 129/128, C(67)61: Commonwealth Secretary's memorandum on his tour of the Far East, 17 March 1967.
61. PRO, CAB 129/129, C(67)63: Commonwealth Secretary's memorandum on Commonwealth interests affected by EEC membership.
62. PRO, CAB 133/342: Commonwealth Office brief on EEC for Commonwealth Prime Ministers' Meeting, 24 August 1966.
63. PRO, PREM 13/1037: Bowden to Wilson, 15 November 1966.

64. PRO, PREM 13/907: minutes of a meeting between Mansholt and Thomson, 28 June 1966; PRO, EW 5/6: Ford to Shillito, 18 July 1966; Wall to O'Neill, 3 August 1966; PRO, EW 5/9, p. 201: Hannay to Beale, 29 September 1967.
65. Wilson, op. cit., note 27 above, p. 251; PRO, PREM 13/729: Johnston (Canberra) to CRO, 9 July 1966; Mackilligin to Palliser, 8 July 1966.
66. PRO, CAB 129/128, C(67)35: memorandum by the President of the Board Trade on the Kennedy Round, 21 March 1967.
67. PRO, EW 5/6: DEA brief for visit of Prime Minister Holt, 23 June 1966.
68. PRO, CAB 133/329, p. 130: Commonwealth Office brief for visit of Prime Minister Holt, 12 June 1967; PRO, CAB 129/128, C(67)37: memorandum by Commonwealth Secretary on his tour of the Far East, 17 March 1967.
69. PRO, PREM 13/905: handwritten comment on Stewart to Wilson, 26 January 1966.
70. PRO, PREM 13/905: Wright to Wilson, 28 January 1966.
71. PRO, CAB 133/329, p. 5: minutes of a meeting between Holt and Bottomley [then Commonwealth Relations Secretary] in London, 8 July 1966; PRO, CAB 130/462, p. 33: minutes of a meeting between Wilson and Pearson in Ottawa, 19 December 1965.
72. PRO, EW 5/6: Hampshire (Port of Spain) to CRO, 14 April 1966.
73. PRO, EW 5/6: Commonwealth Office to Britten (Kingston), 25 May 1967.

9
A Matter of Preference: the EEC and the Erosion of the Old Commonwealth Relationship

Stuart Ward

The history of Britain's search for a viable relationship with the European Community, and contemporaneous changes in the British Empire and Commonwealth, are usually treated as two quite distinct and separate fields of historical enquiry. It is as though the division of responsibilities in Whitehall in the 1950s and 1960s has marked out the territories of imperial historians and European integration specialists respectively. This has been unfortunate, in that it has tended to obscure the extent to which developments in the one area of British foreign policy influenced events in the other.[1] This chapter looks at the way in which Britain's decision to seek membership of the European Economic Community in 1961 served to alter the ideological foundations of the 'old' Commonwealth relationship. The EEC membership crisis was a sobering experience for Australia, Canada and New Zealand. The Macmillan government's European aspirations underlined the discordance of sentiment and self-interest long inherent in Britain's ties to the old Dominions, eroding the sense of mutual identification and organic community that had traditionally characterized Commonwealth relations.

At the time of Britain's first EEC membership bid, Canada, Australia and New Zealand had long functioned as fully sovereign, independent nation-states. But there had always been something faintly anomalous about Dominion independence. None of the Dominions had ever formally severed their ties to the Mother Country, and none of them celebrated any kind of 'national independence day'.[2] Rather, the ongoing ties of sentiment and self-interest ensured that Dominion independence was achieved in a gradual, piecemeal, almost imperceptible manner. As a result, the Dominions retained a sense of 'dual loyalty': on the one hand vigorously defending their own distinctive interests, often in outright defiance of the Mother Country, while at the same time retaining a broader cultural allegiance to the worldwide community of the 'British race'. Right down to the early 1960s, the political evolution of all three Dominions was profoundly influenced by the ideology of 'British race patriotism'. London formed the centre of an imperial imagination in which the Dominions were firmly cast as loyal outposts of British culture and British civilization.

The ideological relationship between Dominion nationalism and British race patriotism revolved around two key assumptions. On the one hand, there prevailed the idea that the Dominion nation-states had distinctive interests, priorities and aspirations, which might not always converge precisely with those of the Mother Country. It was this sense of a potential conflict of interest that underlined Australian, New Zealand and Canadian vigilance against the encroachments of the British government in their own affairs. But at the same time, these distinctive national aspirations were viewed through the sentimental prism of British race patriotism, which promoted the idea that the wider interests of the British Empire ultimately transcended the more narrow, particular interests of any single Commonwealth country. Thus, beyond the more immediate awareness of the potential for conflict with the Mother Country, there prevailed a powerful sentimental assumption that the interests of the British world *ought* ultimately to coincide. When it came down to the survival of the British race, it was axiomatic that the Dominions and the Mother Country were mutually bound by blood and sentiment to join each other's interests as their very own. It was this assumption that provided the ideological cement of the old Commonwealth relationship through countless imperial crises. And it is the fate of this assumption that is central to understanding the demise of British race patriotism in Australian, Canadian and New Zealand political culture.

In this chapter it is argued that the United Kingdom's first attempt to join the European Community was a pivotal moment in reorienting all three Dominions away from the British race patriot outlook on the world, and towards a more limited, exclusive conception of their nationhood. This is not to suggest that Britain's EEC membership bid of 1961–63 was the fundamental cause of the parting of the ways between Britain and the old Dominions. The postwar years had seen profound economic and political changes on the international scene, which had subtly undermined the traditional precepts and practices of the old Commonwealth relationship. The transformation of the British Empire into an increasingly discordant 'new' Commonwealth, the advent of the Cold War and the emergence of the 'superpowers', and the relative decline in Britain's economic capacity had all contributed to a steady weakening of the practical ties between Britain and the old Dominions. But the gradual and piecemeal nature of these changes meant that their impact on the public imagination and political culture in all three Dominions was somewhat muted. The occasional rifts in Commonwealth relations, such as Britain's exclusion from the ANZUS Alliance in 1951, or Canada's refusal to support British actions at Suez in 1956, were invariably papered over by loud, ostentatious affirmations of the British blood ties. More searching reflection, discussion or debate were extremely rare. The ongoing sense of an organic, British cultural community, embodied in the endless round of Royal tours, Royal titles, test matches (in the case of Australia and New Zealand), Oxbridge scholarships and the like, tended to obscure the nature of the changes taking place. There was no episode of sufficient magnitude to activate the press, the parliament, and public opinion in such a way as to reshape the core assumptions of Anglo–Dominion relations.

The British decision to seek membership of the European Community, however, provided a key focal point around which many of these issues converged. The British government's painful choice between the communities of 'Europe' and 'the British world' provoked a crisis of British race patriotism throughout the 'old Commonwealth', and fatally undermined the core ideological precepts of Anglo–Dominion relations. The British decision to join in the economic obligations of a European common tariff and to face the long-term political implications of European unity signalled a conflict of interest of an entirely different kind to those which had disrupted Commonwealth harmony in previous years. Far from posing a mere transitory conflict of interest with old and familiar Commonwealth partners, the EEC problem involved the fundamental question of how future 'British' interests would be conceived, delineated and pursued. It seemed to imply a fundamental and permanent reorientation of the British conception of 'community', away from the former imperial conception of Britain's world role and towards a new basis for great power status as a leading player in an economically dynamic and politically united Europe. Thus, the EEC became a prime catalyst for long overdue discussion and debate, which played a vital role in redefining national assumptions and resetting national priorities. More specifically, it marked a point of explicit recognition that the sentimental assumptions of British race patriotism were no longer tenable in a world dominated by political and economic self-interest.

Throughout the 1950s, Britain's approach to the interlocking problems of Europe and the Commonwealth had been characterized by an attempt to reconcile the growing conflict between sentiment and self-interest in British priorities. Quite apart from Britain's obvious commercial interests in retaining as great a share of Commonwealth markets as possible, successive British governments were also influenced by the moral imperatives of British race patriotism in their approach to the EEC problem. The issue was widely regarded as a question of British honour, and political orthodoxy held that no British government could be seen to abandon the Commonwealth and survive. It was these considerations, as much as commercial factors, that underpinned the Macmillan government's approach to the Free Trade Area negotiations of 1957–58, and the subsequent 'bridge building' rationale behind the creation of the European Free Trade Association in 1959. Even in 1960, the year of Whitehall's major reappraisal of the EEC question, Macmillan continued to think in terms of 'reconciling' the Commonwealth trading system with British membership of the European Community.[3]

It was not until early 1961 that the British government began to recognize fully the stark conflict that had emerged between the ideological precepts of British race patriotism on the one hand, and the national aspirations of the United Kingdom on the other. In April 1961, Whitehall officials succinctly and unsentimentally assessed the Commonwealth implications of a British move towards EEC membership:

> A decision by the United Kingdom to join the Six would clearly have major political implications for the Commonwealth. We should be entering a relationship with Europe different from, and in some respects closer than, that which we have had with Commonwealth countries since they became independent. It would appear to public opinion in other Commonwealth countries to mark a turning away from them … Although the Commonwealth is a flexible concept, we would find it harder to take their interests into account where these conflict with those of our European partners, and hence more difficult to secure their support for our policies.[4]

Here, British officials pinpointed the key issue at stake for the future of the Commonwealth relationship: membership of the European Community would tend progressively to bind the hands of the British government whenever European interests clashed with those of the Commonwealth. And this, in turn, would fatally undermine the notion of a worldwide community of interest organically binding the British family of nations. Officials had become resigned to the fact that Commonwealth free entry would have to be abandoned and replaced by 'reverse preferences' in favour of European suppliers. Realistically, the government could only hope to gain concessions on items which were 'really vital' to the Commonwealth, which would 'serve to mitigate the damage which some Commonwealth countries, notably Australia, New Zealand and Canada, are bound to suffer'.[5] But in the final analysis, officials were highly pessimistic about the chances of obtaining the kind of safeguards that would be regarded as adequate by Commonwealth countries.[6]

In keeping with this analysis, the Secretary of State for Commonwealth Relations, Duncan Sandys, informed his Cabinet colleagues in June 1961 that the best he could hope to secure for Commonwealth countries in negotiations with the Six would be a progressive elimination of Commonwealth preferences over a transitional period, as a means of cushioning the blow of British entry. He acknowledged that Commonwealth countries would be unlikely to accept such a solution, but suggested that 'they might be brought to do so at the end of a long negotiation in which they had seen that we had done our utmost to secure the best possible terms for them'. In other words, Sandys proposed that Britain should put forward exaggerated demands on behalf of the Commonwealth, knowing full well that these would be rejected by the Six, in the hope that a purely tactical display of loyalty to Commonwealth countries might help to secure their ultimate acquiescence in British entry. He emphasized that 'if we tried to get the Commonwealth to agree to accept what we now thought might eventually be negotiated, we should risk doing serious damage to Commonwealth relations while there was still no assurance that we might negotiate satisfactory arrangements with the Six'.[7] This was an ingenious, if somewhat disingenuous strategy, and illustrated the extent to which the Macmillan government had discarded sentimental notions about Britain's wider duties and obligations to the Commonwealth 'family'.

For Macmillan himself, it was no longer important that Commonwealth leaders should accept British entry into the EEC, but rather that they should 'be *made* to accept' it.[8] Thus he tended increasingly to view these problems in terms of political tactics rather than sentimental notions of British duty towards kith and kin. Macmillan genuinely believed he had a responsibility to 'lead the country away from its traditional approach' to European and Commonwealth affairs, and received occasional reminders from Heath about the need to 're-educate the British people' in this regard.[9] Similarly, Duncan Sandys was bent on inculcating his CRO staff with a new, more exclusively 'national' conception of British interests.[10] Despite repeated British assurances that special safeguards would be negotiated to protect vital Commonwealth interests, it was clear that the discordance of sentiment and self-interest in Anglo–Dominion relations had begun to unravel, as the British strove to disentangle their own distinctive interests from the emotional, historical and cultural ties to the wider British family.

For Canada, Australia and New Zealand, however, the deeply ingrained ideas about wider British community were not so easily dispensed with. All three Dominions stood to suffer substantial economic loss from the dismantling of Commonwealth trade preferences and the erection of 'reverse preferences' in favour of the EEC. And all three were profoundly influenced by the ideology and rhetoric of British race patriotism in their response to the Macmillan government's decision to negotiate with the Six. This manifested itself in a variety of ways, from loud and frequent appeals to British racial sentiment,[11] to naive expressions of faith in British assurances, to more bitter accusations of unrequited loyalty. But above all there prevailed a deeply ingrained reluctance to distinguish clearly between the interests of Great Britain and those of the Commonwealth as a whole. For example, the Australian Prime Minister, Robert Menzies, went to great lengths to reconcile the stark conflict of interest that had emerged. Commenting to the press, Menzies described the forthcoming negotiations as 'the most important in time of peace in my lifetime. They will demand of us both wisdom, patience, and our constant vigilance'.[12] But despite his call for 'vigilance', Menzies' remarks in the House of Representatives on 16 August 1961 betrayed a deep confusion in distinguishing precisely whose interests Australia should be looking out for:

> …we are both British and Commonwealth. But our first duty is to protect what we believe to be the proper interests of Australia, whose future development will be a considerable factor in Commonwealth strength, and will in particular produce economic advantages for Great Britain herself. We do not doubt that this is understood and accepted by Great Britain. There is therefore much common ground on which to stand.

Menzies' reasoning was ideologically rooted in the British race patriot view of Australia's ties to Britain. By emphasizing the traditional theme of the 'common ground', Menzies failed to grasp the essence of Britain's shift towards Europe. The Macmillan government's decision to seek entry into the EEC was essentially a tacit acknowledgment of the declining economic and political utility of the Commonwealth as a vehicle for British interests. It came as a direct challenge to the fundamental notion of 'mutuality of interest' which had for so long permeated the conduct of Commonwealth relations. But rather than confront this new set of circumstances, Menzies insisted that the problems associated with the Common Market could be dealt with 'on a proper Commonwealth level; our common interests never forgotten, but our particular interests zealously expounded and upheld'. For Menzies, the solution was essentially a matter of sticking to the tried and true method. Although there would inevitably be 'intense arguments' and 'conflicts of opinion', these need not be feared because 'such matters are in the British tradition'. Interestingly, Menzies went to great lengths to emphasize that 'the problems will not be solved by saying that we have common objectives'.[13] Yet this seems to have been precisely his state of mind. He could not conceive, given the long tradition of cooperation and compromise in Empire relations, that a solution ultimately satisfactory to all parties would not be found.

Another typical response to Britain's EEC membership bid took the form of an angry protest against the morally dubious actions of a thoroughly un-British government. In Australia, this standpoint was personified by the Deputy Prime Minister and Minister for Trade, Jack McEwen, who, although less sentimental in his comments than Prime Minister Menzies, made claims which derived from much the same conception of Australia's place in the British world. In particular, his angry assertion that it would be 'unthinkable' for Australians to contemplate that 'foreigners' should obtain a preferred position in the UK market,[14] reveals how the pervading sense of an Anglo-Australian community of culture underpinned an ongoing attachment to the organic ideal of an Anglo-Australian community of interest. Although McEwen was more willing to face up to the conflict of interest than Menzies, he fundamentally shared the Prime Minister's instinctive belief that Australia ought not to be abandoned. The main difference between the two was that for McEwen, finding a satisfactory solution was essentially a question of loud and forthright protest. The British would have to be compelled to see the seriousness of Australia's plight, and this could only be achieved if Australia's voice was clearly, even painfully heard. He therefore viewed the forthcoming negotiations as 'a fight ... a fight for stakes which for us are very, very high'.[15]

In Canada, the government of John Diefenbaker reacted in a particularly hostile manner when Macmillan first broached the question of

British EEC membership in mid-1961. Diefenbaker was convinced that the British were prepared to 'write off the Commonwealth',[16] and like McEwen he tended to view this as an act of betrayal on the part of the Macmillan government. British Commonwealth Secretary, Duncan Sandys, was therefore greeted with a cool response when he visited Ottawa in July 1961 to explain his government's position. The press communiqué from these talks stated bluntly that 'Canada's assessment of the situation is different to that put forward by Mr. Sandys',[17] and the Canadian press described the government's stance as 'frigid', 'angry', 'terse' and 'the stiffest of the older Commonwealth countries'.[18] Relations between the British and Canadian governments deteriorated further at a meeting of the Commonwealth Economic Consultative Council in Accra in September 1961, when the Canadian Finance Minister, Donald Fleming, launched an all-out assault on Britain's EEC membership aspirations. He not only expressed his 'disappointment' and 'grave apprehension' about the British decision, but also poured cold water on the idea that the UK would gain any benefit from membership of the Six. In British eyes, Fleming's performance was 'a tirade as much as a speech', and served to provoke other Commonwealth members into airing their grievances.[19] British Chancellor of the Exchequer, Selwyn Lloyd, reported the 'rather sad feeling' among Commonwealth ministers 'that we had made up our minds and although we would try to solve what we could, we were in effect jettisoning the Commonwealth as it had developed up to now'.[20]

This point of view was not universally shared, however. Beyond the bitter protests of McEwen and Fleming, there prevailed in all three Dominions a seemingly endless reservoir of trust in the assurances of the British government that 'vital Commonwealth interests' would be safeguarded. Indeed, in New Zealand this blind faith in the Mother Country became formalized as government policy. The National Party government of Keith Holyoake was well aware that New Zealand's trading future was ultimately dependent on British goodwill, and it was therefore decided that any formal challenge to Britain's EEC membership bid would be counterproductive. The New Zealanders felt that their best chances for economic survival lay in establishing New Zealand as a 'special case', by emphasizing their overwhelming economic dependence on the United Kingdom market. This could best be achieved through a policy of helpless 'reliance' on British assurances, which would serve to accentuate the dire nature of their predicament in the eyes of the Six. This did not preclude them from occasionally criticizing Britain's approach in strict confidence (Heath commented to US Ambassador David Bruce that the New Zealanders were 'polite in public and rude in private'[21]) but their attitude was, on the whole, far more cooperative than that of Australia or Canada. Nonetheless, behind New Zealand's vote of confidence in the British negotiators lay a brooding suspicion that more aggressive measures might ultimately be necessary to hold the British government to its promises. As New Zealand Deputy Prime Minister, John Marshall, commented in February 1962: 'New Zealand puts her trust in British assurances but is keeping her powder dry'.[22]

Far less equivocal were leading newspapers such as *The New Zealand Herald*, who refused to believe that Britain would ever join the European Community on terms that might weaken the Commonwealth.[23] Similar views appeared in certain sections of the Australian press. *The Sydney Morning Herald*, for example, saw no reason to doubt British assurances, claiming that 'it would be churlish to believe that the British Government will not try hard and persistently to win from the present members of the Common Market those special arrangements without which Commonwealth trade would be gravely disrupted, and old links of friendship subjected to strain'. Australia, it was argued, should acknowledge Britain's 'dire necessity' and applaud Macmillan's commitment to European unity 'without pernickety reservations'.[24] This profound reluctance to conceive that Britain might abandon Commonwealth interests was the other side of the coin of the pervasive British race patriotism in the response of the Dominions to the Common Market crisis. Regardless of whether one considered British entry an unmitigated disaster or took a more complacent sentimental view, the prospect of a major rupture of the old Commonwealth nexus was widely thought to be unthinkable.

In Canada, public faith in British government assurances was even more pronounced, and became a major thorn in the side of the Diefenbaker government in its efforts to secure a fair deal for Canadian trade interests. *The Toronto Globe and Mail* was among the most vociferous critics of the Canadian government, accusing them of 'screaming before she is hurt', and claiming that it would 'be wiser for Ottawa to reserve judgment until the actual effect on Canadian trade is known'.[25] The British High Commissioner in Ottawa, Derick Heathcoat Amory, was positively embarrassed by the degree of understanding and support in Canada for the British decision to enter into negotiations with the EEC.[26] He informed Macmillan in March 1962: 'I think public opinion has been almost unreasoningly favourable to our case, with a tendency to oversimplify the issue and underestimate the effects of exchanging a preference in favour for a tariff against on some Canadian products'.[27] The Liberal Opposition, led by Lester Pearson, quickly took advantage of this situation by declaring their unconditional support for Britain's EEC membership application. In this political climate, Finance Minister Fleming was forced to repudiate vehemently the suggestion that Canada had behaved in a hostile manner towards the United Kingdom. He explained his government's response to the EEC question in terms that echoed the British race patriotism of Robert Menzies. 'Like all families', he declared in a speech at Winnipeg, 'we have had our differences; like all human associations ours is not a perfect one, but by and large our aims have been common, and where they have diverged we have brought our differences to the conference table and discussed them as members of a family'.[28] Thus Fleming was placed in the absurd situation of having to defend himself against the charge of disloyalty to the British race patriot ideal. There could be no clearer illustration of the way in which the idea of an organic community of interest with the Mother Country remained one of the core ideological precepts of Dominion political culture at the time of Britain's first EEC membership bid.

The course of Britain's EEC membership negotiations soon revealed the inadequacy of the traditional ties of culture and sentiment as a means of securing the vital trading interests of Commonwealth countries. The Six proved to be completely averse to the idea of granting meaningful trade concessions to relatively affluent countries like Australia and Canada, although some sympathy for New Zealand's special problems was occasionally in evidence. The Europeans were unimpressed by Britain's arguments about the importance of the Commonwealth as an element of peace and stability in the non-Communist world, and remained more concerned that British accession to the European Community should not be to the detriment of European farmers. Moreover, they remained sceptical about the alleged political benefits of a Commonwealth association that showed more signs of atrophy than real cohesion or unity. The French, in particular, were at a loss to understand 'what common ideology unites men of such different nature as Mr. Nkrumah, Archbishop Makarios, and Mr. Menzies', and felt that much of the 'nostalgia' that underpinned Britain's arguments about Commonwealth unity amounted to little more than 'une certain sympathie amusée'.[29] Thus, to the extent that the Europeans were willing to grant special terms to protect the interests of Commonwealth countries, they were overwhelmingly more concerned about the plight of the newly independent states of Africa and Asia. Any concessions to the relatively affluent 'white Dominions' would have to be 'temporary, restrained, and kept to the utmost minimum'.[30]

As the intransigence of the Europeans on the Commonwealth question became increasingly apparent, the Macmillan government stepped up its efforts to wean the older Commonwealth countries off their traditional attachments to the Mother Country. For example, in early 1962 Heathcoat Amory sought guidance from London about the content of his official speeches in Canada on the EEC question. In particular, he sought permission to include certain remarks about the contribution of the Commonwealth during the Second World War, and to conclude one of his speeches with the words: 'Today the British people owe it to their sense of honour to send a message no less loyal to the Commonwealth ... for at the end of the day we go into the Common Market if and only if we believe we can get a square deal for you'.[31] The response of Britain's chief negotiator, Edward Heath, to Amory's request reveals the direction of British thinking at this time. 'I am doubtful about this', Heath cautioned; 'our main purpose now must be to bring the Commonwealth public along with us as we go – not hoist the banner even higher'.[32] Amory soon got the message, and his subsequent communications with the CRO were littered with references to his progress in 'bringing the Canadians along' to the new realities of the Commonwealth relationship.[33] In much the same way, Amory's counterpart in Wellington, Sir Francis Cumming-Bruce, spoke in rather condescending terms about the need gently to 'guide the New Zealanders in blinkers' towards a more mature conception of Anglo–New Zealand relations.[34] He complained frequently about the New Zealanders' stubborn attachment to the old British race patriot outlook:

> The body politic here moves more slowly than the speed of events elsewhere requires. As with one of the smaller dinosaurs having slow moving limbs and a small head, no amount of kicking and pricking or even the risk of destruction will make the animal move much faster than its habit. But we will do all we can here to push it along from behind.[35]

Meanwhile, the British were growing impatient with the slow progress of the negotiations in Brussels. The general feeling among the British Delegation was that they were negotiating with one hand tied behind their backs, which in turn served as a serious drain on British sympathy and support for Commonwealth interests. By mid-March 1962, Heath was at his wits' end trying to find some basis for a workable compromise. He even raised with his Cabinet colleagues whether 'it would be possible to come to some arrangement with [the Europeans] that would lead to the United Kingdom appearing to be asking for a position in advance on what they were eventually prepared to accept in the hope of being able to demonstrate to the Commonwealth that we had gone some way to meet their representations'. Heath wisely concluded that 'a fudged arrangement of this sort would be certain to leak', but the fact that such a ludicrous idea was even considered reveals the anxious state of mind of British ministers at this time.[36] Moreover, it is significant that the only objection raised to a 'fudged arrangement' was the danger of leaks, rather than any notion that the idea was inherently distasteful or inappropriate to relations among the British family of nations. Clearly, the imperative of EEC membership had fundamentally altered the Macmillan government's ordering of British priorities, which in turn had seriously shaken any genuine sense of obligation to the Commonwealth. In these circumstances, the Commonwealth was bound to be regarded as something of a nuisance, and an unwelcome hindrance to the legitimate pursuit of British interests.

The dwindling British resolve to protect the interests of the old Commonwealth did not pass unnoticed, and all three Dominions communicated their concerns to the Macmillan government in trenchant terms.[37] But at the same time, the Dominions were forced to consider whether there was in fact any point in persevering with their complaints in the face of British and European indifference to their economic needs. At the very outset of the Brussels negotiations in October 1961, Australian officials had begun to ponder the fundamental issue at stake: 'How far is it really possible to reconcile the interests of the Six, the United Kingdom and Australia? Can we assume that there is a basis for a mutually acceptable reconciliation of interests?'[38] The Australians acknowledged that Britain's desire to join the European Community was 'quite reasonable, or at least understandable'. The conclusion therefore was inescapable: 'Given that each country's first duty is to itself… there is a real and fundamental clash of interests'.[39] One might easily dismiss this assessment as little more than a statement of the obvious. But it carried a far deeper resonance for a country where conflict with the Mother Country had generally been reconciled within the traditional British race patriot paradigm. Far from representing a mere transitory difference of opinion or an expression of 'particular' interests, the EEC issue challenged core ideological assumptions about the organic unity of the British world.

The futility of pressing the British to secure adequate safeguards for Commonwealth interests was underlined further during the course of McEwen's tour of Britain and Europe in March–April 1962. In continental Europe, McEwen was politely informed that the Treaty of Rome required that all 'third countries' be treated on a non-discriminatory basis.[40] And in London, he was infuriated that British ministers and officials were unable to provide any indication of their objectives in the Brussels negotiations. He remained convinced that this was due to deliberate deception on the part of Edward Heath, prompting him on one occasion to announce indignantly that if it were Britain's intention 'to treat the Australian Government as opponents, well and good; but [we] would like to know'.[41] Years later, McEwen reflected on the disappointing outcome of his overseas tour:

> It became increasingly clear that the existing members of the Common Market were determined to prevent Australia getting special treatment if Britain should succeed in joining the Market. I also came to realise that the British were having so much trouble looking after their own interests in the negotiations that they were not going to complicate things further by trying very hard to defend Australia's position ... So we were left without a friend in the world.[42]

At around the same time, opinion in New Zealand and Canada began to recognize the futility of relying on British assurances to safeguard their national interests. *The Wellington Evening Post* observed that 'not the slightest reassurance for New Zealand, or anyone else in the Commonwealth, can be derived from the present atmosphere in Whitehall'.[43] In Canada, there were signs of a more resigned approach. *The Montreal Gazette* cast doubt on the political value of the modern Commonwealth and posed the question: 'What is really left but the ties of sentiment?'[44] The comments of *The Toronto Globe and Mail* were typical:

> We live in a world of change – changing trade, changing alliances, changing balances of power – and we must be adventurous and adaptable to survive. It is unthinkable that Canada, through lack of vision and selfish insistence upon present advantage, should attempt to resist great and beneficial changes in Europe.[45]

Indeed, by this stage the Canadian government had recognized the inevitability of Canadian trade sacrifices in the Brussels negotiations, and were already looking for ways of evading the charge of 'selling particular interests down the river'.[46] To this end, Canadian ministers entered into a clandestine agreement with Edward Heath to the effect that Britain should refrain from asking the Canadians for their official views on developments in the Brussels negotiations. The Canadians, in turn, would refrain from criticizing the performance of the British negotiators, either in public or in private. The point of this deal, from the point of view of the Diefenbaker government, was to try to cloak the EEC issue in a shroud of silence and thereby remove it from the agenda in the forthcoming election campaign.[47] Thus in an appalling display of political expediency, the Canadians offered to keep their mouths shut in return for British cooperation in making the Common Market a non-issue in Canadian electoral politics. Heath could hardly believe his good fortune, and quickly accepted the offer on the condition that the Canadian government would not attempt to veto any decisions agreed in Brussels, nor claim at any future date that they had not been properly consulted. The outcome of this extraordinary deal was a subtle, but nonetheless significant change in the tone and frequency of Canadian statements on the EEC issue. Rather than openly criticize the British government, Canadian ministers preferred to emphasize Canada's reliance on British assurances, and deferred judgment on specific points until a more complete package of terms had emerged.[48]

With the Canadians and New Zealanders taking a softer line, the views of the Australian government assumed greater prominence, particularly during the much publicized visit of Prime Minister Menzies to London in June 1962. But despite Menzies' success in promoting wider public awareness in Britain about the nature of Australia's problems, there were mounting anxieties within the Australian government about the dangers of pushing Australia's case too far. Upon Menzies return to Australia, his Cabinet colleagues actually expressed concern about the heightened international press attention which he had attracted during the course of his trip. Unless care was taken, Australia might find itself regarded as the 'leader' of Commonwealth opposition to British entry into the EEC. The Cabinet agreed that 'Australia must be on guard not to be manoeuvred, in fact or even in appearance, into any such role'.[49] The Menzies government had become acutely anxious that Australia might be held responsible should the Brussels negotiations end in failure. At a time of growing political unrest in the South

East Asian region, any serious damage to Australia's traditional strategic alliances could be far more serious than the economic damage arising from British EEC membership.[50]

These pressures soon prompted signs of a more resigned Australian approach to the EEC problem at official level. In the Department of External Affairs in particular, there was a growing feeling that the horse had already bolted as far as Australian trade interests were concerned, and the time had arrived to consider the alternatives. This view was most clearly articulated by Australian Ambassador to Paris, E. Ronald Walker, in the immediate aftermath of Menzies' world tour:

> I feel that the time has already come when serious thought must be given to the adjustments that will be required, both in our national economic life and in our external relations with various other countries. Whatever the outcome of the Brussels negotiations, Australia is moving into a new phase of her history, requiring adaptation to entirely new conditions.[51]

Even more significantly, on 12 July the Prime Minister himself delivered a major speech that marked the first clear signs of a fundamental revision of the government's public stance. Here Menzies offered an entirely new perspective on the significance of British EEC membership for Australia's future:

> If Britain goes into the Common Market on any terms that are now comprehensible by me, we are going to be faced, not with disaster, dear me, no, but with a challenge to get cracking, to discover new ways in which we can build up our income abroad, and therefore, new ways in which we can increase our development at home.[52]

Menzies' speech marked the first occasion where he publicly conceded that the old Anglo–Australian relationship was in for some major restructuring, and that Australia would be increasingly drawn economically towards new markets, particularly in the Asia-Pacific region. But far from representing a sudden conversion from his renowned Anglophilia, Menzies' call to Australia to 'get cracking' was more a reflection of his concern to establish a new political footing for a more cooperative Australian stance on the Common Market issue.

Meanwhile the New Zealand government had all but lost faith in the assurances of the British government,[53] but they remained nonetheless highly reluctant to enter into dispute with the United Kingdom.

By this stage they clearly recognized the sheer futility of raising further complaints against the British, and were more anxious to find some way out of what had become an awkward political bind. Prime Minister Holyoake himself had come to see the entire EEC issue as a problem of presentation. As Francis Cumming-Bruce observed, 'He recognises that eventually New Zealand will have to face some changes obnoxious to farmers, but he does not see how he can appear to acquiesce'.[54] Holyoake was finally relieved of this dilemma on 5 August, when the Italian Minister for Industry and Trade formally declared from the chair of the Brussels negotiations: 'There is an awareness on the part of the Six of the problem of New Zealand and a willingness to reach a solution'.[55] Although this undertaking remained typically vague and raised more questions than it answered, it nonetheless allowed Holyoake sufficient political justification to soft pedal New Zealand's grievances.

The dwindling Commonwealth resistance to Britain's EEC aspirations prompted the Macmillan government, at the end of July 1962, to abandon formally any remaining hopes that Commonwealth trading arrangements might be preserved beyond a transitional period. Duncan Sandys wrote to all three Dominion Prime Ministers: 'We are being reluctantly forced to the conclusion…that there is virtually no prospect of retaining the existing Commonwealth preferences after the transitional period and that we shall probably have to accept that they should be phased out by 1970'.[56] This amounted to the clearest admission on the part of the British that they would be unable to meet the requirements of the Dominion governments in the Brussels negotiations. And by implication, the British government conceded that they did not consider this sufficient reason to remain outside the EEC. Sandys' tactics accorded precisely with his original objective of bringing Commonwealth governments around gradually, after the experience of negotiation had demonstrated the futility of pressing for genuine safeguards. The Dominions were given clearly to understand that the Macmillan government could ill afford to be deflected from what had become a primary national objective. Within two weeks of Sandys' message, the British government reached a broad outline of agreement with the Europeans for a phasing out of virtually all Commonwealth preferences by 1970. The only encouragement for the Dominions was a commitment on the part of the Europeans to work towards 'world-wide commodity agreements' as a long-term solution, combined with a hopelessly vague undertaking to 'offer reasonable opportunities' for exporters of temperate foodstuffs.[57] It had thus become painfully clear that where fundamental British interests collided with those of Commonwealth countries, the former would naturally prevail.

The Commonwealth Prime Ministers' Meeting of September 1962 effectively marked the end of Dominion resistance to Britain's EEC membership application. The Dominion Prime Ministers struck a deliberate balance between advocating their national interests, without going so far as to block British entry into the EEC – a strategy which *The Observer* aptly described as 'trying to find a way of fighting without hurting Britain'.[58] Although the earlier sessions of the meeting featured some harsh judgments of the British negotiating performance, particularly from Diefenbaker, the final outcome was nonetheless satisfactory from Macmillan's point of view. The Commonwealth Prime Ministers' conceded that the final decision was one for Britain alone to take, and the London press were generally agreed that the meeting had allowed the Macmillan government full freedom to resume negotiations with the Six.[59] The lasting impression from the Prime Ministers' Meeting was threefold: firstly, the British government was utterly determined to join the European Community, regardless of Commonwealth views; secondly, that Commonwealth countries, although thoroughly dissatisfied with the heavy cost they were expected to bear, were not prepared to press their complaints to the point of outright opposition; and perhaps most importantly, as Miriam Camps observed, there remained a palpable sense that 'the conference had marked a turning-point in Commonwealth affairs and that, even if the negotiations in Brussels failed, a phase in Commonwealth relations was over and a new and uncharted relationship was beginning'.[60]

In the immediate aftermath of the meeting, the discussion about vital Commonwealth interests and the value of British assurances gave way to a widespread feeling of resignation on the EEC question. As Amory reported on the mood in Canada after the Prime Ministers' Meeting: 'The general view seems to be that the Prime Ministers collectively gave the British a hard hammering but had no alternative to propose. That being so, the British have firmly made up their minds to go into Europe and Canada has to make the best of the situation'.[61] Diefenbaker showed every sign of wishing to distance himself from the Common Market issue, even to the point of reaching an agreement with Macmillan that they should refrain from discussing the EEC in any detail at their meeting in the Bahamas, scheduled for December.[62]

Much the same feeling prevailed in Australia, where Prime Minister Menzies revised his thoughts on Britain's impending entry into the EEC:

> I think that twenty years ago I might have become more impassioned about this matter, but the Commonwealth has changed a lot since then. Its association has become much looser. For most of its members, the association is, in a sense, functional and occasional. The old hopes of concerting common policies have gone. Under these circumstances, it may well prove to be the fact that even if federation should be achieved in Western Europe, the anomalous position of Great Britain in the Commonwealth which would then emerge would be regarded as no more anomalous than many other things which have been accepted, and with which we have learned to live.[63]

This undoubtedly represented a profound change of heart from a Prime Minister who, only 14 months earlier, had described Britain's Common Market negotiations as 'the most important in time of peace in my lifetime'.[64] Menzies had obviously undergone a searching reappraisal of his lifelong commitment to the idea of a British family of nations, and was no doubt deeply disturbed by the encroaching realities of the post-imperial world. His grudging acceptance of the modern day 'anomalies' of the Commonwealth was indicative of his feeling of powerlessness to hold back the steady advance of change and his ongoing reluctance to see anything truly positive in Australia's evolving new predicament. Although Menzies had achieved his primary objective of avoiding a head-on collision with Australia's senior alliance partners, it is nonetheless clear that the Common Market episode was for him a sobering experience which continued to cause him considerable sadness.

The general mood of resignation was accompanied by widespread reflection, discussion and debate about the changing determinants of Australian nationality in the post-imperial world. *The Melbourne Age* was typical in presenting the Prime Ministers' Meeting as the end of an era: 'What is clear … is that Australia must now accept the indications of a shift in history. As a nation we can grapple with the consequences without bitterness or fear. But as a member of the Commonwealth we cannot help feeling that an uneasy future lies ahead'.[65] In Sydney, both *The Daily Telegraph* and *The Sydney Morning Herald* viewed the Prime Ministers' Meeting as a pivotal moment in Australia's national development. The *Telegraph* concluded on a more optimistic note: 'This is a step towards national self-reliance that we would have had to take sooner or later; in the long view it might not be wholly regrettable that it has been forced upon us now'.[66] The *Australian Financial Review* ran strongly with this theme, claiming that the developing world situation posed 'considerable new challenges, great new problems':

> The result of this London conference points inexorably to a time when Australia will be increasingly on her own... We may have to stop thinking about Britain as 'Home' and start thinking urgently about getting to know very much more of our Asian neighbours' needs.[67]

In New Zealand *The Wellington Evening Post* echoed Australian press discussion about the changing international outlook, and claimed that New Zealanders were now applying all their 'energy, initiative and enterprise' to the challenges that lay ahead.[68] *The Auckland Star* even suggested that New Zealand should take a leaf out of General de Gaulle's book and develop a clearer, more self-reliant view of the nation's future.[69] Prime Minister Holyoake adopted this new note of optimism to conclude his address to the House of Representatives in October: 'At such a critical time for our nation I earnestly believe that all New Zealanders will respond to the challenge which faces us...I am certain that they will all work together with determination, clarity of vision, and a singleness of purpose as well as with confidence in the future of our country and our people'.[70] The following month he pressed this theme even more earnestly: 'Get this Common Market scare out of your minds. The future is always brighter if you are prepared to look upon it with unjaundiced eyes'.[71] By the end of the year, Francis Cumming-Bruce reported with satisfaction that among New Zealand ministers, officials, the press, and farming interests 'there has been a very substantial advance, even among the most rigid, towards acceptance of the inevitability of change'.[72]

But the broad shift in the outlook of the Dominions on the Common Market was perhaps best illustrated by the parliamentary speech of the Australian Minister for Trade. McEwen had been one of the fiercest opponents of Britain's EEC membership negotiations, and he could not resist a swipe at the British government for its marked change in attitude towards the Common Market since the mid-1950s, referring to a number of earlier British ministerial statements to illustrate his point. He noted wryly that 'had the Australian Government been prepared to endorse the British Government's policy on this matter as it has been expressed over recent years, we here would have been following a pretty winding path'. But he pleaded that he was 'not calling into question the propriety of this change of policy'. Rather, he wished to highlight the most important lesson which he drew from Britain's Common Market negotiations:

> The record of history is that in a sufficiently serious situation those responsible for the political and economic security of a nation, take the course judged to be right for their own people. This has a message for Australians – if Britain goes into the Common Market on terms which seriously weaken our trading position.[73]

McEwen's 'message for Australians' might have seemed self-evident, were it not for the prevailing assumptions about organic 'British community' that had so profoundly influenced the response of all three Dominions to the Common Market problem. McEwen's comments represented by far the most frank, sober and open acknowledgement of the inescapable fact that the interests of Australia and Great Britain did not, and indeed ought not, form part of some higher, indissoluble whole. On the contrary, although Australia and Britain might often see eye to eye on a range of political and economic matters, as independent sovereign nations their political and economic interests were, ultimately, distinct and separate. Australians could no longer afford to assume that their economic and political interests would automatically be joined by others in times of difficulty or crisis. Rather, it was precisely during those times of crisis that Australia's closest allies, even blood relatives, would take the course judged right for their own national interests. In a sense, then, McEwen had pronounced that Lord Palmerston's celebrated dictum, that there are 'no eternal allies, only eternal interests', applied equally to the realm of 'kith and kin'.

The breakdown of the Brussels negotiations on 29 January 1963 at the hands of General de Gaulle in no way signalled a return to the comfortable precepts of British race patriotism. On the contrary, all parties proceeded on the assumption that Britain would, sooner or later, join the EEC, and that Commonwealth interests would not be allowed to stand in the way. In Australia, Canada and New Zealand, de Gaulle's veto was looked upon as a 'temporary respite' allowing precious time for adjustment to the inevitable changes that lay ahead.[74] The shock of Macmillan's EEC membership bid had provoked a more immediate awareness of the changes which had been slowly undermining the traditional conception of Commonwealth relations since the Second World War. Above all, it was the idea that the interests of fellow 'British' countries ought ultimately to be reconciled under a common 'British' destiny that had been most profoundly shaken by the experience of Britain's EEC membership negotiations. As former Secretary of the Australian Department of Trade, John Crawford, remarked in the aftermath of the Brussels breakdown: 'Our psychology has been changed. We will never be the same as we were before we were given a shake-up by Britain's application'.[75]

It has not been suggested here that the EEC membership crisis was the fundamental cause of Britain's fraying ties to the old Dominions. Rather, it provided a prime catalyst for long overdue discussion and debate, serving to redefine national assumptions, and helping to reset the national priorities of all countries concerned, including the United Kingdom. By the end of 1962, the British race patriotism that informed the broad Commonwealth response to the announcement of Macmillan's EEC membership application had given way to a resigned acceptance of Britain's European aspirations, and a new awareness of the changing bases of Australian, New Zealand and Canadian nationality. Although the Common Market crisis resonated in different ways, and to differing degrees, in the three countries concerned, it remains nonetheless clear that as Commonwealth efforts to defend the old order were slowly exhausted, many dated assumptions about the British connection were finally submitted to detailed public scrutiny. The suggestion that it may no longer be appropriate to refer to Britain as 'Home', the likelihood of the declining relevance of sentiment and tradition in foreign and commercial policies, and the notion that the Dominions were mature enough to stand on their own feet were not necessarily new ideas. But they were ideas that unmistakably converged under the impetus of Britain's EEC ambitions in such a way as to leave an indelible mark on the political culture of all three 'British' Dominions.

Notes

1. Recently, the work of Catherine Schenk has addressed this problem, identifying the ways in which the European question forced British governments to confront the changing relationship with the colonies in Asia and Africa. See Catherine Schenk, 'Decolonization and European Economic Integration: The Free Trade Area Negotiations, 1956–58', *Journal of Imperial and Commonwealth History*, 24/3 (1996) 444–63.
2. To this day, most Australians, Canadians and New Zealanders are unable to identify the precise origins of their national independence.

3. As Macmillan instructed Duncan Sandys on appointing him to the post of Commonwealth Secretary in August 1961, 'I rely on you to put your excellent brain to the task of working out how the Commonwealth's interests can be reconciled with some association between the seven and the six, or even their amalgamation': Churchill Archives Centre, Cambridge (CAC), Duncan Sandys Papers, DSND 15/5, Macmillan to Sandys, 17 August 1960.

4. Public Record Office, Kew, London (PRO), CAB 134/1821 EQ(61)4: European Economic Association Committee, Implications of Signing the Treaty of Rome, 26 April 1961, p. 5.

5. PRO, CAB 134/1821, EQ(61)18: European Economic Association Committee, The Implications of Signing the Treaty of Rome: Commonwealth Free Entry, 12 June 1961.

6. CAC, Duncan Sandys Papers, DSND 8/18: Meeting in the Commonwealth Secretary's room, Europe and the Commonwealth, 12 June 1961.

7. PRO, CAB 134/1821: Minutes of ad hoc Cabinet Meeting at Chequers, Europe and the Commonwealth, 18 June 1961.

8. PRO, PREM 11/3325: Memorandum by the Prime Minister, 29 December 1960–3 January 1961, p. 25 (original emphasis).

9. See Heath to Macmillan, 7 February 1961, quoted in Wolfram Kaiser, *Using Europe, Abusing the Europeans* (London: Macmillan Press – now Palgrave, 1996) p. 150. See also Macmillan's remarks on his responsibility to 'lead the country away from its traditional approach' during his talks with President Kennedy in April 1962 in *Foreign Relations of the United States, 1961–63*, Vol. XIII (Washington, DC: Department of State) p. 85.

10. Sandys' appointment as Commonwealth Secretary in July 1960 was clearly intended to shake up the CRO, who were widely thought to be dragging the chain on the EEC question. See the account of former Permanent Under-Secretary of the CRO, Joe Garner, *The Commonwealth Office, 1925– 68* (London: Heinemann, 1978) pp. 397–401.

11. The comments of the New Zealand Governor-General, Lord Cobham, were typical: 'We have shed our blood together on many fields, and that is a bond between the countries that no trade difficulties should ever be allowed to sever. When old friends fall out, rogues and ruffians come into their own, so let us try to sort out our difficulties together, and keep our powder dry for the vast problems that only a united Commonwealth can tackle'. Quoted in PRO, DO 159/64: *Australian and New Zealand Weekly*, 3 March 1962.

12. *Sydney Morning Herald*, 1 August 1961, p. 1.

13. Menzies, Commonwealth Parliamentary Debates (*CPD*), House of Representatives (H. of R.), Vol. 32, pp. 134–41.

14. National Library of Australia (NLA), McEwen Papers, MS4654, Box 122: Extract of Speech by the Minister for Trade and Federal Leader of the Australian Country Party, Mr. J. McEwen, at the Official Opening of the NSW Country Party Annual Conference, Lismore, 21 June 1961; ibid., Review of Trade Problems by the Rt Hon. J. McEwen, 5 August 1961; see also *The Australian Financial Review*, 22 June 1961, p. 3.

15. McEwen, *CPD*, H. of R., Vol. 32, 17 August 1961, pp. 257–63.

16. PRO, PREM 11/4016: Amory (British High Commissioner, Ottawa) to Macmillan, 23 March 1962.

17. UK–Canada joint communiqué, 'The Common Market', 14 July 1961.
18. Quoted in John O'Brien, 'The British Commonwealth and the European Economic Community: The Australian and Canadian Experiences', *The Round Table*, 340 (1996) 479–93, 486.
19. PRO, PREM 11/3211: Summary Record of Discussion at Accra, 15 September 1961.
20. PRO, PREM 11/3211: Lloyd to Macmillan, 14 September 1961.
21. National Archives and Records Administration, Washington DC (NARA), RG59, 375.800/5-2562: Bruce (London) to Department of State, 28 May 1962; see also for example PRO, PREM 11/4016, Marshall to Sandys, 30 March 1962.
22. Quoted in PRO, DO 159/64: Francis Cumming-Bruce (UK High Commissioner, Wellington) to Sandys, 21 February 1962.
23. See, for example, *The New Zealand Herald*, 24 March 1962, 4 May 1962.
24. *Sydney Morning Herald*, 2 August 1961, p. 2. Former Australian Foreign Minister, Lord (R. G.) Casey made similar remarks about the wider Commonwealth benefits of a politically and economically strengthened Britain, and expressed his faith that 'Britain will not enter this Common Market unless she can get conditions which very largely protect the trade of her Commonwealth countries'. Quoted in *The Age*, 2 August 1961, p. 5.
25. *The Toronto Globe and Mail*, quoted in *The New Commonwealth*, February 1962.
26. PRO, DO 159/52: Amory to Joe Garner (Commonwealth Relations Office), 15 February 1962.
27. PRO, PREM 11/4016: Amory to Macmillan, 23 March 1962.
28. Fleming, speech at Winnipeg, 19 January 1962. Text in PRO, DO 159/52.
29. Historical Archives of the European Community, Florence (HAEC), MAEF48/OW Microform 321: Jean Chauvel (French Ambassador, London) to Maurice Couve de Murville (French Foreign Minister), 'La Grande Bretagne et le Commonwealth', 26 February 1962.
30. HAEC, BAC24/1967 E13, Rapport fait au nom de la Commission du commerce extérieur sur les aspects commerciaux et économiques de la demande d'adhesion du Royaume–Uni à la CEE, 16 January 1962; PRO, CAB 134/ 1512 CMN (62) 4, Lord Privy Seal's Account of the Ministerial Session of the Negotiations on 22–23 February, 5 March 1962.
31. PRO, DO 159/52: Amory to CRO, 13 February 1962.
32. Quoted in PRO, DO 159/52: F. G. K. Gallagher to J. R. A. Bottomley (CRO), 26 February 1962.
33. See, for example, PRO, DO 159/54: Amory to Sandys, 9 May 1962.
34. PRO, DO 159/64: Cumming-Bruce to Sandys, 21 February 1962.
35. PRO, DO 159/64: Cumming-Bruce to Lintott (CRO), 16 March 1962.
36. PRO, PREM 11/4016: Record of a Meeting in Admiralty House, 23 March 1962.
37. See PRO, PREM 11/4016: Marshall to Sandys, 30 March 1962; PRO, CAB 134/1512, CMN (62) 5, 14 March 1962; National Archives of Australia, Canberra (AA), A4940/1 C3368, Pt. 3, Sixth Report of the Inter-Departmental (Common Market) Committee, 27 March 1962.
38. AA, A4940/1 C3368, Pt. 3: PM's Department (Salter & Foxcroft), memorandum to Menzies, 'Common Market', 18 October 1961.

39. AA, A4940/1 C3368, Pt. 3: PM's Department (Salter), memorandum to Menzies, 24 October 1961.
40. AA, A3917/1, Vol. 7: McEwen to Menzies, 7 April 1962; McEwen to Menzies, 28 March 1962.
41. PRO, DO 159/57: Record of a Meeting in the Lord Privy Seal's Room, 21 March 1962.
42. John McEwen, *His Story* (privately published, 1983) p. 61.
43. *Wellington Evening Post*, 4 April 1962.
44. Quoted in *The Sunday Times*, 8 April 1962.
45. *Toronto Globe and Mail*, 3 May 1962.
46. PRO, PREM 11/4016: Record of Meeting between the Lord Privy Seal, the High Commissioner, Mr Fleming, Mr Hees, and Mr. Hamilton in Ottawa, 26 March 1962.
47. Fleming insisted that the agreement should apply to confidential as well as public statements because of the danger of government leaks. He explained that all senior Canadian officials had been trained by the Liberal Party during its 22 years of power, and all of them still had the closest connections with the Liberal leaders. Therefore any written views on the merits of particular British proposals, even at the most confidential level, would be brought to the notice of their political opponents 'within a matter of minutes': ibid.
48. PRO, PREM 11/4016: Amory to Macmillan, 23 March 1962. Amory described Diefenbaker's tactics as 'a convenient electoral stand as he can't really lose'.
49. AA, A4940/1 C3616: Cabinet Minute (Decision no. 275), 25 June 1962; Bunting (Secretary, PM's Dept) to Tange (Secretary, External Affairs), 2 July 1962.
50. See AA, A1838/283 726/1: Harry (Deputy-Secretary, External Affairs) to Tange, 23 March 1962; AA, A5819/2 Vol. 5/Agendum 164, Cabinet Submission no. 164 (Barwick), ANZUS Council Meeting, 26 April 1962; Cabinet Minute (Decision no. 204), 1 May 1962.
51. AA, A571/161 1961/791, Pt. 37: E. Ronald Walker to Barwick (Australian External Affairs Minister), 27 June 1962.
52. Speech by the Prime Minister, the Rt Hon. R. G. Menzies, to the Greater Wollongong Chamber of Commerce and Industry, 12 July 1962, text in AA, A1838/275 727/4/2, Pt. 5.
53. PRO, DO 159/65: Cumming-Bruce to Sandys, 3 August 1962; Cumming-Bruce to Lintott (Commonwealth Relations Office), 10 August 1962.
54. PRO, DO 159/65: Cumming-Bruce to Commonwealth Relations Office, 27 August 1962.
55. PRO, FO 371/164815: Statement by Sig. Colombo in Brussels, 5 August 1962.
56. PRO, DO 159/60: Sandys to Menzies, 24 July 1962. Practically identical messages were sent to Holyoake and Diefenbaker.
57. British White Paper, Cmnd. 1805, August 1962.
58. *The Observer* was referring specifically to the performance of Australian Prime Minister Menzies, but the remark was equally applicable to Canada and New Zealand: 14 September 1962.
59. *The Times*, 20 September 1962. *The Financial Times* concluded that the government had achieved its two main objectives: 'It has avoided any new

commitments which would tie the hands of Mr. Heath in Brussels', and 'It has for all practical purposes averted the possibility of a second Prime Ministers' conference once the final terms have been settled with the Six', 20 September 1962. *The Daily Mail* described the final press communiqué as a 'tremendous triumph' for Macmillan, and said that the Commonwealth had given a 'full-steam-ahead signal' to Britain's negotiations, 20 September 1962; *The Daily Telegraph* (20 September 1962) said that 'Britain can resume negotiations with the Six in Brussels without the incubus of open Commonwealth disapproval', while *The Guardian* (20 September 1962) said that although the British government had failed to win the approval of the Commonwealth, it had avoided any precise commitment to reopen matters already covered in the Brussels negotiations. Only Beaverbrook's *Daily Express* (20 September 1962) remained critical, describing the attitude of Commonwealth Prime Ministers as 'ice-cold', and declaring that most of the leaders were leaving London 'as they arrived, hostile or disturbed'.

60. Miriam Camps, *Britain and the European Community, 1955–1963* (London: Oxford University Press, 1964) p. 444.
61. PRO, DO 159/54: Amory to Sandys, 2 October 1962.
62. PRO, PREM 11/4099: CRO to Ottawa, 30 November 1962; Garner to Amory, 14 December 1962.
63. Menzies, *CPD*, H. of R., 19 October 1962, pp. 1553–61.
64. Menzies, quoted in *The Sydney Morning Herald*, 1 August 1961.
65. *The Melbourne Age*, 21 September 1962.
66. *Daily Telegraph*, 21 September 1962.
67. *Australian Financial Review*, 25 September 1962.
68. *Wellington Evening Post*, 4 October 1962.
69. *Auckland Star*, 15–16 January 1963.
70. Holyoake, Speech in the New Zealand House of Representatives, 11 October 1962.
71. Holyoake, Speech at a New Zealand Chamber of Commerce meeting, Palmerston North, 13 November 1962. Text in PRO, DO 159/65.
72. PRO, DO 159/65: Cumming-Bruce to Lintott, 14 December 1962.
73. McEwen, *CPD*, H. of R., 18 October 1962.
74. See AA, A4940/1 C3368, Pt. 4, Cabinet Minute (decision no. 638), 5 February 1963; *Australian Financial Review*, 31 January 1963, 5 February 1963; *The Melbourne Age*, 25 January 1963, 31 January 1963. On the British side see, for example, PRO, DO 159/11, Treasury Paper, Policy in the Event of a Breakdown in the Brussels Negotiations, 23 January 1963; *Financial Times*, 1 February 1963.
75. NLA, Crawford Papers, MS4514, Box 196, Folder 18: J. G. Crawford, Termination of Common Market Negotiations, Notes for address to Summer School of Business Administration, Melbourne, 28 February 1963.

Index